Flickering Empire

Flickering Empire

HOW CHICAGO INVENTED THE U.S. FILM INDUSTRY

Michael Glover Smith and Adam Selzer

WALLFLOWER PRESS
LONDON & NEW YORK

A Wallflower Press Book
Published by
Columbia University Press
Publishers Since 1893
New York • Chichester, West Sussex
cup.columbia.edu

Cover image:
Charlie Chaplin with Francis X. Bushman and "Broncho Billy" Anderson.
Courtesy of the Chicago History Museum.

A complete CIP record is available from the Library of Congress

ISBN 978-0-231-17448-0 (cloth : alk. paper)
ISBN 978-0-231-17449-7 (pbk. : alk. paper)
ISBN 978-0-231-85079-7 (e-book)

Columbia University Press books are printed on permanent
and durable acid-free paper.
This book is printed on paper with recycled content.
Printed in the United States of America

c 10 9 8 7 6 5 4 3 2 1
p 10 9 8 7 6 5 4 3 2 1

For Jillian and Ronni

Table of Contents

IT ALL CAME CRASHING DOWN

Acknowledgments

The authors wish to acknowledge the following individuals and institutions for their generous help during the writing of *Flickering Empire*: Yoram Allon and everyone at Wallflower Press; Lisa Wagner for her invaluable advice, editorial work and tireless championing of this book from the beginning; George Walsh for his proofreading, editing and good taste in French bakeries; Jeff Look, the great-nephew of Colonel William Selig, for having us over for dinner and allowing us access to the family archives; Diana Dretske and the Lake County Discovery Museum in Wauconda, IL; the Chicago History Museum; the Library of Congress in Washington, D.C.; Gary Keller, Vice President, Essanay Centers and Strategic Initiatives at St. Augustine College; and the residents of 3900 N. Claremont Avenue.

Michael Glover Smith wishes to acknowledge: my wife Jill whose love and support made this project possible; Adam for showing me the ropes in researching and writing non-fiction; my father David; my mother Corrine (who accompanied me to the Chicago History Museum in 2010 — a trip that proved to be an important part of the genesis of this book); my brother Drew (who read an early draft of the manuscript and offered

helpful feedback); Susan Doll and Sara Vaux for their friendship and men-
torship in the field of Film Studies; and all of my colleagues and students
at Oakton Community College, Harold Washington College, the College
of Lake County and Triton College.

Adam Selzer wishes to acknowledge: the kind staff at the George Eastman
House in Rochester who arranged for screenings of a handful of early films
that could be seen nowhere else, and the organizers of the Teen Book Fest
in Rochester who sponsored my trip there. To Ronni for putting up with
my endless rambling, to Aidan for sitting through my experiments to see
whether nine-year-olds still find century-old slapstick funny (results: affir-
mative!), and to Mike, whose hard work and dedication made the project
possible. Thanks also to Hector Reyes, my partner in podcasting, for
accompanying us on our expeditions to the remains of the old studios.

FOREWORD
by Susan Doll, PhD

I lived in Chicago for 25 years, and, in that time, I discovered it to be a city of contradictions. It is a city that earned fame for the contributions of progressive thinkers in social sciences, education, and religion, but ignominy for its legacy of political corruption. A beacon for clever entrepreneurs such as Cyrus McCormick and Aaron Montgomery Ward, Chicago also attracted con men like Joseph "Yellow Kid" Weil. Righteous Billy Sunday, who preached about the evils of alcohol during Prohibition, is buried in a Chicago suburb called Forest Park, five miles due east from the Hillside grave of ruthless Al Capone, who became rich and infamous for selling illegal liquor during the same period of time. A "city on the make," to quote writer Nelson Algren, Chicago was the perfect place for the burgeoning film industry to develop and prosper.

Flickering Empire: How Chicago Invented the U.S. Film Industry offers the full story of Chicago's enormous contributions to the history of cinema. Like Chicago, the film industry was a modern wonder that attracted as many notorious characters as it did innovative entrepreneurs. And, sometimes those contradictory impulses were represented in the same person! Readers will learn about Colonel William Selig, who not only was a phony medium in Dallas when he saw his first motion picture but also was a phony colonel. Selig returned to Chicago to jump into the business of manufacturing motion-picture equipment, in which enterprise he became a key figure. The 1893 *World's Columbian Exposition* is a celebrated event in Chicago's history and also a notorious one, because of the escapades of serial killer H.H. Holmes, though *Flickering Empire* focuses on the fair's influence on the beginning of the film industry. It was at the fair where George Spoor, Selig's rival for many years, saw the Tachyscope, a rotating wheel with photographs mounted around the periphery. When spun, the images were animated, suggesting the illusion of movement, which intrigued Spoor.

The failures and successes of Chicago's film pioneers are not the only scandalous events in early cinema history recalled in *Flickering Empire*. Readers will discover the truth behind Thomas Edison's role in the invention of the motion-picture camera and the establishment of the cinema industry. Authors Michael Glover Smith and Adam Selzer provide details of Edison's penchant for taking credit for the innovations of his assistants, including the work of W.K.L. Dickson, the man who made the inventor's ideas for a camera that captured movement actually work. They expose Edison's ruthless tactics in suing rivals for control of film production and distribution, his bootlegging of European films, and even his lack of interest in improving the production values of his films. Edison's tactics stunted the development of the industry on the East Coast, which helped studios and distributors in Chicago to expand and dominate production and distribution for a short while.

The authors effectively paint the big picture of the pioneering days of cinema history and then carefully place Chicago's major contributions within it. But the devil is in the details, and their incredible research in primary sources pinpoints dates, people, and films to carefully support their argument about the central role of Chicago-based film entrepreneurs and the superior production values of their movies. Indeed, the detailed descriptions of films in the chapters on the Essanay and Selig Polyscope Studios are among the most fascinating segments in a book written in a direct, entertaining style. In 1907, cross-eyed comic Ben Turpin, later a part of Mack Sennett's Keystone Studios, skated his way into a movie career in Essanay's first official movie, *An Awful Skate*. This stunt comedy featured Turpin, who did not know how to skate, careening and crashing through Chicago's Old Town neighborhood in a quasi-improvised narrative. *An Awful Skate* was directed by Gilbert Anderson, later known as

Broncho Billy, who by 1909 had turned his talents to making westerns, including the film *The James Boys in Missouri*. Jesse and Frank James had been romanticized in dime novels and newspaper accounts since they began hitting banks and trains shortly after the Civil War. In the first decade of the new century, they were still memorialized in dime novels, and Frank James had been touring in Wild West shows and popular theater as late as 1907, exploiting his notoriety. Illustrator N.C. Wyeth had returned from a trip out West in 1906 and may have painted his illustration with a similar title, *The James Brothers in Missouri*, about this time. In this context, Anderson's decision to turn the story of Frank and Jesse into Essanay's first western was timely, and his sympathetic perspective of the brothers was in keeping with other popular representations. However, glorifying the lives of outlaws got the film banned in several cities, including Chicago. Meanwhile, over at Selig Polyscope, the Colonel collaborated with author L. Frank Baum on the first film to be based on the *Wizard of Oz* novels. Baum toured the country with the film, which was a handcolored spectacular.

This "reel history" of Chicago is relatively unheralded. Long ago, I studied film history at Northwestern University and, despite the school's proximity to events and locations described in *Flickering Empire*, the city was barely acknowledged in class or in textbooks. Little has changed through the decades. A few years ago, I attended a screening of a multiepisode documentary series on the history of the American film industry presented by the director. Though the contributions of such forgotten pioneers as French filmmaker Alice Guy-Blaché were acknowledged in order to "right the wrongs" of standard film histories, Chicago was represented by a single photo of the Selig Polyscope Studio. The director of the documentary — and the audience — did not appreciate my question: Why was there so little about Chicago? Annoyed, he dismissed what he perceived as a criticism, answering that he couldn't possibly include every detail of film history, as though Chicago's contributions were too minor. Apparently, neither he nor the audience wanted me to spoil their preconceived ideas about the history of American cinema as a tale of two coasts and two cities — New York and Hollywood.

Standard textbooks for film history classes are no better. If Chicago is included in texts, it is generally a brief acknowledgement of Essanay and Selig as members of the Motion Picture Patents Company, a trust founded in 1907 to control production, distribution, and exhibition. But, after Michael and Adam's painstaking research and comprehensive detail in

Flickering Empire, the textbooks need to be rewritten. There can be little debate that Chicago was absolutely instrumental in the development of distribution and as a production center in the pioneering days of the film industry. Any text that does not reference Michael and Adam's work and research will be guilty of distortion by omission. *Flickering Empire* is the link that has been missing in standard film histories.

When I lived in Chicago, I often visited the sites and locations associated with the early days of cinema. I lived near the intersection where the Selig studio once stood; I walked past the Essanay buildings that are still standing on Argyle Street; I tracked down the address of Oscar Micheaux's office; I tried to find the apartment building where Chaplin lived for only a few weeks. I thought these sites could transport me back in time so that I could understand what it was like to make movies in gritty, turn-of-the-century Chicago. I live in another state now, but I can still fulfill that wish by leafing through *Flickering Empire*.

PERSONS DISCUSSED
IN FLICKERING EMPIRE

George Ade (1866–1944)
John Alcock (18??–19??)
Edward Amet (1860–1948)
Gilbert M. "Broncho Billy"
    Anderson (1880–1971)
Otto Anschutz (1846–1907)
Maclyn Arbuckle (1866–1931)
Thomas Armat (1866–1948)

Richard Foster "Daddy" Baker
    (1857–1921)
Ephraim Banning (1849–1907)
Thomas Banning (1851–1927)
Theda Bara (1885–1955)
L. Frank Baum (1856–1919)
Beverly Bayne (1894–1982)
Wallace Beery (1885–1949)
Alexander Graham Bell (1847–1922)

Don J. Bell (1869–1934)
Arthur Berthelet (1879–1949)
J. Stuart Blackton (1875–1941)
Francis Boggs (1870–1911)
Hobart Bosworth (1867–1943)
Charles Brabin (1882–1957)
Hazel Buddemeyer (1893–1973)
John Bunny (1863–1915)
Luis Buñuel (1900–1983)
Francis X. Bushman (1883–1966)

E.H. Calvert (1863–1941)
Al Capone (1899–1947)
Wallace A. Carlson (1894–1967)
Bill Cato (1887–1965)
Charles Chaplin (1889–1977)
Syd Chaplin (1885–1965)
Herma Clark (1871–1959)

Charles Clary (1873–1931)
Jean Cocteau (1889–1963)
William F. "Buffalo Bill" Cody
   (1846–1917)
Henrietta Crossman (1861–1944)

William Emmett Dever
   (1862–1929)
William Kenndy Laurel Dickson
   (1860–1935)
John Dillinger (1903–1934)
Bess Dunn (1877–1959)
Frank Dyer (1870–1941)

Paul Edgerton (19??–19??)
Thomas Alva Edison (1847–1931)
Elmer Ellsworth (18??–19??)
Charles Eyton (1871–1941)

George Fabyan (1867–1939)
Louis Feuillade (1873–1925)
Michael Figliulio (18??–19??)
F. Scott Fitzgerald (1896–1940)
John Ford (1894–1973)
William Foster (1884–1940)
William Fox (1879–1952)
Metellus Lucullus Funkhouser
   (1864–1926)

Joe Gans (1874–1910)
Morris Gest (1875–1942)
William Gillette (1853–1937)
Francis J. Grandon (1879–1929)
D.W. Griffith (1875–1948)
Alice Guy–Blaché (1873–1968)

John Hardin (18??–19??)
William Randolph Hearst
   (1863–1951)

William Heise (1847–1910)
Burton Holmes (1870–1958)
H.H. Holmes (1861–1896)
E. Mason "Lightning" Hopper
   (1875–1964)
Warda Howard (18??–1943)
Albert Howell (1879–1951)

May Irwin (1862–1938)

Charles Jenkins (1867–1934)
Lew Johnson (18??–19??)
Peter P. Jones (18??–19??)

Boris Karloff (1887–1969)
Sam Katz (1893–19??)
Cherry Kearton (1871–1940)
Buster Keaton (1895–1966)
Kitty Kelly (1886–1965)
J. Warren Kerrigan (1879–1947)
Dimitri Kirsanoff (1899–1957)
George Kleine (1864–1931)
Peter Kyne (1880–1937)

Carl Laemmle (1867–1939)
Ring Lardner (1885–1933)
Harry Lauder (1870–1950)
Stan Laurel (1890–1965)
Florence Lawrence (1886–1938)
Margaret Leslie (18??–1906)
Max Lewis (18??–19??)
Robert Todd Lincoln
   (1843–1928)
Max Linder (1883–1925)
Samuel Long (18??–1915)
Siegmund Lubin (1851–1923)
Auguste Lumière (1862–1954)
Claude–Antoine Lumière
   (1840–1911)

Louis Lumière (1864–1948)

Wallace McCutcheon
   (1858–1910)
Terry McGovern (1880–1918)
Scott Marble (1847–1919)
Étienne–Jules Marey (1830–1904)
Frank J. Marion (1869–1963)
William McKinley (1843–1901)
Archer McMackin (1888–1961)
Georges Méliès (1861–1938)
Frank Minematsu (188?–193?)
Tom Mix (1880–1940)
Gene Morgan (18??–19??)
William Morris (18??–1932)
Frank Mottershaw (1850–1932)
J.J. Murdoch (18??–19??)
F.W. Murnau (1888–1931)
Eadweard Muybridge
   (1830–1904)

Tom Nash (18??–19??)
Howard E. Nicholas (18??–19??)
Virginia Nicholson (1916–1996)

Annie Oakley (1860–1926)
Fred Ott (1860–1936)

Paul Panzer (1873–1958)
Lem B. Parker (1865–1928)
Louella Parsons (1881–1972)
Mary Pickford (1892–1979)
Pope Pius X (1835–1914)
Edwin S. Porter (1870–1941)
Evelyn Preer (1896–1932)
Alexandre Promio (1868–1926)

Terry Ramsaye (1885–1954)
George Remus (1874–1952)

Romola Remus (1900–1987)
Tom Ricketts (1853–1939)
John C. Rice (18??–1915)
Jesse Robbins (1885–1973)
Paul Robeson (1898–1976)
Kermit Roosevelt (1889–1943)
Theodore Roosevelt (1858–1919)

Eugen Sandow (1867–1925)
Andrew Schustek (1873–1934)
William N. Selig (1864–1948)
Mack Sennett (1880–1960)
George Shippy (1861–1939)
Upton Sinclair (1878–1968)
Max Skladanowsky (1863–1939)
Albert E. Smith (1875–1958)
George K. Spoor (1872–1953)
Marvin "Major" Spoor
   (1893–1951)
Mary (Mollie) Spoor (1887–1985)
Farida Mazar "Little Egypt"
   Spyropoulos (1871–1937)
Ford Sterling (1882–1939)
Ruth Stonehouse (1892–1941)
Andrew Sullivan (18??–19??)
Gloria Swanson (1899–1983)

Mabel Taliaferro (1857–1979)
Nikola Tesla (1856–1943)
William Hale "Big Bill"
   Thompson (1869–1944)
Otis Turner (1862–1918)
Ben Turpin (1869–1940)

William Vance (19??–19??)
Dziga Vertov (1896–1954)
Erich Von Stroheim (1885–1957)

Raoul Walsh (1887–1980)

Henry B. Walthall (1878–1936)

Bryant Washburn (1889–1963)

John Wayne (1907–1979)

Henry McRae Webster (187?–19??)

Orson Welles (1915–1985)

Theodore Wharton (1875–1931)

Chief Whirlwind (18??–1917)

James H. White (1872–1944)

Robert Wiene (1873–1938)

Billy Wilder (1906–2002)

Kathlyn Williams (1879–1960)

Adolf Zukor (1873–1966)

Preface:
Hollywood Before Hollywood

The Essanay Motion Picture Manufacturing Company's story is a quintessential Chicago story. The story begins as an improvisation; flowers in part due to dubious, ruthless business practices; and ends a few years later with a hazy, oh-well sense of Second City disappointment.

— Michael Phillips, *Chicago Tribune*[1]

You either love Chicago — or else it burns in your memory as a blustering, blistering subdivision of Hell.

— Louella Parsons, *The Gay Illiterate*[2]

T he story of how Chicago served as the unlikely capital of motion-picture production in the United States during the earliest days of cinema has become curiously forgotten in academic circles and in popular fandom alike. Most film history textbooks describe how early American film production developed in the 1890s and early 1900s in New York and New Jersey, the home of the Edison Manufacturing Company and

Filming an Essanay 'western' indoors.

the American Mutoscope and Biograph Company. It has become commonplace for film historians to juxtapose this narrative with the story of how the movies then moved to Hollywood in the second decade of the twentieth century. This version of history completely ignores the story of film production in the Midwest. Chicago, when it is discussed at all, is often treated as an afterthought or a footnote. David Bordwell and Kristin Thompson's otherwise excellent and authoritative *Film History: An Introduction*, for instance, devotes exactly one sentence to major Chicago movie studios like the Selig Polyscope Company and the Essanay Film Manufacturing Company before noting that "poor weather" eventually caused film producers to move farther west.[3]

The astonishing reality is that Chicago filmmakers produced literally thousands of movies between 1896 and 1918, perhaps more than any other single city in the country during this time. It has been estimated that the Chicago film industry at its most prolific, at the end of the first decade of the twentieth century, was responsible for producing the majority of the American movies on the market.[4] Among the major Chicago players were Essanay, Selig Polyscope, and the Kleine Company (a distributor that also dabbled in production), not to mention a copious number of independent production companies, including the American Film Manufacturing Company, the Birth of a Race Photoplay Company, the Ebony Film Company, the Foster Photoplay Company, the Historical Feature Film Company, the Micheaux Book and Film Company, the Peter P. Jones Film Company, and the Unique Film Company. Major studios based in other cities (such as Edison, Biograph, and the American Vitagraph Company) also maintained Chicago offices. This enormous empire employed thousands of men and women in a thriving industry that can accurately be described as "Hollywood Before Hollywood." The biggest of the studios owned lots that comprised entire city blocks, and they released locally shot movies on a weekly basis. Their output totaled hundreds of films every year. Colonel William Selig became known as "the man who invented Hollywood" as a result of his opening the first permanent movie studio in Los Angeles in 1909, but this happened only after he had already produced hundreds of films at his successful Chicago-based studio during the previous ten years.

Among the thousands of movies produced in Chicago during this era, the early Chicago filmmakers can claim many "famous firsts," including:

- the first pseudo-documentary and the first use of special effects "miniatures" (Edward Amet and George Spoor's Spanish–American War movies of 1898)
- the first industrial films made for a corporate client (Selig Polyscope's movies for the meatpacking giant Armour and Company, 1901)
- the first *Wizard of Oz* films (Selig Polyscope's *The Fairylogue and Radio Plays*, 1908, and *The Wonderful Wizard of Oz*, 1910)
- many pioneering westerns, including the first movie about Jesse James (Essanay's *The James Boys in Missouri*, 1908)
- the first American film version of Charles Dickens's *A Christmas Carol* (Essanay's *A Christmas Carol*, 1908)
- the first movie adaptation of Robert Louis Stevenson's *Dr. Jekyll and Mr. Hyde*, which is also probably the first American horror film (Selig Polyscope's *Dr. Jekyll and Mr. Hyde*, 1908)
- the first biographical picture about a U.S. President (Essanay's *The Life of Abraham Lincoln*, 1908)
- the first "two-reeler" (Selig Polyscope's *Damon and Pythias*, 1909)
- the first slapstick comedy to feature the famous "pie-in-the-face" gag (Essanay's *Mr. Flip*, 1909)

- the motion-picture debut of western superstar Tom Mix (Selig Polyscope's *The Cowboy Millionaire*, 1909)
- the first film directed by an African-American (the Foster Photoplay Company's independently produced short *The Railroad Porter*, 1912)
- the first American "cliffhanger" serial (Selig Polyscope's *The Adventures of Kathlyn*, 1913)
- the first successful weekly newsreel (*The Hearst-Selig News Pictorial*, 1915)
- the first feature-length movie to showcase Sir Arthur Conan-Doyle's beloved Sherlock Holmes character (Essanay's *Sherlock Holmes*, 1916)
- the first feature film directed by an African-American (the Peter P. Jones Film Company's independently produced *The Slacker*, 1917)

In addition to its invaluable contributions to early motion-picture production in the United States, Chicago was also an important center for film distribution and exhibition. Carl Laemmle, who would go on to found Universal Studios, got his start as an exhibitor when he opened a nickelodeon in the Second City in 1906. George Kleine, the most successful American importer and distributor of European movies in the early twentieth century, had his headquarters in Chicago. The success of these and other distributors and exhibitors benefitted the local production studios – and vice-versa. The first issue of the trade publication *Show World* in June 1907 claimed "Chicago leads the world in the rental of moving picture films and in the general patronage of the motion view."[5] This claim was backed up two months later by a *Billboard* article that stated that Chicago companies had commanded an incredible *two-thirds* of the American motion-picture rental business in the early part of the year.[6]

There are amazing stories from this era that have been buried by the passage of time, and many undoubtedly great Chicago movies have been lost forever because the nitrate film stock was melted down for its silver content. Fewer than one percent of Selig Polyscope's movies still exist, and Essanay's output has fared only marginally better, a circumstance that partly accounts for Chicago's neglected status in various film histories. Film historian Susan Doll refers to Chicago's history as the original Hollywood as "Chicago's best-kept secret."[7] This book, the first ever devoted solely to the rise and fall of the major Chicago studios, is an attempt to help redress the balance and to bring some of these forgotten stories to light.

For, unlike many of the movies themselves, the stories do survive. There are endless humorous anecdotes about the era: filmmakers being arrested while shooting a bank robbery scene, battles with censors, all-night parties with stars, wild excess, and, in the case of short-term Chicago resident Charlie Chaplin, extreme thrift. There were dreamers who made bad decisions, crooks who changed the world, artists with unstoppable visions, and goofballs who happened to be in the right place at the right time. The North Side of Chicago was a prototype Beverly Hills, where stars would gather at the Green Mill Gardens night club, later a favorite of Al Capone, to see and be seen. Francis X. Bushman, the first true matinée idol and a future star of the original epic production of *Ben Hur: A Tale of the Christ* (1925), would cruise through town in a purple limousine with a spotlight on the dashboard so that everyone could see him.

In 1910, there was plenty of local acting talent from which the Chicago filmmakers could choose to populate their movies. The city's enormous theater industry employed about 4,000 actors and 3,500 vaudevillians.[8] In an era when it was believed that a steady supply of fresh faces was good for the industry, many of these performers appeared before motion-picture cameras. Still other non-professionals were plucked off the street and became unlikely stars: Romola Remus, an eight-year-old girl, was cast by the author of *The Wonderful Wizard of Oz*, Chicagoan L. Frank Baum, to play Dorothy in the first of the Oz movies. She stayed home from school to earn five dollars per day for the role.

A young Gloria Swanson used her connections (her aunt was a nanny for the infant daughter of Essanay co-founder Gilbert M. Anderson) to get a tour of Essanay Studios. Swanson was hired as an extra, and she hoped to earn enough money to buy a dill pickle at the drug store afterwards. She was thrilled to find that her pay, $3.25 for an hour's work, was enough to buy all the dill pickles she could ever want. She eventually became one of Hollywood's most glamorous stars, acting in some of the most famous, and infamous, movies of the entire silent era. The Chicago studios would also serve as a launching pad for the careers of many other stars and behind the scenes players: actors such as Tom Mix, Wallace Beery, and Gilbert Anderson himself (performing under his cowboy moniker, "Broncho Billy" Anderson), as well as screenwriters such as journalist Ring Lardner, humorist George Ade, the future directing great Allan Dwan, and Louella Parsons who would become a future Hollywood gossip columnist and feared power broker.

The story of early film production in Chicago is also a story with uncanny parallels to that of the early twenty-first century. The concerns about patents, intellectual property, piracy, and big business that drove the creation of the early movies continue to resonate with us in the Digital Age today. The Faustian bargain that the Chicago studios engaged in with Thomas Edison and his infamous "Trust," which would ultimately be responsible for bringing about their downfall, serves as a cautionary tale for contemporary movie studios whose business practices likewise teeter dangerously close to the monopolistic.

Above all, though, it is a quintessential Chicago story about three visionaries, the larger-than-life figures of Colonel William N. Selig, Gilbert M. "Broncho Billy" Anderson, and George K. Spoor. These pioneers were the ones most responsible for building a film empire in Chicago, helping to turn motion pictures from a vaudeville novelty into an artistic medium that would define the twentieth century more than any other. For a brief period these men would rise like titans and then, as the world changed around them, crumble back into dust.

PART ONE

THOMAS EDISON, INVENTION AND THE DAWN OF A NEW CHICAGO

Thomas Edison and the phonograph, 1878. (Photo courtesy of the Library of Congress)

CHAPTER ONE

Edison's Kinetoscope and Pre-Motion-Picture Entertainment

The late nineteenth century was an era of astounding innovation. Photography was still relatively new, as were the railroads. Steam and electricity were just beginning to show what they could do. Being able to send messages hundreds of miles instantly via the telegraph was exciting, but in 1876 Alexander Graham Bell eclipsed the telegraph and stunned the world with the introduction of his "electrical speaking telephone." People had known about electricity for decades, but only now were they starting to see for themselves its awesome possibilities.

In many ways, motion pictures would be the climax of this flurry of invention. Although Chicago may not have been the center of the film world in the very beginning, two factors guaranteed that it would become just that in the decade prior to the rise of Hollywood: the *Columbian Exposition* of 1893 and the megalomania of Thomas Alva Edison.

Even in this age of invention, Edison stood out. A self-educated young man from Port Huron, Michigan, Edison wore long lab coats, often caked in mud and grime, in an age when most scientists still dressed to the nines. He slept only two or three hours at a time, and not always at night. He would simply go to sleep whenever he was too exhausted to continue working. So intense was his work ethic that his wife would have to leave scraps of food around his laboratory in places where he was likely to bump into them if she wanted him to eat at all. "He is a strange chap, this Edison," wrote a correspondent for the *Chicago Daily Tribune*. "He has more peculiarities to the square inch than any man in America."[1] Upon his death, the Serbian inventor Nikola Tesla, a one-time Edison assistant, said that his former boss had "lived in utter disregard of most of the elementary rules of hygiene."[2]

The phonograph, introduced in 1877, was the first of Edison's inventions to truly capture the public's imagination, and it made the inventor a star. Prior to the phonograph, when a famous singer died, the sound of the singer's voice could never be heard again. Great orators' skills died with them; there was no record, other than written transcripts, of any speech, conversation, performance, song, event, or, indeed, any other noise that had happened in the past. The fact that sound was as ephemeral as the wind that carried it had been true for the whole of human existence.

When Edison casually announced that he could record, store, and play back a human voice, the public was awestruck. The phonograph seemed so wondrous that prominent magicians came to Edison's lab planning to debunk the invention, confident that he was really just a ventriloquist. Edison's staff played a trick on one, rigging the phonograph with a "matrix" that had been pre-made, so that when the magician read some scripture into the machine, then tried to play it back, the voice emerging from the loudspeaker said, "Louder, old pudding head!"[3]

Reporters began to descend on Edison's lab in droves, fascinated by the unkempt inventor. A *New York Sun* reporter said, "He looked like anything but a professor, and reminded me of a boy apprentice to an iron-moulder. His hands were grimy with soot and oil, his straight, dark hair stood nine ways from Sunday … but the fire of genius shone in his keen gray eyes."

Since the reporter had never seen the phonograph at work, Edison eagerly demonstrated, turning the crank and reciting into the microphone:

> Mary had a little lamb
> Its fleece was white as snow
> And everywhere that Mary went
> The lamb was sure to go – to go – to go
> Ooh ooh ooh – ah!
> Cockadoodle doo-ah!

Tuck-a-tuck-a-tuck
Tuck-ah! Tuck-ah![4]

Edison then gleefully laughed as he played it back — first at the normal speed, then comically faster and slower to the amazed reporter, whose headline simply consisted of one word: "Marvelous."

Edison was quick to see how much could be done with the machine. Songs, speeches, and sounds could be recorded and copied. A statue in a wax museum could play the voice of the character it imitated, if a matrix were placed inside. Dolls could be made to recite nursery rhymes. Poor churches, Edison said, could have the greatest preachers of the era recite their sermons every Sunday. Young couples could dance to waltz music long after the local dancehall closed. Recordings of arias, speeches, and even full orchestras could be sold for five dollars apiece.

Reading now about his performances for reporters (for they certainly were performances, part of Edison's shameless, and brilliant, self-promotion), it seems almost as if Edison were predicting what the twentieth century would be like. In hindsight, his talk about the possibilities of recorded sound makes him seem as if he were a psychic describing Watergate. "I could fix a machine in a wall," he said, "and by resonation any conversation in a room could be recorded. Political secrets and the machinations of Wall Street pools might be brought to light, and the account charged to the devil. Kind parents could lie in bed and hear all the spooney courtship of their daughters and lovers."[5]

Having made the recordings, Edison had even devised a means to play them back loud enough so that they could be heard distinctly at a distance of four miles. Ships' captains could communicate directly with each other. Trains could announce themselves and where they were going.

"Why," he said, "I could put a metal diaphragm in the mouth of the Goddess of Liberty that the Frenchmen are going to put up on Bedloe's Island that would make her talk so loud that she could be heard by every soul on Manhattan Island."[6]

The public could only read in amazement. This was a man who could make statues talk. He seemed not only to have imagined a futuristic world far more advanced than anything conceived of in the works of the writers of "scientific romance," as science fiction was then called, but also to know exactly how to make it all come true. Ideas seemed to burst forth through his very ears. All of these accomplishments, keep in mind, happened *before* he invented the first practical light bulb or started building the power stations that would bring electricity to ordinary people for the first time.

When talking about the possibilities of the phonograph in 1878, an invention that he would continue to refine for years to come, he came tantalizingly close to describing the advent of television, and talking movies, before anyone had ever seen a silent motion picture at all: "A man in Europe has invented a machine that takes instantaneous photographs," he said, his voice sparkling with excitement. "Let us suppose that he photographs Dr. (E.H.) Chapin every second, and we take down his sermon on the matrix of the phonograph. The pictures and gestures of the orator, as well as his voice, could be exactly reproduced, and the eyes and ears of the audience charmed by the voice and manner of the speaker ... whole dramas and operas can be produced in private parlors."[7]

It was not, however, Edison who invented the movies. Indeed, it could be argued that Edison never truly invented anything in his life, other than the larger-than-life inventor's persona that reporters found so fascinating. This persona also fascinated many of the budding movie pioneers, including Edward Amet, who created a primitive film projector by combining Edison's Kinetoscope with a magic lantern. In Chicago, Amet and his business partner George Spoor, along with their movie-producing rival William Selig, would in many ways invent the "film industry."

Chicago is where so many innovations began, where concepts of moving pictures and their possibilities came together. It happened a few clicks at a time. The *Columbian Exposition*, the massive "World's Fair" that put Chicago on the map in 1893, was originally planned by Edison to be the event that would introduce the movies to the world. Moving pictures, albeit not in projected form, had already existed for some time by 1878, when Edison began teasing reporters about the idea. Throughout the 1860s, various mechanisms that made a series of images appear to be a single moving image, such as the Zoetrope, were marketed. In 1877, the photographer Eadweard Muybridge, the "man in Europe" of whom Edison spoke, took a series of "instant" photographs to settle a bet as to whether all four hooves of a racehorse were ever off the ground simultaneously when the horse was in full gallop. The answer was yes.

Spurred on by his success, Muybridge went to work using instant photographs to study bodies in motion. When viewed in quick succession, these photographs appeared to come to life. From the photos, he found that many long-held notions about what humans and animals look like in mid-motion, as shown in countless works of art, were dead wrong.

However, Muybridge seems to have lacked the foresight to understand the wide-ranging possibilities of moving pictures. From all available evidence, it would seem that he was interested in the technology only as a form of studying motion and advancing science, not as a way to amuse people or create art. One would think it must have occurred to him that the many studies he made of nude women walking down stairs, picking up jugs, and jumping on one foot had broad appeal outside of the scientific community, but he certainly never tried to market any of his moving pictures as entertainment.

Muybridge's photographs, however, which were typically captured by a series of 24 cameras set up in a row, were not originally seen by the public as "motion pictures." Instead, they were printed onto glass plates that were shown one at a time in slideshows. In 1882, the French scientist Étienne-Jules Marey improved upon Muybridge's breakthrough by inventing a "chronophotographic gun," a single camera that could take twelve photographs every second on a strip of flexible film. This was the prototypical movie camera that Edison would modify and ultimately patent as his own.

Edison's work on the phonograph, and the possibility of adding moving pictures to his recorded sounds, floundered, as did his work on nearly every other invention that he dangled at this time in front of breathless reporters. Despite his around-the-clock work ethic, he found it always difficult to keep his attention on any given project long enough to perfect it. By 1888, when he finally got around to working on motion pictures in earnest, Edison was a fabulously wealthy man. His progress on the light bulb had been eagerly watched by newspaper reporters (and his rivals), and his efforts to build power stations in every major city to supply electricity to the buildings and streets had made him a household name.

In 1889, Paris staged its *Exposition Universelle*, a world's fair to commemorate the 100th anniversary of the storming of the Bastille. The fair was a huge accomplishment, featuring hundreds of new buildings and crowned by the enormous Eiffel Tower. Countries from all over the world sent their finest technological innovations and works of art, but America, by many accounts, stole the show. "Buffalo Bill" Cody and Annie Oakley played their Wild West Show to packed houses, and Thomas Edison was given an acre of space to showcase 493 of his inventions.

It was during the exposition that Edison came to be seen not only as the greatest inventor of the age but also as a symbol for American individuality and ingenuity, an image that he carefully honed. Equally well crafted were his modesty and embarrassment at the honors bestowed upon him. When he attended a gala performance of an opera in Paris, the orchestra played "The Star Spangled Banner" as he entered his box. "Whereupon," he said, "I was very much embarrassed." At the end of the exposition, he was made a commander of the Legion of Honor and given a diamond-studded emblem. Publicly, he modestly stated "they tried to put a sash on me, but I could not stand for that."[8]

Privately, though, he stated that the Parisians had "upped my ante." He emerged from Paris as an international star, the master of electricity, the very symbol of everything that was good and right about the United States of America, a country that was transforming from its image as an odd, dangerously progressive experimental nation (and, since the 1860s, an experiment that had gone awry) into one of the leading nations of the world, a bastion of creativity and innovation that the "Old World" could not match.

A darker side of Edison, however, was also emerging. Although they did not bother people much at the time, stories of how Edison treated his staff were occasionally alarming. He was notorious for taking personal credit for work done by his employees and for working the men an almost inhuman number of hours. His top staff was known, for obvious reasons, as "the insomnia squad." Edison brushed off these criticisms, and so did many of his most loyal employees. "I hear men tell of playing poker for 40 hours at a stretch," one staff member said. "Well, experimenting has the same fascination for us as poker has for others."[9]

To be sure, there was a lot of experimenting to be done. Edison's oft-repeated maxim that genius is 1% inspiration and 99% perspiration was one by which he lived. For every idea, he would order every possible experiment to be done, preferring trial and error to mathematics or "book learning," an attitude that was a holdover from his own nearly complete lack of formal education. Nikola Tesla, then a young Edison employee, found it exasperating, describing Edison as "inefficient in the extreme ... just a little theory and calculation would have saved him 90 percent of the labor."[10] Tesla was a genius in his own right. Many believe that he far surpassed Edison in his abilities as a scientist. For his part, Edison simply did not understand the importance of treating his top talent well, a problem that would plague him later, along with many of the other pioneers of the movie industry.

When Tesla began work as an electrical engineer, Edison told him, perhaps with a chuckle in his voice, that if he could improve upon the Edison Company's direct-current brand of electricity, there was $50,000

Thomas Edison and most of his Orange, Massachusetts, laboratory staff, 1893. (Photo courtesy of the Library of Congress)

in it for him. When Tesla did improve the brand, he expected to be paid. Perhaps he should have realized that Edison's offer was a joke; $50,000 amounted to more than fifty years of his $18-per-week salary. Perhaps he should have realized that when Edison offered, instead, to raise his salary more than 30% to a rate of $25 per week, he was actually being rather generous. Edison, however, certainly could have handled the situation better too. When Tesla confronted him, Edison's reply was, "Tesla, you don't understand our American humor."[11]

Tesla promptly resigned his position and spent a few months as a ditch-digger before being snapped up by the Westinghouse Electric Company, with whom he developed alternating-current electricity. The innovation would become the greatest rival for Edison's direct current, and it would eventually overtake it. Edison was always vulnerable to having his innovations overtaken by more creative rivals. He was often able, however, to retain the credit for himself. The same sleight of hand would occur with the movies.

The idea of marrying moving images with recorded sound stayed with Edison, and so he bought some of Muybridge's instant photographs and told the Insomnia Squad to get to work. Edison and his crew knew

Nikola Tesla, age 34, 1890.
(Photo courtesy of the Library
of Congress)

that a series of slightly different images that passed by the eye quickly enough would appear to be a single moving picture, but synchronizing it to a phonograph recording proved difficult. Edison wanted to imprint instant photographs on a spinning cylinder, but his crew estimated that thousands of images would be required to create a moving picture that would be worthwhile to view, more than would fit on any cylinder then in existence.

Edison seemed to lose interest in the project personally, but he recruited William Kennedy Laurel Dickson, a Scottish-English immigrant and his company's official photographer, to develop the optical and photographic aspects of the invention, while he himself focused on the electromechanical side. Dickson knew that the Eastman Kodak Company had recently developed a new celluloid film stock that could be rolled up, as opposed to the then-common sheets, making it possible to take images more rapidly than ever before (Étienne-Jules Marey's prototypical camera had never been able to take more than forty photographs at a time).

Dickson ordered some of Eastman Kodak's film, experimented for a few months, and devised a new camera, the Kinetograph, that drew the roll of film across the lens by using toothed-sprocket wheels that grabbed the perforated edges along both sides of the film frame. The Kinetograph was the first motion-picture camera to utilize the soon-to-be standard, and by now familiar-looking, perforated rolls of 35mm film. Once the camera was in working order, Dickson and the crew began work on an exhibition device that came to be known as the Kinetoscope, a wooden box that contained a 50-foot loop of film that could be rolled by an electric motor. Viewers could put a nickel in a slot (right from the first, the devices were designed to make money), bend over and peer into a hole to see about thirty seconds of film.

In 1889, Edison went off to preside over his exhibition at the Paris Expo. When he returned, Dickson proudly directed him to look into a box, where Edison saw a moving picture of Dickson, allegedly synchronized with a phonograph recording of Dickson welcoming him back from his trip. By most accounts Edison was not particularly impressed, but work continued, and in 1891 he exhibited the work-in-progress to a typically astonished *Chicago Daily Tribune* reporter, whose subsequent headline read:

LIGHT AND SOUND UNITED: EDISON OUTDOES HIMSELF WITH THE KINETOGRAPH.

"From the laboratory of the wizard in Menlo Park there is coming an invention which out-Edisons Edison," he wrote. "With it the opera can be carried into the parlor … the new wonder will be called the 'kinetograph,' a strange-sounding title to the ear today, but destined perhaps soon to be as familiar as locomotive or telephone, both strange words in their infancy." He spoke of Edison as "the greatest inventor of the day," and used the terms "wizard" and "genius" freely.[12] (The reporter apparently got his terms mixed up: the Kinetoscope was the name given to the machine that exhibited the movies, while the Kinetograph, also less commonly known as the Kinograph, was the name given to Edison's motion-picture camera.)

The reporter described Edison's prototype as a wooden box with a hole in the top the size of a silver dollar, through which he saw a negative image of a man bowing and raising his hat. Like other reporters of the day, the *Daily Tribune* staffer immediately realized that this new device could be used to capture prizefights. When talking about the new medium, nearly every reporter of the day pondered that the device would soon record sermons, operas, and boxing matches. No one seemed to speculate that fictional narratives could also one day be produced.

Though most of the credit really belonged to Dickson, Edison proudly talked up the wonders of the new device. "I wrote an article some years ago hinting at this very invention," he said. "The papers made fun of me — said I had better stop talking. This made me mad, and I determined to carry the conception to a successful issue ... this I have done. ... Do I expect to make money out of it? Well, I have never thought of that."[13]

Here was Edison as a consummate, practiced performer, projecting the image of a rugged American individualist, determined to show the people in high places what this scrappy young fellow could do, without even caring about money. Though he did privately doubt that motion pictures would ever be a big moneymaker, and even referred to them in papers as "one of my new novelties," he instinctively grasped that being the man who made pictures move and talk would be good for his image, not to mention his bankbook, and spoke of the movies far more excitedly in public than he seems to have done in private. The model shown in 1891 was a simple prototype, but improvements were being made.

"I intend," he said, "to have it ready and in practical working shape for the Chicago Exposition."[14]

CHAPTER TWO

The Columbian Exposition

E ven as the *Exposition Universelle* was under way in Paris, Americans were making plans to stage a similar extravaganza in the United States. America was still a new country in those days. The Constitution was barely a century old. For much of its history, America had been seen as a weird, experimental little nation. Although some progressives overseas spoke of it as a veritable wonderland that had corrected the problems of the Old World, far more people saw it as a nation of disgusting slobs and of people with no sense of their place in the world. That the cries of freedom were coming from a land whose economy had once been (and to an extent still was) based on slavery was an irony that escaped hardly anyone. Charles Dickens had imagined America as the Promised Land but, when he sailed there as a young man, he found a dirty, grimy land full of shysters, hucksters, savages, thieves, con artists, and people who lived in poverty and misery, a country in which the national pastime seemed to be spitting. The experience shook him so badly that some commentators feel that he never really recovered his former optimism.

As the Civil War raged, the popular perception of America began to shift from that of a potentially promising experiment to that of an experiment that had failed. Other people felt differently. As the wilderness was

Exposition grounds, World's Columbian Exposition, Chicago. (Photo courtesy of the Library of Congress)

tamed and the age of invention brought untold progress, some commentators thought that this vast land could emerge as one of the most powerful nations in the world. Chicago's 1893 *Columbian Exposition* would be the way that America introduced the twentieth century, and itself, to the world.

Chicago was barely a generation old, but no city had ever grown so fast or so high in such a short span of time. Tens of thousands of years of human civilization had been, in the past, required to produce a single city with a population of more than a million people, but by 1890 Chicago had gone from a few thousand inhabitants to more than a million in fewer than fifty years. Even the devastating fire of 1871 had failed to halt the progress. Indeed, after the city had burned to the ground, many Chicagoans seemed determined to roll up their sleeves and make their city better than ever. Skyscrapers throughout the city were soon stretching more than two or three hundred feet towards the sky; not so high as the Eiffel Tower, but a sight to behold.

Chicago's reputation around the country was still mainly that of a city of crime, corruption, and prostitution, but there was no denying the progress there. Where only decades before there had been little more than the "mudhole of the prairie," a frontier town on the edge of an unimaginable wilderness, there now stood a huge, elegant city, with elevated trains zipping citizens and tourists from the downtown area to the *Exposition's* sparkling fairgrounds. Only in America could a city barely more than twenty years old have been the home of the convention that nominated Abraham Lincoln for president. Though graft and corruption surely played their role in Congress's decision to choose Chicago as the site of the *World's Columbian Exposition*, there was also no denying that the city was a quintessential example of the can-do American spirit.

It is difficult today to impress upon people just how big the *Columbian Exposition* was. It covered more than twice the space of the *Exposition Universelle*. More than two hundred gleaming white buildings were specially constructed, several of which were then among the largest buildings in the world. There were some 27 million paid admissions to the fair between May and October of 1893, roughly the equivalent of half the population of the United States at the time.

To imagine the impact of the fair on the people who passed through the gates, consider how many of the attendees came from small farming communities. Many of them had never seen a building larger than a two-story barn, and may have never been higher off the ground than the time they climbed up a haystack. Of course, such attendees would never have seen a light bulb before, and now they were confronted with a vast city-

Entering Midway Plaisance to the World's Fair Grounds, Chicago. (Photo courtesy of the Library of Congress)

within-a-city of gleaming white buildings, every one of which was covered in brilliant electric lights. Amazingly, these lights made the fairgrounds seem just as bright at night as they were during the day.

Electricity, indeed, would be the star attraction of the fair, pointing the way to a new century in which electricity would bring previously unimagined change and progress to every aspect of daily life. Long before the fair even opened, the *New York Advertiser* stated that the electrical exhibits alone would make a trip to Chicago worthwhile.

One of the major innovations of the fair was the building of a "Midway," a section of the fair for the "amusements" that would be separate from the halls where the great thinkers of the day would hold forth and where different countries would show off their achievements in technology, agriculture, manufacturing, and the fine arts. On the Midway, you could ride the massive Ferris Wheel, watch "Little Egypt" (the stage name of belly dancer Farida Mazar Spyropoulos) dance the "hootchie coo," tour a Bedouin encampment, or attend what amounted to the first movie theater in history — though hardly anyone noticed this theater at the time.

Situated in an inconvenient location at the end of the Midway, Eadweard Muybridge was granted a concession for his "Zoopraxigraphical Hall." By this time, Muybridge had developed a device he called the "Zoopraxiscope," a sort of primitive movie projector. Muybridge had printed a series of images onto the edges of glass discs that would rotate inside his machine; the images, only line drawings, would be projected onto a canvas screen by a light. As the glass discs rotated inside of the Zoopraxiscope, the images on the screen appeared to move. Muybridge's Hall probably deserves to be called the first commercial movie theater in the world.

Muybridge, however, utterly failed to realize the potential of what he had created. Though he was placed on the Midway, where he would give lectures about the Zoopraxiscope, his focus was strictly on the "science" of what he was doing. Given the choice between watching Little Egypt dance the hootchie coo and seeing Professor Muybridge present a lecture on animal locomotion, nearly everyone went with Little Egypt. If projection had developed to the point where he could have shown his images of the naked woman jumping up and down on one foot as moving pictures, one suspects the lectures would have been better attended. As it was, the Zoopraxigraphical Hall was a total flop. The nearby "Street in Cairo" exhibit made more money than Muybridge's Hall by a margin of more than a thousand to one.[1]

Midway Plaisance, home of Eadweard Muybridge's 'Zoopraxigraphical Hall', the world's first movie theater. (Photo courtesy of the Library of Congress)

Elsewhere at the fair was a slot machine known as the "Tachyscope." Invented by Otto Anschutz of Germany, it was similar to the Zoopraxiscope in that it created the illusion of a moving picture by displaying images on a spinning disk. The images were faintly lit and, as with Edison's Kinetoscope concept, visible to only one or two people at a time through a window in the machine, which was mounted on the wall. The Tachyscopes were not much more advanced than Muybridge's Zoopraxiscope, and even though they could not be shown to a whole crowd at once, they still outdrew Muybridge fifteen to one.[2] One thing, however, was missing from the fair: the planned pavilion of twenty-five Kinetoscopes.

Throughout 1891, 1892, and 1893, Thomas Edison and W.K.L. Dickson had worked hard to perfect their machine, and a single, mostly working prototype was completed and used for a demonstration in Brooklyn in May 1893. Edison's methods of managing his lab, however, were taking their toll. Dickson had suffered a nervous breakdown earlier in the year, and he had taken a leave of absence to recuperate. Another employee was given a contract in late June to create twenty-five Kinetoscopes for the fair based on the prototype; unfortunately, it was rumored that this employee found it difficult to stay sober. The Kinetoscopes would ultimately not be ready in time for a grand public unveiling at the fair.[3]

The Chicago writer Herma Clark wrote a column in the *Daily Tribune* from 1929 to 1959 titled "When Chicago was Young." It consisted of fictional letters written by one Martha Freeman Esmond to her childhood friend, Julia Boyd, although many of these letters were merely thinly disguised accounts of real encounters Clark had observed while working as a secretary to a socially prominent Chicago family in the late nineteenth century. In a letter dated August 24, 1893, "Esmond" wrote to "Boyd," telling her of the time she had spent with her grandson in Chicago that summer. She, her husband, Will, and grandson, Esmond, had visited (though "stalked" may be a better term) Edison at his hotel, saying that young Esmond "desired the privilege of gazing at him for a few minutes." Edison greeted them kindly and had a pleasant chat with the three of them. Will asked if he had "any more wonders like the phonograph," and Edison replied that he was working on a "kinograph," a method of producing moving photographs. "I can't quite understand how it's done," Martha wrote, "nor what good it will be when perfect ... [it] seems to me rather useless ... but Will and Esmond had caught some of the inventor's enthusiasm and were full of excitement over it ... Mr. Edison said it is very hard to get the grimaces of a man's face, or the working of a man's hands playing the piano, but the method has really been perfected. He was anxious to have the invention exhibited at the fair, but it was not ready for that."[4]

Indeed, the fair was, for Edison, something of a flop. Although electricity was the star of the show, it was not Edison who was providing it. He had bid fiercely for the contract, but was outbid in the end by Westinghouse and Tesla, whose alternating current was proving to be far superior to Edison's direct-current system.

In a relentless quest to squash alternating-current electricity, which his rivals supplied in competition with his own direct current, Edison had spent years doing everything he could to encourage rumors that "AC electricity" was terribly dangerous. He made speeches and published lengthy pamphlets telling stories about people whom AC had killed, and he had even arranged to provide a demonstration of his theories. In one of the more despicable marketing stunts in history, Edison arranged for his rivals' alternating-current electricity to be used to execute a convicted murderer. (Even ten years after the fair, when vast improvements had been made at capturing and projecting moving images, Edison would notoriously make a film depicting an elephant being electrocuted by AC.) At the World's Fair, Nikola Tesla, now dubbed the "Wizard of Physics," demonstrated how safe his electricity actually was by using himself as a conductor: sparks and bolts of lightning were shot right through his body.

By this time, however, Edison had won the publicity war: around the country, people thought of Edison when they saw an electric light of any sort. Though Westinghouse's logo was the one prominently displayed in the electrical building, it was Edison who the public wished to credit, and he was only too happy to let them, even though he had personally seen to it that none of his light bulbs were used with Tesla's system. When the World's Fair also emerged as the place where the public first saw and paid for moving images, they linked Edison's name to that too. (There are many references in works of historical non-fiction to the Kinetoscopes actually being present at the fair, including in Erik Larson's *The Devil in the White City*, which describes the notorious serial-killer H.H. Holmes admiring movies on Edison's machines.[5] These references, however, are most likely based only on the advance publicity that insisted that the Kinetoscopes would be there.) Edison would be careful to ensure that people continued to link his name to motion pictures for the next twenty-five years as well.

Most everyone involved in the *Columbian Exposition*, including Edison, in his grand quest to present himself as a role model, would have said that the true purpose of the World's Fair was not to show off innovations but to inspire the fair-goers to create, to invent, and to dream. Sure enough, over the course of the fair, one by one, many of the men who would create the American motion-picture industry filed through the gates, and were inspired — indeed profoundly changed — by what they saw.

George Spoor, who would co-found the Essanay Film Manufacturing Company, perhaps the most enduring of the Chicago studios, would later claim he had first seen moving pictures on the Tachyscope machine at the World's Fair. He would go on to team up with suburban Chicagoan Edward Amet to become a pioneer in the film exhibition business in the 1890s before starting his famous Chicago studio with Gilbert M. Anderson in 1907.

The original automobile, the steam-powered "horseless carriage," was introduced at the fair and would eventually be purchased by Colonel William Selig with the money he made from the Selig Polyscope Company, whose studio was on the Northwest Side of Chicago. The Colonel would use the carriage as a prop for chimpanzees in his popular animal pictures.

He would also use the replicas of Christopher Columbus's ships that had been built for the fair in a 1912 movie, *The Coming of Columbus*, which was among the first feature-length motion pictures. The film would earn him a medal from Pope Pius X, despite the fact that Selig was not even a Catholic. After building a small empire in Chicago, the Colonel would also eventually open the first movie studio in southern California.

L. Frank Baum, a writer, oil salesman, and photographer, was dazzled by the "White City" built on the fairgrounds, and it would reportedly inspire him to create the gleaming "Emerald City" in the book that made him famous: *The Wonderful Wizard of Oz* (originally published in Chicago in 1900). Fifteen years after the fair, Baum would also use the Selig Polyscope studio in Chicago to film the first of the *Wizard of Oz* movies.

Chicagoan Burton Holmes (no relation to H.H. Holmes), an explorer and photographer who gave wildly popular illustrated lectures on his world travels and is credited with coining the term "travelogue," visited the Midway and was inspired to begin incorporating motion pictures into his appearances. He eventually became an important documentary film-maker himself. In an illustrated lecture at Chicago's Central Music Hall in 1897, Holmes told of a recent trip to a primitive and remote area in the mountains of Algeria. Holmes said he had been startled there one day when he found himself addressed in "good Chicago slang." "Ah, there!" a voice called out to him. "Seems to me I saw you on the Midway?" Incredibly, the voice belonged to a "fakir" who had driven "a thriving business in the shadow of the Ferris wheel."[6]

Across the street from the fairgrounds, "Buffalo Bill" Cody had rented an adjacent park to stage his famous Wild West Show. "Buffalo Bill" was hardly an old frontiersman himself (though he claimed to have been injured countless times fighting Indians, his wife insisted he was mak-ing up nearly all of these stories), but many performers in his show were authentic. The show represented a borderline between the days when the Old West was still real and the days when it would exist only in myths put forth by the genre of film that would dominate the industry for much of the twentieth century. Thomas Edison and his crew may have had the popularity of the Wild West Show in mind a decade later when they made *The Great Train Robbery*, the first significant "western" movie.

Meanwhile, back at the lab, Edison's team was beginning to film subjects for their eventual commercial launch of the Kinetoscope. The popularity of strongman Eugen Sandow at the World's Fair made the bodybuilder an obvious choice for a motion-picture subject, and a film was made of him flexing his muscles; he would soon be a prototypical movie star, helping to propel the popularity of the Kinetoscope across the sea, where photographer Claude-Antoine Lumière would see it in Paris and challenge his sons, Auguste and Louis, to make a better machine.

All of these innovations would come together, be broken apart, and come together and break apart again. For a brief period when movies were in their infancy, on the borderline between novelties and works of art, Chicago would be the film capital of the world. Building up the industry in a place like Chicago, rather than the East Coast, was something of a necessity: the early American film pioneers had to stay far away enough from New York and New Jersey to stay under Thomas Edison's radar.

CHAPTER THREE

The Dawn of Exhibition

The origins of commercial film exhibition as we now know it can be traced to April 1894, when the first of Edison's Kinetoscope "parlors" opened in New York City, exhibiting the devices that had originally been planned for Chicago and the *Columbian Exposition*. A month later, more parlors sprang up in other cities, including Chicago, Atlantic City and San Francisco. An advertisement in the *Chicago Daily Tribune*, probably the first real "movie ad" to appear in a local paper, simply stated:

THE KINETOSCOPE.
EDISON'S LATEST MARVEL
Out at Last and on Exhibition at
148 STATE-ST.[1]

One has to love that "at last," a reference to the device having been long-hyped in the Chicago press, tinged with, perhaps, a hint of ruefulness over the missed opportunity of having it premiere at the World's Fair.

Chicago had officially become America's "second city" in 1890 when census records showed its population had surpassed a million residents for the first time and it had thus overtaken Philadelphia. This growth was in part due to Chicago's annexation of surrounding townships although the city's most densely populated neighborhood remained the downtown business district known as "the Loop," an area bounded today by Adams Avenue, Lake Street, Wabash Avenue and Wells Street. It made sense that this teeming neighborhood would host Chicago's first Kinetoscope parlor – although determining its exact location on State Street is somewhat problematic.* Numerous sources place it in Burnham and Root's Masonic Temple at the corner of State and Randolph Streets (the site of the Joffrey Tower today), though 148 State Street would actually be at the northwest corner of State and Erie Streets, several blocks north, prior to the 1909 re-numbering of the city; the 1905 Sanborn Fire Insurance Maps clearly mark 148 at this location. The Masonic Temple is listed on those maps at 57–63 South State Street.

An 1894 edition of the *Western Electrician* magazine states that ten Kinetoscopes were at 148 N. State Street, and explained that when "46 distinct views" pass by per second (though the projection was probably closer to sixteen frames per second), "the eye is unable to retain separate impressions ... and the pictures blend together, giving life-like motion to the figures and objects portrayed." Among the films being displayed, according to the magazine, were those involving a barbershop, a blacksmith's forge, and wrestlers, but one movie was particularly singled out: "The best is a representation of a cock fight, which is very spirited."[2]

Though a building at 148 N. State Street in contemporary numbering would be at the corner of State and Randolph (albeit across the street from the Masonic Building site, near where the Gene Siskel Film Center stands today), none of the early newspaper references or ads that use the address "148 N. State" make any mention of the Masonic building, which was then a notable landmark, towering more than twenty stories high. More likely, the first Kinetoscope parlor stood in a storefront on the grounds where 664 N. State Street is today.

Furthering the confusion is a 1916 *Motion Picture World* article stating that the first Chicago parlor was in the Ashland Block building located at the northeast corner of Clark and Randolph Streets "early in 1894."[3] This Kinetoscope parlor, however, seems to have opened in December of 1894, by which time there was already another parlor on State Street and yet another on Wabash Avenue.

---

* The street numbering at the time does not correspond to the grid used today; street numbers then were loosely based on a location's proximity to the Chicago River.

Wherever on State Street it stood, the first parlor predictably made a fortune, but showing movies to one person at a time had obvious limitations, and Edison's movies were generally mere "proof of concept" devices that simply showed that pictures could indeed move. These early novelty movies, what film historian Tom Gunning has usefully dubbed the "cinema of attractions," were all less than a minute long, the length of an average roll of film at the time, and they typically consisted of a single, unedited shot. Edison's cinematographers would point their Kinetograph cameras at a given subject and crank the cameras by hand until the film simply ran out. The mostly non-narrative movies that resulted consisted of whatever was happening in front of the cameras during the thirty-odd seconds it took to do this.

Thomas Edison was a great scientist and a good businessman, but he was neither a visual artist nor an entertainer. He was justifiably proud of the Kinetoscope, but he also referred to it in interviews as a "mere toy of no commercial value."[4] This attitude of condescension is arguably reflected in the films themselves, which show a marked lack of rigor on the part of the filmmakers. The earliest movies of the Edison Manufacturing Company typically saw their subjects placed in front of a simple black backdrop with the absolute minimum of sets and props necessary to convey the idea of a given scene.

Edison's early films are interesting to watch for historical reasons, perhaps most of all because of what they illustrate about what early filmmakers thought the first motion-picture audiences wanted to see: then, as now, the movies played to the audience's appetite for sex and violence. Among the popular early subjects of Edison's films were Sandow the strongman flexing his muscles while wearing only a loincloth, a "comical" boxing match, theatrical actors John C. Rice and May Irwin kissing (the first ever screen kiss) and the aforementioned film of two men pretending to gamble while observing a real cock fight.

Then there is the matter of 1897's *Seminary Girls*, a movie about schoolgirls in nightgowns hitting one another with pillows. A description from a motion-picture catalog of the period indicates that the film's distributors were fully aware of its titillating appeal: "A most amusing and life-like scene, in which a number of young ladies clad in their night robes, are seen engaged in a midnight frolic; starting in smoking cigarettes, drinking tonic and ending in a pillow fight. They are suddenly interrupted by the Principal appearing on the scene (with candle in hand) when a general stampede occurs, one girl being very conspicuous in her frantic efforts to

Seminary Girls, 1897. Directed by James H. White.

get under the bed, and thus escape the wrath of the school marm, but the scene ends in the young lady being caught, pulled from under the bed and punished."[5] It looks innocent by today's standards, but yes, it *is* still a movie about Catholic schoolgirls gone wild.

Still, while he has never been anyone's idea of an *auteur*, nobody in 1894 understood the technological side of filmmaking better than Edison. *Seminary Girls*, like the majority of the films produced by the Edison Manufacturing Company, was made in the East Orange, New Jersey studio known as the "Black Maria" (pronounced Ma-RYE-uh), a building with a retractable roof that was also cleverly designed to rotate on a massive turntable. This innovation enabled Edison's filmmakers to move the entire studio in order to get the most sunlight possible at any time of the day in an age when film stock was notoriously insensitive to light. Also impressive at this time was Edison's understanding of the vital importance that marrying image and sound would eventually hold for the future of the motion-picture medium — and the problems that imperfect synchronization between the two could potentially pose.

An 1894 *Chicago Daily Tribune* article states: "Mr. Edison says his purpose is to combine the phonograph and Kinetoscope so that the ear and eye shall both be entertained. This he could easily do with present appliances were it not for the difficulty of making the phonograph and kinetoscope jibe exactly in point of time. Mr. Edison will not take any chances of being made ridiculous by a combination of kinetoscope and phonograph which may get out of harmony. He hopes to photograph the hands of an expert pianist, and have the phonograph so accurately adjusted to the kinetoscope that when the pictured fingers touch the pictured keys the phonograph will give forth the proper notes at the exact instant. Until he has accomplished this he does not regard his work in this direction as done."[6]

Thomas Edison's ingenuity and foresight into methods of motion-picture production, however, did not also extend to their *exhibition*. Exhibitors were clamoring for a way to show the movies to more than one person at a time. The financial benefit of being able to show one film to many people, rather than to a single viewer, was obvious. Edison, however, resisted. The Kinetoscopes had become surefire moneymakers, and he believed that implementing a system of large-scale projection would render his profitable machines obsolete.

Around the world, though, innovations were happening in spite of him. As had happened with alternating current, Edison's insistence on sticking to his original concept for as long as it could make money would allow others the chance to leave him in the dust. On the other side of the Atlantic, Claude-Antoine Lumière, the recently retired owner of a photographic firm, returned from a trip to Paris to his hometown of Lyons. Claude-Antoine told his inventor sons, Auguste and Louis, of a wondrous new invention that he had seen: the Kinetoscope. As impressed as he was, he urged them to improve on Edison's machine. "You can do better," he said. "Try to get that image out of the box."[7]

Very soon, they did. Film historians often cite December 26, 1895, when the Lumière brothers gave the first public presentation, in Paris, of their invention, the "Cinematographe" — a combination movie camera, printer and projector — as the true "birth" of the movies. This presentation is believed to be the first time 35mm film projection occurred before a paying public, as opposed to the movies that had previously been seen only on peep-show machines like the Kinetoscope or as Muybridge-style slide shows. (The German inventor Max Skladanowsky did publicly premiere a motion-picture projector on November 1, 1895, but his machine alternated between projecting two different strips of 54mm film. It was a more cumbersome and less effective device than the Cinematographe and therefore exerted no real influence on the developing cinema.)

Soon, the Lumière brothers were expanding their operations. What is most likely the first motion picture ever shot in Chicago, the still extant *Chicago Police Parade* (*Chicago défilé de policemen*), was made only months after the Lumières' first Cinematographe demonstration, and at the behest of the brothers themselves.

Meanwhile, projectors were also being developed in the United States. In contrast to Europe, where the movies were predictably "invented" in the cultural capital of Paris, the most important early experiments with motion-picture projection in America took place not in New York or Los Angeles (which was then still a sleepy little town), but deep in the heart of the Midwest: Edward Amet of the Chicago suburb of Waukegan built the "Magniscope," an early prototype for the 35mm projector. If Amet's (and George Spoor's) later claims can be trusted, their earliest experiments with projecting 35mm movies in the suburbs of Chicago occurred in 1894 and would have predated the Lumière brothers' similar, and far more famous, exhibition in Paris by a full year.

Having been fascinated by Anschutz's Tachyscope at the World's Fair, George Spoor, then a newspaper vendor, made a journey to downtown Chicago to see Edison's Kinetoscope for himself. In an amusing anecdote that may be apocryphal, Spoor claimed that while he was leaning over and peering into the slot to watch the moving pictures of the kiss, the strongman, and the cock fight, someone picked his pocket. In his anger and frustration, it occurred to him that there had to be a better, safer way to exhibit motion pictures. If they were projected onto a large screen, not only would spectators be left in a less vulnerable position than they were while looking into a hole and turning a crank, but the films could be exhibited to many people at once, not just one at a time.

All of these rapid advances in film production and projection technology were proving a major headache for Thomas Edison, whose scientific and business interests were already scattered far and wide. In April 1895, W.K.L. Dickson, Edison's employee who had done most of the work inventing the Kinetoscope, and actually directed most of the early "Edison films," left his boss to invent a projector of his own and start the successful American Mutoscope Company (which later became the American Mutoscope and Biograph Company, and subsequently the Biograph Company). American Mutoscope and Biograph would remain a chief rival of Edison Manufacturing for more than a decade, producing many significant early films, including the earliest directorial efforts of D.W. Griffith. Edison never forgave Dickson for his defection.

As popular as the Kinetoscope and similar peep-show machines had been, large-scale projection would be another matter entirely, a major technological breakthrough and a revelation to the first astonished moviegoers. In New York City, people were more than happy to line up around the block to see moving images that were "bigger than life" being hurled onto giant canvas screens. Edison's primitive Black Maria shorts of Eugen Sandow posing and his employee Fred Ott sneezing from 1894 and 1895 no longer seemed nearly as impressive. Big screens demanded bigger, more eye-filling images.

While Edison stalled on inventing his own projector, he saw the Lumière brothers' Cinematographe take the world by storm. In 1897, Edison eventually caved; licensing his name to, and taking the credit for, the "Phantoscope," a projector that had been co-invented by Charles Jenkins and Thomas Armat but was promptly renamed "Edison's Vitascope" after Edison bought the patent. Having failed to secure an international patent on the Kinetoscope, Edison vowed never to make the same mistake again and patented "his" new device, ostensibly forcing anyone who wanted to show motion pictures projected onto a screen to pay him a royalty.

Since everyone thought of Edison as the father of movies anyway, the public had no objection. Indeed, most people did not believe that projected movies had truly arrived until Edison's device hit the market. Many exhibitors had even held off on buying a projector until an official Edison model appeared.

Before motion-picture projection had ever occurred in Chicago proper (Edward Amet's experiments had all taken place in the suburbs), the *Chicago Daily Tribune* wrote with breathless excitement about the coming phenomenon: "Electrical experts have arrived from Edison's New Jersey establishment to set up and prepare for operation beginning July 5th, the Wizard's latest and wonderful invention, the Vitascope, the exhibition of which has created a sensation in the East. By the aid of this scientific apparatus entire scenes from life are reproduced in complete realism, every animate movement being thrown with distinctness on a huge screen occupying the stage space. An idea of the magnitude of the work is given in the description of the latest view shown in Boston, a 10-mile panoramic view of Niagara Falls from a moving train, moving at the rate of 50 miles per hour, color and life being represented with perfect exactitude."[8]

The first film review to appear in a Chicago newspaper, in the July 7th, 1896 edition of the *Daily Tribune*, covered movies presented via "Edison's" Vitascope projection system only two days after the machine was first unveiled. Under the heading "Amusements," the following item appeared alongside reviews of stage plays, operas, assorted vaudeville shows and even carnival-style freak shows (e.g., the young man from San Francisco whose hands "span 13 inches across"!):

Edison's wonderful vitascope is deservedly drawing enthusiastic audiences at Hopkins' Theater. It is a decidedly novel and popular innovation. The scenes thrown upon the canvas include the serpentine dance of Annabelle and her famous wink, a sensational rescue by firemen, the march in the first act of a 'Milk White Flag,' and a vivid reproduction of the ludicrous kissing scene between May Irwin and John C. Rice in 'The Widow Jones.'[9]

Meanwhile, the possibility of motion pictures achieving instantaneous, widespread distribution meant that the world was rapidly becoming a smaller place. The popularity and financial success of the Cinematographe led the Lumière brothers to dispatch cameramen all over the world so that movie audiences could see, for the first time ever, real-time moving images of how people from different countries and cultures lived, worked, and played.

Made in September 1896, the aptly titled *Chicago Police Parade* (Lumière catalog No. 336) is an approximately 45-second-long "actuality" (the term "documentary" did not yet exist) of 144 Chicago police officers walking down a wide street and past a stationary camera. The officers are formally dressed and carrying billy-clubs. Amusingly, it appears that all but approximately three of the officers are sporting large mustaches. Bringing up the rear of the parade is a horse-drawn carriage.

As with other Lumière productions of the period, including their masterpiece *L'arrivée d'un train à La Ciotat* (*Arrival of a Train at La Ciotat*), the camera is positioned at an oblique angle so that the policemen appear to walk "diagonally" from the rear of the frame to the front. This perspective puts greater emphasis on the depth of field of the image, with a clear demarcation of background, middle ground, and foreground, and also serves as a good example of just how well composed the Lumière brothers' first films actually were, especially in contrast to the relatively flat-looking films being produced concurrently by Edison.

Chicago Police Parade, 1896. Directed by Alexandre Promio.

Chicago Police Parade was not, however, made by either of the brothers themselves but was instead created by one of their favorite cinematographers, a Frenchman of Italian descent named Alexandre Promio, whom the *Chicago Post* described in 1896 as having "the reputation of being the greatest scientific photographer in all Europe."[10] That same year Promio would become a major footnote in motion-picture history by effectively inventing camera movement when he took his Cinematographe to Venice and placed it on board of a gondola.

The popularity of the movies, and the attendant good publicity they could generate, was not lost on Chicago's city hall, which had readily agreed to Promio's request to hold a fake police parade by Lake Michigan. A notice in the *Daily Tribune* in October of 1896 covered the production of *Chicago Police Parade*: "M. Promio induced Assistant Chief Ross to marshal 600 policemen on the lake front, and while they were going through a drill the Frenchman took some 6,000 or 8,000 photographs of them. He also took two or three street scenes, including the Ferris Wheel. The photographs will be sent to Paris, where they will be prepared for the cinematographe and in a few weeks will be seen in Chicago."

Unfortunately, the additional footage shot by Promio in Chicago, tantalizingly referred to in the *Daily Tribune* article, no longer seems to exist, assuming that prints were ever made in the first place. (Later ads for Cinematographe exhibitions include references to *Police Parade*, one of which, dating from 1897, also refers to a movie intriguingly titled *Life on State Street*, though this may have been another title for a recent Edison film[11]). Elsewhere in the same article, the *Daily Tribune* staffer covering the production clearly had a field day interviewing one "M. Tett," a Lumière representative who attempted to explain how exactly the Cinematographe operated. Tett's explanation was hilariously rendered with his French-accented words spelled out phonetically. "Eeet ees simple as a baby," Tett is quoted as saying. "I put ze peectures in so, and turn ze crank so and you see, ah, wonderful, b-e-a-utiful things on ze big curtain in ze front. That is all. I cannot explain him better." The *Daily Tribune* staffer helpfully points out that this analogy is "hardly fair," since "nobody ever fully understood the mental and physical makeup of a baby while the Cinematographe is easily described."[12]

The most significant extant film to be made in Chicago after the Lumière brothers' *Chicago Police Parade* is probably the Edison Manufacturing Company's *Corner Madison and State Streets, Chicago*. Made only one year after the Lumières' pioneering effort, the Edison film, copyrighted in July

1897, is a 50-foot long, one-shot actuality that depicts exactly what the title states. Like most of "Edison's movies," however, the inventor's favorite director/cinematographer team of James H. White and William Heise actually made *Corner Madison and State Streets, Chicago*. Although White and Heise had both been prolific in the motion-picture business since the pre-projection days of 1890, it does not appear that their technique had much improved in the intervening seven years. When viewed alongside *Chicago Police Parade*, with its incredible use of depth of field and impeccably composed diagonal lines, *Corner Madison and State Streets, Chicago* offers an object lesson in the difference between Thomas Edison and the Lumière brothers (i.e., the difference between approaching movies as a business versus approaching them as an art).

Corner Madison and State Streets, Chicago shows a jumbled mass of people, horses, and trolley cars in the heart of Chicago's Loop as they hurriedly move in every conceivable direction at the same time. Some of the subjects are carrying large placards that advertise "BOATING" and "ELECTRIC POOL." Just as *Chicago Police Parade* is of interest because it proves that 99% of all Chicago police officers had mustaches in the late nineteenth century, so too is *Corner Madison and State Streets, Chicago* of interest because it proves that 100% of all Chicago civilians, including women, wore hats during this same era (and in the middle of summer no less). In terms of visual style, it appears that White and Heise have taken little care with the composition of the image, which looks particularly chaotic when compared to the clean lines and artful compositions associated with the Lumières.

The complete description of *Corner Madison and State Streets, Chicago* from the official Edison Films catalog emphasizes the documentary value of showing the downtown area of this thriving metropolis: "The busiest corner in Chicago. Cable cars and street traffic of all descriptions. Hundreds of shoppers. Fine perspective view looking north toward the Masonic Temple. 50 feet. $7.50."[13] (Andrew Erish, in his excellent biography, *Col. William N. Selig: The Man Who Invented Hollywood*, claims that *Corner Madison and State Streets, Chicago* was a William Selig film that Edison pirated and copyrighted as his own. Most other sources, however, cite it as an authentic Edison movie. Edison copyrighted *Corner Madison*

---

* This exchange took place in England in 1909, a good indication of how widespread and for how long the belief was held that motion pictures were no more than a flash-in-the-pan novelty.

and *State Streets, Chicago* along with several other Chicago-shot films on July 31, 1897: *Sheep Run, Chicago Stockyards, Armour's Electric Trolley, Cattle Driven to Slaughter,* etc. Selig Polyscope copyrighted a similarly titled movie, *State and Madison Sts., Chicago,* in 1903.)

Although it was around this time that Colonel William Selig explicitly copied the Lumières' Cinematographe design in order to get into the motion-picture business for himself, he seemed to be almost alone in understanding the far-reaching possibilities of the new medium. Founded in 1896, the Selig Polyscope Company would be the first movie studio in Chicago and, eventually, the largest one in the country. When asked by a journalist if he thought that the motion picture had "come to stay," Selig responded with unbridled enthusiasm. "Come to stay!" he exclaimed. "Why it has only just started. I believe that it will become a permanent feature in the amusements of the public."*14 Unlike Edison and even the Lumières, who notoriously claimed that the cinema was an invention "without a future," Colonel Selig was gambling big on the movies. It was a gamble that would soon pay off: in a few years' time, he would be referred to as "the man who invented Hollywood."

Although the projection of moving images had first occurred with Muybridge and Anschutz at the *Columbian Exhibition* — and had not been particularly successful on the commercial front — in the ensuing years using moving pictures for entertainment had proven to be increasingly profitable. Combining the notion of narrative storytelling with motion-picture projection would soon turn the movies into a giant of mass media that would help to define the next century and beyond.

If this kind of future was lost on Edison and the Lumières completely, William Selig and his future rival George Spoor seemed to have grasped it almost instinctively. Setting up shop in Chicago, a city large enough and with enough ambition that it could handle a new industry and provide all of the opportunities and advantages necessary for inventions, innovations, and, of course, paying audiences for products, both men then went to work.

PART TWO

CHICAGO RISING

'Colonel' William N. Selig, circa 1914. (Photo courtesy of the Margaret Herrick Library, Academy of Motion Picture Arts and Sciences)

Colonel William Selig

When one says the 'Selig Polyscope Company' one really means
W.N. Selig himself, who is the presiding genius and leading
spirit of the establishment. His eye is on every detail of the
business at all times.

— Eugene Dengler, *Motography*[1]

William Nicholas Selig (pronounced SEE-lig) was one of the most
successful, and colorful, motion-picture pioneers of the 1890s and
early 1900s. Selig was a native Chicagoan and traveling magician who
conferred the title "Colonel" upon himself while touring the minstrel-
show circuit. He was a large man with a bushy mustache and a friendly,
ingratiating demeanor; an adjective used to describe the Colonel on more
than one occasion was "Falstaffian."[2] In 1895, the thirty-year-old Selig was
in Dallas, working as a phony "medium" in a stage show advertised as "Prof
Selig and his Company of Mediums," demonstrating table-rapping, slate
wiring, table-floating, and other séance tricks, promising "Spirit Power in
Full Gaslight."

To many believers, the phenomenon of mediums talking to the dead, a spectacle that emerged around the same time as the early motion-picture experiments of Eadweard Muybridge and Étienne-Jules Marey, was the wonder of the modern age. It was while in Dallas that Selig first saw a *true* wonder of the age: Edison's Kinetoscope.

Selig soon became obsessed with motion pictures and with finding his own way to create and exhibit them (and, hence, get around Edison's patents). Selig returned to Chicago, where he created, in collaboration with machinist Andrew Schustek, his own camera and projector based on the design of the Lumières' Cinematographe. Selig named his camera the "Selig Standard Camera" and his projector the "Selig Polyscope." In April 1897, operating out of a rented loft at 43 Peck Court (now East 8th Street between State Street and Wabash Avenue) in Chicago's brothel-strewn "tenderloin district," Selig founded the first Chicago studio, and indeed one of the first such motion-picture studios in the world: the Mutoscope and Film Company, which became the W.N. Selig Company, before permanently changing its name to the Selig Polyscope Company.*

The first Selig production (and what is likely the first *narrative* film shot in Chicago), *The Tramp and the Dog*, now lost, was a "backyard comedy" shot in a residential neighborhood on the far North Side of the city known today as Rogers Park. The picture won instant popularity due to an accident that occurred while filming. According to various accounts, *The Tramp and the Dog*, approximately 150 feet long (or less than two minutes in length), featured the character of a tramp knocking on the back door of a residence looking for a handout, only to be met by a bulldog that chased him across the yard and over a fence. Before the genuinely terrified actor could clear the fence, the dog's jaws clamped down on the seat of his pants and, after a brief struggle, the actor tumbled to the other side while the dog came away with a mouthful of pants.[3] Thus began the long tradition of "pants humor" in silent motion-picture comedy, which would arguably reach its apex with the films of future Essanay star Charlie Chaplin.

There is some debate over exactly when *The Tramp and the Dog* was made. There are no known newspaper reports of its first exhibition. Some

---

* Historian Kalton C. Lahue has Selig's first company named the Multoscope and Film Company, and Selig biographer Andrew A. Erish has followed his lead. The additional "l" was almost certainly a typographical error on the part of Lahue (or another writer whose lead *he* followed), however, as the "Mutoscope" was a motion picture device patented in 1894 whereas "Multoscope" has no known meaning.

sources date the production as being from 1896, while others, including Colonel Selig himself, have dated it as late as 1899.[4] It is also possible that the film was shot in late 1896 but not publicly exhibited until the following year. Since the Selig Standard Camera was a modified version of the Cinematographe, and the Lumière brothers' representatives did not bring their motion-picture equipment to Chicago until September 1896, it is a good bet that *The Tramp and the Dog* was not shot until the last quarter of 1896 at the earliest, and probably not until later.

By all accounts *The Tramp and the Dog* was a success, although it is difficult to know to what extent. The movie circulated widely, even playing in Europe (where it was sometimes screened under the abbreviated title *Tramp and Dog*). Selig later stated, "There wasn't a lecturer, carnival company or circus that did not show it."[5] Selig also wrote that he created literally *thousands* of prints of the film, a claim that is probably an exaggeration. He would likely not have had the finances at the time to do so: each print cost approximately $13.50.

What is indisputable is that other filmmakers in the United States, including the Edison Manufacturing Company, and in Europe, borrowed Selig's basic conceit, as a rash of humorous tramp-themed pictures soon appeared. These included such titles as *The Tramp and the Giant Firecracker*, *The Tramp and the Baby's Bottle*, *The Tramp and the Crap Game*, etc. Selig recycled images from the film himself as late as 1904 for his comedic production *Serenade*. Edison Manufacturing titled its 1901 imitation *Pie, Tramp and the Bulldog*, which offered only the slightest variation on Selig's original scenario, and advertised it as "one of the funniest pictures ever put on exhibition." The Colonel got his revenge by duplicating Edison's movie and distributing it himself. For the next several years, however, Selig put on hold any ambitions he had about producing narrative films, and turned his attentions instead to a series of Lumières-like actualities that would be decidedly more exotic affairs.

In 1898, the Spanish–American War was all the rage in the American media. Edward Amet, inventor, filmmaker, and partner of George Spoor, reportedly appealed to the U.S. War Department to be given permission to travel to Cuba and document the battles.[6] His request was denied, and so Amet single-handedly invented the pseudo-documentary genre by recreating and filming the battles himself, based on newspaper reports in Waukegan and nearby Third Lake. Pioneering films like *The Battle of Santiago Bay* (also known as *Spanish Fleet Destroyed*), not to be confused by the better known remake of the same title by J. Stuart Blackton, were among the very first to use special photographic effects such as miniature replicas of naval ships and painted backdrops of Cuba that stood in for "real" war footage.

Taking a cue from Amet, Colonel Selig realized that actualities depicting allegedly distant locales could readily be made without traveling too far from home. Selig's 1898 productions included a series of actualities depicting soldiers training at Fort Tanner in nearby Springfield, Illinois, and that series soon gave way to a slate of Amet-style Spanish War films. Selig even produced a movie about the washing of streets in Puerto Rico, a newly-acquired territory of the United States, in an attempt to capitalize on a then-popular media topic. A Selig catalog from 1903 cleverly describes the 1898 production of *Washing the Streets of Porto Rico* as, "A very unique scene showing the method of washing down the streets in Porto Rico and of special interest now that this country forms part of Uncle Sam's domain. This is a particularly brilliant film, perfect in every detail and being something out of the ordinary has proved very successful."[7] *Washing the Streets of Porto Rico*, like Selig's "Cuban" actualities, was filmed entirely in Chicago or its surrounding suburbs. All of these films, however, were marketed as being "authentic."[8]

Ironically, Selig used bold language to boast of the authenticity of his own films while simultaneously attacking the actualities of other filmmakers for being "fake reproductions," as in this catalog description of *The Gans-McGovern Fight* (1901): "With the exception of this film there are absolutely no genuine moving picture films representing genuine prize fights on the market. The prize fight films, so-called, are either taken by the fight promoters and retained by them for exhibition, not on sale and cannot be procured, or else they are the boldest fake reproductions put up the day following the fight by cheap, so-called fighters, who endeavor, to the best of their ability and under the direction of the enterprising photographer, to represent or reproduce as nearly as possible the scrap which occurred the evening before between the genuine principles. It is easy to see how very little real value films produced in these ways possess for the average public, which [is] quick to see that the so-called principles in the fight are not the men they are advertised to be, and the fight is not the real thing. This is not only a genuine picture taken while the fight was in actual progress ..."[9]

The extant film of *The Gans-McGovern Fight* offers a fascinating window into how the process of early motion-picture production could create unwelcome intrusions upon real life. The much-hyped featherweight title bout occurred on December 13, 1900, in front of an estimated 10,000 to 15,000 spectators. The fight was booked at Chicago's Tattersall's Athletic Association, which had outbid other venues across the country by offering the winner a $7,500 purse *plus* 50% of the box office. The bout was scheduled to last six rounds precisely because this was thought to be an ideal length for William Selig's motion picture. Six powerful arc lights and four giant reflectors were placed around the ring to ensure that there would be enough light for Selig's camera to achieve the proper exposure. The intense heat that resulted required that the giant doors to the hall remain open during the bout. Unfortunately, the median temperature was 24 degrees Fahrenheit in Chicago that night, meaning that patrons close to the doors and patrons close to the ring would have been made equally uncomfortable by experiencing temperatures at opposite ends of the spectrum.[10]

A final irony was that title-holder Terry McGovern knocked out challenger Joe Gans in the second round of a still-controversial fight that many feel had been fixed, bringing to light a scandal that may have been brewing in Chicago for years. "I know of at least five fake fights which have been conducted in this city," said one Alderman Patterson shortly thereafter. "Chicago is becoming the laughing stock of the country because of the ease with which a hippodrome can be managed here."[11] (Newspapers reporting on the fight frequently referred to it as a "hippodrome," a word then going through a brief vogue in which it was a common term not for an arena, its normal definition, but for a fixed fight.) The scandal that ensued resulted in Chicago's mayor, Carter Harrison, Jr., signing an ordinance banning the sport for the next twenty years. If the Gans–McGovern fight was indeed a "hippodrome," how "authentic" does that make Selig's film after all? If the outcome was predetermined, should this ostensible documentary not be classified as fiction?

Also shrewd was the way Selig Polyscope used new catalog descriptions to make old movies seem more current. *Infantry Charge*, a war film from 1898, was being marketed in the 1903 catalogue as a depiction of the Philippine War, which did not actually break out until a year after the movie was shot. To paraphrase Charles Foster Kane, Selig was providing the actualities and was content to let the United States government provide the war. This was exactly the kind of canny business sense that would establish the Colonel as Chicago's most successful film producer at the dawn of the twentieth century. Soon, however, this success would also attract the wrath of Thomas Edison.

The original "Diamond S" logo above the entrance of the sole remaining Selig Polyscope building in Chicago. (Photo: Michael Glover Smith)

The financial success Selig enjoyed with the dozens of shorts he produced in the late nineteenth century, as well as revenues generated by film equipment sales through the catalogs of Sears, Roebuck and Company, made him a wealthy man. He officially incorporated as the Selig Polyscope Company in November 1900 with capital of $50,000. Edison sued for copyright infringement exactly one month later. Selig refused to be intimidated by Edison and hired the law firm of Banning and Banning to fight the suit. In an unusual arrangement, lawyers Thomas and Ephraim Banning agreed to represent Selig until January 1903, a period of exactly two years, in exchange for a large number of shares in Selig Polyscope. It was a wise decision: financial statements show that Selig's profits surged in 1900/01, making his films equal in popularity to any in America, including those being produced concurrently by Edison and the successful Philadelphia-based Siegmund Lubin.[12] Selig would later re-acquire the Banning shares.

For his official company logo, Selig selected the letter "S" inside of a diamond. This decision would generate controversy a few years later when, according to the *Moving Picture World* magazine, Russian border guards "always on the lookout for Nihilists, Anarchists and Socialists," seized Selig materials after mistaking the "diamond S" logo for a "Socialist emblem." *The Moving Picture World* responded by defending Selig in its pages, using language that would not have been out of place in an official Selig Polyscope advertisement: "If Mr. Selig is guilty of anything, it is in trying to educate and elevate the nations by means of decent, clean and moral pictures."[13]

Later in life, Selig would describe his 1903 production of *Arrival of Humpty Dumpty* as his first "real" movie. However, the most significant Selig film from the turn of the century was the even earlier *The Life of a Fireman* (1901), an impressive, multi-shot narrative made at a time when most fictional movies still consisted of a single shot. Clocking in at 450 feet (or between five and six minutes in length), the film was a relative epic in comparison to other releases of the day. The influence of *The Life of a Fireman* could immediately be felt on the developing cinema in terms of both form (the ambitious editing of multiple shots together to create a more complex cinematic experience) and content (the dramatic depiction of a daring "fire run"). Among the important motion pictures influenced by Selig's early fire-fighter epic were the far more famous, and still extant, *Fire!* (1901), directed by James Williamson and *Life of an American Fireman* (1903), directed by Edwin S. Porter.

Though the film itself is now lost, Selig Polyscope's 1903 catalog description indicates *The Life of a Fireman* consisted of at least three different shots and possibly more: "This picture, in its complete form, shows the firemen sitting in front of a fire house, when suddenly an alarm is sounded. You see the [firemen] rush and break for the inside of the fire house, to get to their respective places on the apparatus before going to the fire. The next picture shows them leaving the fire house; the mad dash out of doors, and the most realistic fire run ever shown on canvas. Twenty-eight pieces of fire fighting machines madly rushing and plunging down a thoroughfare on the way to the fire."[14]

Not all of Selig's early efforts were as innovative or ennobling, however. William Selig was, first and foremost, a businessman, and he had known the importance of generating a steady income since his days as a carnival huckster. The Colonel thus augmented his income by purchasing prints of European films by Georges Méliès and others, making duplicate copies, and selling them for distribution himself. He thereby earned royalties on intellectual property that legally belonged to others. (Selig was, however, hardly alone in this "bootlegging" of pirated pictures. The practice was widespread at the time, especially since it was virtually impossible for filmmakers from other countries to know if and how their movies were being distributed in the United States.)

Still other Selig endeavors pandered to the lowest common denominator: the minstrel shows that were popular at the time, with their "comical" racial stereotyping, provided the basis for films with titles like A *Night in Blackville*, *Who Said Watermelon* and *Something Good – A Negro Kiss*. The last of these is described simply in the 1903 Selig catalog as "a burlesque" on Edison's famous *The Kiss* from 1896 (i.e., the very notion of seeing African-Americans or, more likely, white actors in blackface make-up, kissing, was meant to be humorous). It is worth pointing out that, in the 1890s, Selig co-owned a minstrel company with a black barber from San Francisco named Lew Johnson. Although that arrangement does not excuse the racial stereotyping found in Selig's films, it was still a remarkably progressive partnership for the era.

Such racial stereotyping in film would eventually lead to African-Americans' independently producing their own motion pictures, ones that offered alternative and more authentic images of black American life. African-American filmmaking pioneer William Foster has been quoted as saying, "Nothing has done so much to awaken race consciousness of the colored man in the nation as the motion picture. It has made him hungry to see himself."[15] Chicago too would be home to the first significant movies made by African-Americans, like the Foster Photoplay Company's short *The Railroad Porter* in 1912 and the earliest feature films of Oscar Micheaux, the most important of the early "race film" directors (see Post-Script).

In spite of Selig's best efforts, however, Chicago was not yet the capital of motion-picture production it would become later in the decade. In the first years of the twentieth century, Chicago's role in the movie industry, as it was in so many other U.S. industries, was to function primarily as a center for distribution throughout the Midwest. In addition to Chicago's Sears and Roebuck, who sold projectors and slide presentations in their catalogs (with which traveling men like Burton Holmes could launch a career giving illustrated lectures), many other local companies catered to the burgeoning motion-picture market by selling films and film equipment. These companies included Montgomery Ward (who had set up a special department catering to the "optical trade"), the Kleine Optical Company, the Stereopticon and Film Exchange, the Chicago Projecting Company and the Enterprise Optical Company.

Thomas Edison sued or threatened to sue all of these companies. The only entrepreneur who capitulated was George Kleine, who was able to pacify Edison by agreeing to exclusively sell Edison's films and projectors beginning in 1899.[16] All of the other companies resisted, with some following Selig's lead and hiring the firm of Banning and Banning to fight the suits. This resistance was significant. Almost all of the motion-picture production and distribution companies in New York and New Jersey, because of their close proximity to Edison and his patent-enforcing "Goon Squad," agreed to pay licensing fees to use and/or sell equipment that resembled any of the devices Edison had patented. If they did not pay up, they were soon discouraged from continuing in the movie business. These practices allowed Edison to have a virtual monopoly on filmmaking in the northeastern United States, but arguably they also stunted the growth of the film industry there. That stagnation, in turn, allowed the Chicago companies, by virtue of being farther away from Edison geographically, to gradually build themselves up over the next several years.

In 1901, Selig embarked on an ambitious series of movies that documented the local meatpacking giant Armour and Company. There were sixty films in the series, which were co-productions between Armour and Selig Polyscope, featuring such blunt titles as *Weighing Mutton*, *Stunning Cattle*, *Stuffing Sausage* and *Canned Meat Department, No. 6: Painting and Labeling*. These are the earliest known "sponsored films," a term coined by archivist Rick Prelinger to refer to movies made by a sponsor for a purpose other than art or entertainment and designed to have a limited shelf life (though one of the Lumière brothers' earliest films also functioned as an advertisement for a beer company owned by a friend of their father). The movies in the Selig/Armour series were essentially the first commercials.*

In the coming years, Selig continued to produce locally-shot movies while also expanding his operations to include film production in Florida and Colorado, where the climates were more conducive to shooting in the winter than was that of Chicago. (This was also the kind of thinking that would eventually lead to Selig's opening a permanent studio in southern California in 1909, the beginning of Hollywood as we now know it.) The most significant Selig Polyscope pictures of this period were

---

* It would also not be long before motion-picture studios began the more insidious form of advertising that would come to be known as "product placement." Essanay's 1912 production of *Back to the Old Farm*, for instance, uses a fictional narrative as a thin pretext for showing off the efficiency of the International Harvester Company's farming equipment.

actualities filmed outside of Chicago, such as the inauguration of President Theodore Roosevelt (inaugurations always proved a popular draw — and were one of few big news events for which filmmakers could prepare in advance), and fictional westerns filmed on location out west, the most prominent of which was probably the incendiary, Colorado-shot *Tracked By Bloodhounds; or, A Lynching in Cripple Creek* from 1904.

In 1906, Selig Polyscope generated unwanted publicity when one of its contracted actors, Howard E. Nicholas, murdered one of its contracted actresses, Margaret Leslie. The two had co-starred in six films (including *The Tomboys*, a comedy directed by Gilbert Anderson shortly before he split with Selig to found Essanay) and were scheduled to appear in a seventh, a Colorado western, when Nicholas strangled Leslie in a Chicago hotel room. A newspaper article cited jewelry theft as the motive but Andrew Erish's Selig biography identifies it as a likely "crime of passion." It was the first of many such scandals to plague the burgeoning motion-picture industry.[17]

Even as Selig's rate of production dramatically increased, however, so too did his legal troubles. His battles with Edison had never gone away and, by 1907, they actually threatened to bankrupt the Selig Polyscope Company. On October 24 of that year, a Chicago District Court Judge ruled that Selig Polyscope's motion-picture cameras infringed on patents that belonged to Edison.[18] Fortunately for the Colonel, aid soon arrived in the unlikely form of his former partners at Armour and Company.

In 1905, the socialist newspaper *Appeal to Reason* had published a serialized version of *The Jungle*, a novel by Upton Sinclair that functioned as a damning exposé of the unsafe, unsanitary, and downright corrupt practices of the Chicago meatpacking industry. The novel was based on Sinclair's own experiences while working in the Chicago stockyards as an undercover journalist in 1904. (Previous journalists found that the meat packers went out of their way to cover up anything unpleasant when they toured the premises; Sinclair found that by just showing up with a lunch bucket he could sneak right in and never be questioned.) When Doubleday, Page and Company published the novel as a single volume in early 1906, it reached a wide audience and caused an immediate sensation with the public. To combat Sinclair's unflattering account of the industry, Armour and Company waged an all-out public relations war. This effort involved re-releasing their Selig promotional films, as well as providing financial and legal backing to Selig in his lawsuit with Edison.

The legal arm of Armour and Company worked towards reaching a settlement with Edison that would lead, in 1908, to Selig reluctantly

Selig Polylscope movie set of a building's exterior, *Chicago Daily News*, 1914. (Courtesy of the Chicago History Museum)

entering into an agreement with Thomas Edison's Motion Picture Patents Company, which oversaw royalty payments to Edison while simultaneously allowing Selig to focus on his own company. With his legal battles with Edison seemingly behind him, Selig expanded his studio to include a massive lot on the corner of Irving Park Road and Western Avenue on Chicago's Northwest Side. The Colonel had already opened a second office there in the late nineteenth century but could now afford to snap up all of the surrounding land so that his new studio facilities, bounded by Claremont Avenue and Byron Street to the south and east, would encompass several city blocks. These new facilities included outdoor stages, artificial hills, a giant man-made lagoon, "jungle trees" and an interior studio with a glass roof. Selig made his old friend Tom Nash superintendent of the plant.

Because the concept of a "movie star" was still at least a couple of years in the future (it began with the Biograph Company marketing their leading lady Florence Lawrence as the "Biograph Girl" in 1909), the main draw of the early Selig Polyscope films was simply their production values. Early advertisements used the impressively large "Selig Motion Picture Plant" itself, often illustrated in a hand-drawn picture, as the main point of interest of the movies, and only afterwards mentioned the skilled but unnamed "pantomimists" in Selig's employ. One such ad earnestly read, "This plant is one reason why Selig films are the best. It gives no idea, however, of the great stock company of well-trained actors employed in making our films. We have hundreds of actors regularly employed — skilled pantomimists and others are on call so that there can be no monotony in Selig films. We take more pains than anybody else to make our scenery and properties correct. The result is that we draw the largest crowds and give complete satisfaction. The making of our wonderful up-to-date pictures has been described by the biggest newspapers and magazines."[19]

As that ad indicates, the public at this time was still ignorant about how movies were made. An amusing item that appeared in the *Daily Tribune* in late 1907 recounts the story of the filming of a bank robbery scene in a Selig Polyscope production. A woman who lived across the street from the suburban bank where the film was being shot thought that the actors playing "masked and heavily armed bandits" were acting suspiciously and called the police. A half-dozen Oak Park police officers soon arrived, arrested the cast and crew and took them all to the city lockup. The presence of the bank president was eventually required to get them out.[20] Perhaps this story is what Chicago outlaw John Dillinger had in mind years later when, according to legend, he successfully pulled off a *real* bank robbery by making it look as if he were filming a movie.

With more money and renewed confidence, Colonel Selig was prepared to ramp up the pace of his film production for the 1908 season. Selig Polyscope's membership in the Motion Picture Patents Company seemed to be advantageous to both Edison and Selig in the short term, but in many ways it would also signal the beginning of the end of the local Chicago film industry.

CHAPTER FIVE

George Spoor, George Kleine, and the Rise of the Nickelodeon

George Kirke Spoor, like William Selig, had a theatrical background that made him a natural for the movie business. Spoor was an enterprising young man who, along with a friend, had leased and successfully managed the Phoenix Opera House in Waukegan, Illinois, beginning in 1892 when he was barely twenty years old. Although his main business was running a newspaper stand in Chicago's Old Town neighborhood on the Near North Side, Spoor was a newly married man, and he had decided to manage the suburban Opera House as a means of making extra income. His experience booking vaudeville and theatrical acts in Waukegan soon whetted his appetite for show business.

Some years later, Spoor met Edward Amet, a local inventor ten years his senior who had been developing a motion-picture projector in the workshop of his employer, the Chicago Recording Scale Company. Like many early film pioneers Amet was inspired by seeing Edison's Kinetoscope, an event that happened in 1894, and he was determined to invent a device that could show 35mm films like those being exhibited in the Kinetoscope but on a much larger scale. (Perhaps Spoor told him he had the same idea after having his pocket picked in the Kinetoscope parlor on State Street.)

George Spoor and his most
famous discovery, Gloria
Swanson, revisiting Essanay
Studios, in the early 1930s.
(Photo courtesy of the
Chicago History Museum)

Amet had run out of funds for his experiments, but, with Spoor's financial backing, which some sources claim was as little as $25, he successfully completed his projector. In their short-lived partnership, Amet was the creative one; Spoor took care of the business end. (This would be the exact same role Spoor would play in his successful partnership with Gilbert "Broncho Billy" Anderson when they founded Essanay together several years later.)

In interviews later in life, Spoor claimed that Amet's prototypical film projector was fully operational in late 1894 and that they used it to exhibit movies to paying audiences at the Phoenix Opera House during that time. If the projector was being demonstrated in 1894 by one or both men, it would have been a full year before the Lumière brothers first publicly displayed their Cinematographe in Paris, which would also have likely made this demonstration the first time 35mm motion pictures were ever projected *anywhere*. For his part, Amet recalled that he was using an early version of this projector to exhibit films to church groups and other informal gatherings of spectators in 1894, but noted that he did not actually become Spoor's partner until 1896. Unfortunately, there are no contemporaneous newspaper articles or other "smoking gun" evidence that can definitively establish that these 1894 exhibitions actually took place, though the town of Waukegan made a concerted effort in later decades to establish itself as the birthplace of the movies. Even as early as 1897, in a sworn statement in the possession of the Lake County Discovery Museum, Amet stated that he had come up with the idea for the projector "sometime in 1893," and that he had begun work in March 1896, and "reduced the invention to practice in the early part of May, 1896."[1]

Far more tantalizing, though, are the memories Amet recorded in the 1940s. In a hand-typed letter (also in the possession of the Lake County Discovery Museum), he states, "I conceived the idea of making the life-size motion picture in 1893. I made a small camera which could also be used as a projecting machine in the winter of 1893/94. This I demonstrated to Mr. Leon Douglas and his backer, Mr. Charles Dickinson. They both said it would not be a success as a means of entertainment and decided not to back the camera financially for me. I had a great deal of respect for their opinion and let the matter rest. ... About three months after showing the camera ... I showed it to Mr. [Henry S.] Clark. After thinking it over a few days, Mr. Clark said, 'If you say you can do it, the Electrical Advertising Scale Company will back you' ... I did not have a really marketable machine until August of 1895. The company started on a lot of 25 machines, which they thought was a large quantity. I put an advertisement in a theatrical newspaper, and we had a standing order with a cash deposit of $100.00 on more than 150 machines in two weeks. This machine was advertised as the Magni-Scope ... during my experiments in making the Magni-Scope I would give showings of pictures to Sunday School, church festivals, and to the public schools under the direction of Mr. John Bogatt, principal of Waukegan Schools ... Our company had sold more than 250 machines before I ever met George K. Spoor. He had nothing to do with the conception or development of my Magni-Scope motion picture machine ... I met ... George K. Spoor in the spring of 1896."

Elsewhere in the letter, Amet notes that the first pictures he took with his 1893 camera were of a horse-drawn milk wagon going down the street after a snow storm: "The photography was excellent, and their [sic] was lots of motion — motion in all directions. The horse trotted o.k., but the picture danced all over the wall."[2]

In late 1895, Amet built his "laboratory," a two-story wooden building at 421 North Avenue in Waukegan. Local papers would eventually call it, with little hyperbole, the world's first film studio; unfortunately, the city ordered the building torn down in 1965.

Local motion-picture shows were certainly popular by 1897, though attendees seemed more impressed by simply seeing pictures move than they were by the specific subjects on display; a letter from that year in the county archives from someone named "Verne," addressed to his or her uncle, reads: "Enclosed you will find a piece of the strip used in the Magniscope for producing living pictures … the strips are about 70 feet long and take about 30 or 50 seconds to go through the camera. The pictures are reproduced by stereopticon at the same speed. Please write and let me know if you get this."[3]

In his partnership with Amet, Spoor's new business began to thrive and he quit the Phoenix Opera House in the fall of 1896 to devote himself full-time to making motion pictures. He incorporated as the National Film Renting Company, and opened an office at 62 North Clark Street in downtown Chicago. The "Amet Magniscope Projector," so named by its distributor George Kleine, went on sale around the country and was first purchased by vaudeville houses in New Orleans, St. Louis, and, naturally, Chicago. The Magniscope was also popular with "itinerant showmen" who followed the lead of Burton Holmes and carried the relatively lightweight projector (it weighed about 70 pounds) from town to town to exhibit the movies, accompanied by lectures and/or theatrical acts, in the manner of a traveling carnival.[4]

In a 1943 interview with the *Chicago Daily News*, Spoor said "In Waukegan I got to know a man named Armat [sic]. He was a mechanic … but in the evenings he, too, had a hobby. He was working on a projection machine that could show the strange motion pictures both he and Edison had worked upon. Armat [sic] wanted to take the picture out of the (Kinetoscope) box and throw it upon a larger screen. … I lent him $100 to complete his machine. In February of 1895 the awkward but effective projector was ready. The first screen projection was in a factory in Waukegan … from 1897 until 1902 we had to work out our problems of production as well as promoting Armat's [sic] projector. The films we made were 25, 50, 100 feet long, and their subject was almost always some simple action shot. Big parades, McKinley's inauguration, films showing trains rushing along a track, all of these were big hits with the people."[5]

Amet remembered in the 1940s how "Children and funny subjects went best at first. I had one picture of an old pig — black as coal — and her 10 little white piglets at dinner called 'Mamma and Her Pets' which was always good for a laugh … Train scenes, Panoramas, Magic and Kissing Pictures seemed to go best. Then the launching of ships went good. Then came the Spanish–American War and the movement of troops, pictures of embarking and street scenes and everything of interest. I made a fleet of Men of War and pictured many of the engagements."[6]

By far the best remembered of the Amet/Spoor films are these re-creations of battle scenes from the Spanish–American War, such as *The Battle of Santiago Bay*, a 25-second excerpt of which survives today. Traveling "war shows" depicted these films as actual battle scenes. Amet noted in the 1940s that "the public never questioned the authenticity of the pictures. The several scenes produced great applause. The Spanish Government purchased two complete sets of the naval engagements to use in the Court Martial of Geneva." Remembering this remarkable event in 1943, Spoor said, "The films were a sensation. Why, at the end of the war, the Spanish Government used our pictures of their fleet running the blockade at the harbor at Santiago as evidence in the trial of the admiral who was held responsible for that disastrous defeat. He was acquitted, but we never knew whether the Spaniards thought those were newsreel pictures or were paying us a compliment for our authentic research."

For the era, the Amet/Spoor Spanish–American War films were not only the first of their kind but also the best. The "miniature" ships Amet constructed were actually quite large, 3½ x 5½ feet in length (or 1/70 the scale of the actual ships) and constructed of sheet metal. The ships were photographed in a water tank 18 x 24 feet in length. Arduous feats of engineering were required to create the illusion of real naval battles. According to Lake County historian Diana Dretske, "The models were constructed with firing-gun turrets and smoking stacks and flags. The gunfire was replicated with blasting caps, and gunpowder and camphor-soaked cotton wadding, which was electrically ignited and provided smoke for the ships' smokestacks. All of these effects were controlled from an electrical switchboard off-camera. Additionally, waves were created by underwater jets and a large fan off-camera."

By contrast, J. Stuart Blackton's more famous, New York-shot remake of *The Battle of Santiago Bay* used tiny wooden ships in a tub and featured cigarette smoke blown in from off camera by an assistant. "If Amet saw this film," Dretske speculated, "he probably rolled his eyes and laughed." In any event, the end result of Amet's meticulously made pseudo-documentaries was so convincing to audiences at the time that he was invited to screen his "war movies" at the opening of the new Naval Station in Great Lakes, Illinois, more than a decade later. (Today, Amet's impressive model of the USS *Olympia* and a digital transfer of *The Battle of Santiago Bay* are both on permanent display at the Lake County Discovery Museum in Wauconda, Illinois.)[7]

With regard to these productions, on which his cousin, Billy, assisted, Amet noted, "We had some laughs. One of the funny happenings was when my great St. Bernard dog got loose just as we were making a picture. The firing made him angry, and he broke down the door of the room we had him in for safety. Rushed out growling like mad, jumped into the tank, grabbed one of the Spanish fleet ships and shook it to pieces."[8] Another time Billy dropped a ship when he got a drop of solder on his arm, wryly noting that "I would drop it for half a drop; no pension in this navy." These comments suggest that Amet had every intention of presenting the war movies as genuine: if not for the threat of blowing his cover, the scene of the dog tearing the ship to pieces conceivably could have made a popular comedic film.

In addition to their Spanish–American War movies, Spoor and Amet had also filmed real actualities, beginning with modest subjects with titles such as *Chicago Fire Department Runs* and *Mamma's Pets* (the film of piglets suckling on their mother that Amet had misremembered as *"Mamma and Her Pets"*). Soon, however, they expanded their scope by filming the presidential inauguration of William McKinley in 1897, which became a hit because of its famous subject. (Indeed, it was one of the first known instances of a movie's being advertised explicitly on the basis of its content rather than on the novelty of showing that pictures could move.) Although Spoor was technically Amet's partner in the production of these films, he appears to have been a very "hands-off" producer at this stage of his career; Spoor's only real interest in these movies seemed to be in making sure that anyone who purchased their projector would also have something to project along with it. While Amet oversaw the actual production of the films, typically shot in his backyard or laboratory, and using local actors, Spoor's job was to negotiate the contracts with the vaudeville houses that would exhibit the Magniscope and the movies.

Spoor, unsurprisingly, did not always remember it this way. In a 1943 interview with the *Chicago Daily News*, he presented himself specifically as a director: "I remember one of the first films we made," he said. "I got

... the railroad office to get permission to use a new, deluxe, million-dollar train. Down a long hill on the outskirts of Waukegan came the train, with Armat [sic] set up on some pilings at the bottom of the grade with the camera and me opposite him directing a group of laborers. Well, one of the workmen misunderstood my waving arms and was almost clipped by the train. I had to run him off the track myself at the last moment. You can imagine what a thriller that was back in the old days. Armat [sic] and I had some fun with those crude films."[9]

Waukegan took pride in its local inventor and enjoyed his productions. An article from the November 15, 1898 edition of the *Waukegan Daily Gazette-Register* gives some idea of what a typical presentation of motion pictures would have been like. Three hundred people attended "Magniscope Entertainment" at the Congregational Church and "passed a most enjoyable and interesting evening in viewing the attractive scenes of home life, war and travel flashed upon by the canvas by the wonderful mechanism that has made Mr. Amet famous."

As is often the case when reading early accounts of now-lost films, one gets the impression that if the movies were rediscovered, we could re-write some of what we know about cinema history: the Gazette article tantalizingly describes some of the entertainment as "colored war and comic pictures," suggesting that some of the scenes may have been tinted, making the presentation at the church a very early display of color films. Another movie is clearly described as a multi-shot narrative ("in six pictures"). The films shown included: "Explosion of the Maine, Lieut. Hobson, Dewey on the Bridgee [sic] at Manila, Sinking of the Merrimac, Surrender of Santiago, Darkey Town Fire Brigade (Comic), Landing of the Cavalry at Cuba, Dewey and his fleet, Battle of El Caney, Death of Capt. Capron, Starving Cubans, Milking Scene, 'Fighting Bob' Evans, Bombardment of San Juan, A Temperence [sic] lesson in six pictures (a) Wife lecturing husband, (b) She empties his jug of whiskey in trough, (c) Cow takes drink, (d) She milks the cow, (e) She prepares supper (which consists chiefly of milk), (f) Effect on wife and child, Cow in distance, Picnic scene (comic), Col. 'Teddy' Roosveldt [sic], Columbia."

Following some "illustrated songs" (in which a local singer sang a couple of songs while slides were projected on the wall), more motion pictures "taken by Mr. Amet for his Magniscope" were shown, some thirty-three in all. These included "Two north side Waukegan Belles engaged in their favorite amusement, i.e., Boxing (the expression, grace and agility of the contestants was of special notice)," "Dog Saving Child from Drowning,"

"The 'Heavenly Twins' Bury Grandpa With Leaves," some fire brigade and parade scenes, several home scenes, "Excitement at North Chicago — party waving at train run down by another — one man (supposedly) killed," "Accident at nutting party (society gentlemen's trousers suffer irreparable injury)," "Dr. Killern's Busy Day (comic)," and other various scenes from around town.[10] By the account of the paper, the individual films were shown to great applause.

The boxing-women picture survived until at least the early 1950s, when it was a popular exhibit at the Lake County Museum of History. In 1951, one of the stars, Bessie Dunn, then 81 years old, remembered the shooting of the film: "Edward Amet asked Isabelle Spoor and me to come to his house so he could take our pictures. He was our town inventor. Back in those days he was fooling around with something new — a movie camera. We thought he would take a nice portrait of us, but when we got there, he announced 'Here are some boxing gloves. Put them on and go to it.'"

Neither one of them had actually boxed before, or even seen a prize-fight. But they went at it as directed. "We whipped those long skirts out of the way and had a fine old time," Bessie recalled. Both women thought the film would be something that only Amet ever saw, and Bessie was initially horrified when the movie was exhibited, but then decided that it was "to the good of Waukegan." As late as 1909, Bessie later claimed, an usher at a theater in Spokane, Washington recognized her from the film.[11] In 1939 she remembered having received marriage proposals based on it, but scoffed at suggestions that she was the original "Glamour Girl." "Glamour?" she asked. "There was no such word in my day; it had not yet come to the movies." She noted at the time that she had never even been to Hollywood.[12]

By 1902, Spoor was almost certainly producing color-tinted films. He recalled that, when Mount Pelée erupted in April of that year, he used a newspaper photo of the volcano to construct a miniature replica for yet another pseudo-documentary: "With compressed air, soapsuds, gravel, ashes, and big stones, we had our own explosions of a mountain. That was the film, too, that Fred Mytinger, who had an office in the McVicker's Theater Building, colored for us. He had 20 girls, and they worked four weeks coloring our eruption of Mount Pelée."[13]

Whether Spoor was still with Amet at this time, though, is in doubt. Some sources state that the two went their separate ways in 1898. According to a speech given by Spoor at the Waukegan Chamber of Commerce in 1944, he was annoyed when Amet sold most of his equipment to the Philadelphia company of Williams, Brown and Earle in 1900 (they turned around and sold it to Thomas Edison). Bessie Dunn said that it was in 1900 that Amet decided there was "no future" in movies, and other sources make similar claims about his comments at the time, sometimes portraying him as a shortsighted fool who did not realize the lucrative future of the medium. The truth, more likely, is that he simply preferred inventing to making movies.

There is also evidence that Amet *did* have a good idea where the medium was heading. An 1897 article in the *Chicago Daily Tribune* states, "Mr. Amet is convinced that the production of moving pictures is yet in its infancy, and hopes for great things. The introduction of some successful method of color photography … will greatly add to the attractiveness of the views. By a possible phonographic attachment these colored views may be run with the sounds which actually accompany them … resulting ultimately in the one of the greatest sources of popular amusement ever devised."[14]

In any case, Amet had moved on to other projects by the end of 1902, and he seems to have stopped making new films in 1899, though he did not leave the film world entirely. In 1904 he was exhibiting motion pictures at the *Louisiana Purchase Exposition* in St. Louis, and in 1912 he filed U.S. patents for a camera that could record both image and sound. Spoor's memory of working with Amet through 1902 is probably inaccurate: although a few sources (including the inventor himself in his own later reminiscences) give 1902 as the date when Amet sold his film equipment, 1900 seems the more likely date. Certainly Spoor was making plans to move forward and improve the state of the art of motion-picutres — without Amet — well before 1902.

In the fall of 1897, Spoor had enlisted Don J. Bell and Albert Howell, founders of the future motion-picture equipment giant Bell and Howell, to make a new projector that he christened the "Kinodrome." The projector was ready in 1899 and became an immediate hit, far outpacing the sales of the Magniscope. (Any connection between Spoor and Amet beyond that date is unlikely.) Distribution of the new projector included not just the machine itself but also films to exhibit along with it, as well as a projectionist to operate it. The Kinodrome was more advanced than either the primitive Magniscope or the Polyscope, which had the unfortunate tendency to mutilate the film prints that ran through it.[15] The Kinodrome soon became famous throughout the country, and it made Spoor a fortune. Vaudeville houses were so eager to snap up the Kinodrome that

Spoor's supply could not keep up with the initial demand.[16]

A smart businessman, Spoor has been described as possessing "the calm reserve of an expert poker player."[17] His newfound success soon allowed him to re-incorporate as the George K. Spoor Company. He took out print advertisements touting an "astounding increase" in business that necessitated conserving his distribution ("Rental Department") and exhibition ("Complete Services Department") concerns under the new corporate umbrella name.[18] Although, on his own, Spoor was not particularly interested in the production of movies at this time, he still needed films to distribute with the Kinodrome. The films he acquired were mostly pirated "dupes" of European movies that he purchased from a New York importer and, ironically, considering the litigation that lay ahead, Thomas Edison.[19]

Although Edison may still have regarded motion pictures primarily as a novelty (the films he continued to make were still "proof of concept" films, such as one in which he pretended to be at work in his lab), he appears to have been alone in understanding the importance of copyrighting motion pictures. Edison had also jumped on the Spanish–American War actuality bandwagon in 1898, copyrighting more than a hundred such films over the next two years. By contrast, most other filmmakers of the day, including Spoor, Amet and Selig, never bothered to copyright any of their late nineteenth-century productions.[20] (Because the vast majority of their films have been lost, it is difficult to know exactly how prolific these early filmmakers were. Their filmographies in reference books and in online databases are all woefully incomplete.)

The issues of "intellectual property" and "copyright law" in the motion-picture industry at the turn of the twentieth century were as complex and thorny then as they are in the early twenty-first. The initial thinking at the time was that if you a bought a print of a motion picture, it was yours to keep, and you were free to exhibit it whenever and however often you liked. (A properly maintained 35mm print could be screened approximately three hundred times before becoming unusable.) This was a line of thinking that would soon change as distribution companies realized there was more money to be made in a system of licensing the rental of film prints for a finite period of time. Although he had gone into the motion-picture business mainly as a distributor, George Spoor would soon shift his energies to production, ceding the distribution duties to his colleague George Kleine, who soon established himself as the undisputed king of film distribution in the United States.

The story of the George Spoor/Edward Amet relationship is a good illustration of how, in the film industry of the late nineteenth century, the divisions between artist and inventor, scientist and businessman, producer and distributor, were often blurred. If you were in the business of making movies at the time, you probably also sold them, along with the projectors to exhibit them. In the following years, the lines between production, distribution and exhibition would become more clearly drawn. The most important development in the film-distribution business in the early twentieth century was in the founding of "film exchanges." These companies were so named because they specialized in renting or trading film prints exclusively (i.e., without the projection equipment to go along with them).

George Kleine had a leg up on the competition in the movie-distribution business because he had set up the Kleine Optical Company in Chicago in 1893, selling optical devices and stereopticons, before the advent of motion-picture projection. In 1896, the company began selling filmmaking equipment and, in 1901, it became the main "selling agent" not only for local Chicago filmmakers but for Biograph and Edison as well.[21] Among the Edison films that Kleine distributed were pirated "dupes" of European films. In 1903, the French company Pathé Frères, the leading film studio in Europe, successfully curtailed the bootlegging of their films by opening offices in New York and overseeing their own distribution in the United States.

Beginning in 1904, Kleine began distributing films directly from Pathé on a regular basis, much to Edison's dismay, and the import of European films would remain Kleine's bread-and-butter until he retired a wealthy man in the late 1920s. The deal with Pathé led to a serious falling out between Edison and Kleine. Kleine had been responsible for a whopping 30% of Edison film "sales" in 1903, but Edison was willing to sever all business ties over what he saw as Kleine's betrayal. On October 1, 1904, Edison revoked the special discount he had given Kleine since their exclusivity agreement of 1899, and then he quickly established his own Chicago offices under the management of John Hardin, the former head of Montgomery Ward's "optical department."

Kleine countered by first firing off a letter addressed to his "Good Customers" that explained the rift. He then publicly denounced Edison's piracy in a print ad that began "There are various kinds of 'Dupes.' The dictionary describes one kind as a 'Victim of deception ...'" and concluded "In no case will 'Dupes' be delivered to our customers when the original can be obtained. In some instances the originals can be purchased at the same prices as the 'Dupes,' in others at a slightly advanced price."[22] Kleine would resume distribution of Edison's films in 1908 with the advent of the Motion Picture Patents Company, but Edison would never again be his primary client. In fact, Kleine would look increasingly to European filmmakers from whom he could directly import. Soon, there were more than fifteen "film exchanges" operating in Chicago, which controlled an astounding 80% of the nationwide distribution market.

The other serious shift that occurred in the film industry in the first decade of the twentieth century was the transition of exhibition away from the vaudeville halls and penny arcades and towards the newly established storefront theaters known as "Nickelodeons" (so named because of their five-cent admission price). As it became increasingly obvious that the movies were more than a passing fad, enterprising exhibitors began opening theaters in metropolitan centers, most of which were converted storefronts, exclusively for the purpose of showcasing motion pictures. Once again, Chicago would be at the forefront of this new phenomenon.

Carl Laemmle was a hardworking 39-year-old German immigrant who owned a successful clothing store in Milwaukee and became involved in the movie business by chance after a business trip to Chicago in 1906. Tired of the clothing business, Laemmle originally ventured to the Second City with the purpose of investing in a chain of five-and-ten-cent stores. After attending a motion-picture show at a nickelodeon near his downtown hotel, however, the entrepreneur changed his mind.

In an unpublished manuscript written in 1927, Laemmle colorfully described his excitement at seeing movies in a theater for the very first time more than twenty years earlier: "Not only was every seat occupied, but the right and left sides were jammed with standing patrons. The rear was also filled, and after waiting ten minutes, the duration of the performance, at which time people trickled out, I was finally able to secure a seat." Laemmle estimated there were 500 people in attendance at his first picture show.[23]

Only one month later, Laemmle opened his own nickelodeon in Chicago, a 214-seat theater on Milwaukee Avenue that he painted white and named, rather unimaginatively, the "White Front Theater." Laemmle's masterstrokes as an exhibitor, however, were to open this theater in a residential neighborhood far from the Loop, where all of the other nickelodeons were concentrated, and to keep it immaculately clean in order to entice more female patrons. Both gambles paid off. According to historian

Bernard F. Dick, "Located next to a milliner at 909 North Milwaukee Avenue (1257 N. Milwaukee Avenue in contemporary street numbering), the White Front was accessible by trolley. Since Saturday was a shopping day, Carl thought that by mid-afternoon shoppers might want a diversion before returning home, and with sundown so early, observant Jews could drop in later. The gimmick worked; when the doors closed, Carl had taken in $200 – not bad, considering the price of admission. Thereafter, the White Front operated on a regular morning-through-evening schedule, which meant the difference between 1,400 paid admissions on February 24 and 4,000 the next day."[24]

Laemmle's great financial success with the White Front Theater would mark the beginning of an empire, as he gradually expanded his operations to include film production, founding the Independent Moving Pictures Company in 1909, which became Universal Pictures in 1912, one of the oldest and most durable film studios in the history of Hollywood. (The boy Laemmle hired to play piano at the White Front Theater, Sam Katz, with his partners the Balaban brothers, went on to build some of Chicago's greatest movie palaces, including the Uptown Theater and the Chicago Theater, both of which still stand.)

Carl Laemmle in Chicago in 1916, *Chicago Daily News* (Photo courtesy of the Chicago History Museum)

1907 saw an explosion of nickelodeons in Chicago's Loop and on the Near North and West Sides. There were at least 158 such theaters in operation in Chicago that year and more than three hundred the following year. This was *in addition* to the vaudeville houses that still regularly screened motion pictures. Film historian Lauren Rabinovitz earthily describes the city's early nickelodeon scene: "there were nickel storefront theaters along State Street to the South (the vice district known as "Whiskey Row") and strung out on Halsted to the west in neighborhoods that were filled with storefront brothels, penny arcades, dime museums, winerooms and saloons; on North Clark to the north of the Loop; and along the main thoroughfares of immigrant and working-class neighborhoods."[25]

Rabinovitz believes that the phenomenal success of the movies in Chicago at the time was directly attributable to the sharp rise in immigration. From 1890 to 1910 the foreign-born population of the U.S. had risen by an astonishing fifteen million people.[26] Chicago was a central destination for many European immigrants who were constantly arriving and contributing disproportionately to the city's population growth. The movies, with their purely visual and universal language, were the best form of cheap entertainment for newly arrived immigrants who did not speak English.

With the proliferation of film exchanges and nickelodeons, Chicago had distinguished itself as the most important city in the United States for film distribution and exhibition. This success would prove a boon to local producers: the Chicago filmmakers grew increasingly confident and ambitious. In 1907, George Spoor teamed with Gilbert Anderson to form the formidable Essanay Studios. The same year saw William Selig considerably expand the scope of his own production empire. When both studios agreed to join Thomas Edison's Trust, it seemed as though they would have a monopoly on film production in the Midwest. For the next several years, Chicago would be America's filmmaking capital. This golden age would be short-lived, however: no sooner were the owners of the Chicago movie studios granted a glimpse of paradise than they found the gates of heaven being slammed shut in their faces for good.

CHAPTER SIX

Gilbert "Broncho Billy" Anderson

In the silent-film era, trains and movies were a match made in heaven. The early filmmakers knew that movement itself was what most excited movie audiences and nothing symbolized movement in the industrial age like the locomotive. From the Lumière brothers' *Arrival of a Train at La Ciotat* in 1896, which, according to legend, caused early audiences to flee in terror as a train progressed towards the camera (and therefore, by extension, also towards the viewer*), through the simple panoramic films dubbed "phantom rides" that saw cameras being placed aboard trains to create a "you are there" effect, to the incredible locomotive imagery in late silent masterpieces as disparate as *The General* (1926) by Buster Keaton and *Man with the Movie Camera* (*Chelovek s kino-apparatom*, 1929) by Dziga Vertov, no other single image is more closely associated with silent cinema than that of the high-speed train.

---

* Anecdotal evidence strongly suggests that at least *some* viewers were genuinely scared by early movies; in a 1977 hand-typed memoir, Eloise Webb-Johnston (Adam Selzer's great-grandmother) remembered being a little girl in her father's theater, the Lyric, which opened in Seymour, Iowa around 1905: "I have a vague memory of seeing a lot of horses on the screen of our picture show and, fearing that they were really going to run over me, I went to the stairs and sat on the top step until the show was over."

Undated publicity photo of "Broncho Billy" Anderson. (Courtesy of the Chicago History Museum)

In 1896, there were at least six theatrical plays being produced in different parts of the United States that involved trotting out onstage an elaborate puffing locomotive. Thomas Edison, who had dabbled in the development of electric trains before turning his attention to motion pictures, saw one such play in New York City, a four-act melodrama entitled *The Great Train Robbery* by Scott Marble. Impressed by the play's narrative as well as by its special effects, Edison mentally filed it away as a potential subject for a future motion picture. Seven years later, he would realize this ambition.[1]

Movies in the early twentieth century were slowly making the transition from one-shot actualities into more complex multi-shot narratives. The European "story films" that were being duplicated (not always legally) by Edison, Selig, Spoor and others, were widely distributed in the United States and had become increasingly popular with American audiences. This was especially true of science-fiction/fantasy movies showcasing trick photography and special effects, such as Georges Méliès's *A Trip to the Moon* (*Le Voyage dans la lune*, 1902), and crime films involving exciting chases between police officers and criminals, such as *A Daring Daylight Burglary* (1903) by the English director Frank Mottershaw.

In order to compete, the American movie studios soon found it neces-sary to imitate both the form and content of their European counterparts. A few years later, it would be the Europeans who would be copying the Americans. This kind of back-and-forth influencing, spurred on by wide-spread piracy, meant that the language of cinema had begun to develop at a very rapid pace, and would become extremely sophisticated by the end of the decade.

In 1903, W.K.L. Dickson's American Mutoscope and Biograph Com-pany strengthened its commitment to using motion pictures as a vehicle for telling stories. In September, they began producing the first "west-erns," a genre that combined the narratives of the English crime films of the day with the purely American iconography of the popular dime nov-els and stage shows about cowboys and Indians and the "settling" of the west. This time, though, it was Thomas Edison who would be behind the blockbuster movie that effectively inaugurated the new genre and estab-lished its core conventions.

In 1899, former projectionist Edwin S. Porter joined the Edison Manufacturing Company as a camera operator and director. By the time he made *The Great Train Robbery* at the end of 1903, Porter had already directed at least forty-five short films and served as the cinematographer on many more. In this astonishingly prolific run of movies, Porter proved himself a true pioneer (if not quite the "father of the story film" that some histories have claimed): he was responsible for popularizing many of the rules of movie grammar that turn-of-the-twentieth-century audiences were experiencing for the very first time. A good example is *Life of an American Fireman* from early 1903, a "rescue film" that renders space cin-ematically, as opposed to theatrically, by showing the same event from multiple perspectives in consecutive scenes.

In the fall of 1903, Porter teamed up with Gilbert M. Anderson, the stage name of a theatrical actor born Maxwell H. Aronson, who would soon become one of the most significant figures in Chicago's nascent movie scene. Tall, handsome, and only in his early twenties at the time, Anderson was a natural in front the camera, but he also worked behind the scenes as an "ideas man," helping Porter to conceive motion-picture stories. The two collaborated on multiple film projects for the remainder of the year, culminating in their final 1903 production, *The Great Train Robbery*, which was shot in November and released one month later.[2] This game-changing movie would ultimately alter the destinies of both men forever.

Although set in a nameless frontier region of the American west, *The Great Train Robbery* was filmed entirely in New York and New Jersey on studio sets as well as actual locations. The film tells the story of a group of bandits who rob a telegraph office at a train station, then board the train, where they proceed to rob both the safe and the train's passengers before making a daring getaway. Meanwhile, in an attempt to recover the stolen loot, the telegraph operator enters a saloon and rounds up a posse to go after the robbers.

Among the innovative techniques employed by Porter are parallel editing (cutting back and forth between the bandits and the telegraph operator to suggest simultaneous action), double-exposure composite editing (an early "special effect" that allowed information from multiple shots to be combined within a single frame), camera movement (tilt, pan and tracking shots are all utilized), as well as a primitive but delightful use of color tinting on some prints (because each frame was tinted by hand and prints were typically projected at 16 frames per second, this was an extremely painstaking process).

One of the most unusual aspects of the film is its ending. After a shootout in the woods in which all of the bandits have been killed, Porter unexpectedly cuts to a close-up, the only one in the movie, for his final shot: one of the dead bandits has mysteriously reappeared to point his gun directly at the camera and "shoot" into the audience. The End. (A now-famous letter sent by the Edison Manufacturing Company to exhibitors across America actually gave them the option of projecting this shot at either the end or the beginning of the movie. All versions of the film on home video, however, place the shot at the end, where its impact is undoubtedly most effective.)

In contrast to the Lumière brothers, who had scared audiences unintentionally with *their* train film, Edwin S. Porter clearly *intended* to incite a frenzy with his more calculated assault on the audience. This shot would become one of the most iconic images of the early silent cinema, right alongside of the rocket ship hitting the man in the moon in the eye in *A Trip to the Moon*. Porter's image would also be widely imitated: it served as an inspiration for the opening of the James Bond movies as well as the ending of Martin Scorsese's *Goodfellas* (1990).

In an interview in the late 1950s, Gilbert Anderson recalled Porter's rapid pace of production: "We made it all in two days. Then it was finished and taken to the reviewing room. After it was reviewed, they all looked up and they were dubious whether it would go or not. And Porter said, 'Well, the only way we can find out is to try it out in a theater.'"[3]

The Great Train Robbery had its world premiere at Huber's Museum in New York City on December 1, 1903, where it played at the end of a vaudeville show. Legend has it that the audience was so enthusiastic that they demanded the film be run again and again before they would leave the theater. The following week, it opened in eleven theaters in the greater New York City area. It is impossible to know the exact box office figures but, by all accounts, the movie was a commercial phenomenon. After watching the film with one of these early audiences and noting their rousing reception, Anderson said to himself, "That's it. It's going to be the picture business for me. The future had no end."[4]

The Edison Manufacturing Company likewise quickly realized that they had something special on their hands, as this description from a 1904 catalog indicates: "This sensational and highly tragic subject will certainly make a decided 'hit' whenever shown. In every respect we consider it absolutely the superior of any moving picture ever made. It has been posed and acted in faithful duplication of the genuine 'Hold Ups' made famous by various outlaw bands in the far West, and only recently the East has been shocked by several crimes of the frontier order, which fact will increase the popular interest in this great Headline Attraction."[5]

One of the side effects of the movie's popularity was that other filmmakers immediately began to copy its techniques (one of them even remaking it shot for shot) as well as its individual moments: train robberies, fights on the tops of trains, and scenes of men being made to dance by having their feet shot at — these moments all soon became standard conventions of the western (many years before John Ford's *Stagecoach* made it a respectable "A-list" genre in 1939). Another residual effect of the film's popularity was that many people associated with the production soon found themselves in demand for future motion-picture productions. Although *The Great Train Robbery*, like all movies of its era, does not feature credits, a future movie star was nonetheless born: Gilbert M. Anderson, who played three different roles in the film (a robber, a train passenger who dies a spectacularly melodramatic death, and the man who is "made to dance"), would eventually change his moniker again, to "Broncho Billy" Anderson: he became the cinema's first true cowboy star.

Historian Kalton C. Lahue notes that it was both ironic and fitting, given the "make believe" nature of the movies, that its first western star was born with the "unlikely" (and, though Lahue does not say it, Jewish) name of Aronson and that, at the time *The Great Train Robbery* was made, he could not ride a horse and had never travelled "west" of Chicago.[6] This

Undated publicity photo of "Broncho Billy" Anderson. (Courtesy of the Chicago History Museum)

irony is probably what Clint Eastwood had in mind when he directed and starred in the poignant and highly personal 1980 comedy *Bronco Billy*, the fictional story of a New Jersey shoe salesman who decides to become the headliner of his own modern-day "Wild West show." In an age of mechanical reproduction, long after the American west had actually been settled, the story of the original "Broncho Billy" must have resonated with many of the aspiring "authentic" cowboy actors who followed in Anderson's footsteps.

After *The Great Train Robbery*, Anderson starred in three more Edison westerns in 1904 and 1905 (*Western Stage Coach Hold Up*; *A Brush Between Cowboys and Indians*; and *Train Wreckers*), all of which were variations on the basic formula of their first big hit. Anderson, however, had his own ideas about what constituted "western authenticity," and he wanted more creative control. In 1905 he left Edison Manufacturing to work for one of its chief competitors, the American Vitagraph Company. It was there that Anderson directed his first film, *Raffles, the Amateur Cracksman*. Anderson claimed to have taken the name "Broncho Billy" from a western story by Peter Kyne but it is also worth noting that Vitagraph produced a film about a character with that same name starring Paul Panzer around the time that Anderson worked there.

The financial success of Anderson's directorial debut led to an offer the following year from William Selig in Chicago, who was willing to allow Anderson to both direct and star in his own movies. After making a few successful Chicago-shot shorts, Anderson traveled west to shoot a series of Selig Polyscope westerns and "stunt comedies" on location in Colorado. All of these films were released in the spring and summer of 1907 and considerably boosted Selig Polyscope's profits. (Of these movies, only *His First Ride* and *The Bandit King* still exist today, and only as fragments.) Anderson and Selig, however, were not a good fit. Anderson thought his brief but successful run at Selig Polyscope meant that he deserved more money (or, by some accounts, deserved to be made a partner in the company), but Selig thought differently. Anderson promptly quit.[7]

Upon returning to Chicago from Colorado, Anderson met George K. Spoor, who had already made a fortune in the distribution business following his partnership with Edward Amet. In a 1915 interview with *Motion Picture Magazine*, Anderson recalled convincing Spoor to start a Chicago-based studio that would rival the Selig Polyscope Company. According to Anderson, the agreement was that Spoor would put up the cash and Anderson would do "the work."[8] Spoor agreed to an initial investment of $2,500 — a hundred times the amount he had allegedly invested in Edward Amet's Magniscope a few years earlier. Again, this investment proved to be a sound one; the income from the very first Spoor/Anderson production would more than double Spoor's initial investment.

In the summer of 1907, Spoor and Anderson incorporated as the Peerless Film Manufacturing Company, setting up headquarters at 501 N. Wells Street (1300 N. Wells in modern numbering). They recruited their cross-eyed janitor, Ben Turpin, who had been hired at fifteen dollars a week to sweep the floor, to star in their first movie, the Anderson-directed stunt-comedy *An Awful Skate; or, The Hobo on Rollers*. The scenario, reminiscent of *His First Ride*, features Turpin crashing into various people and objects while roller-skating around Chicago's Old Town neighborhood near the Peerless office. The scenes may have been staged, but there was little acting involved: Turpin really had no idea how to skate, and his inexperience is apparent in the film as he careens helplessly through the streets.

In 1943, Spoor remembered the film vividly. "We started out right downtown in Chicago," he told the *Chicago Daily News*. "Anderson had only one actor, a tangle-eyed comedian named Ben Turpin. Anderson would take a camera, cameraman and chauffer, and Turpin, and they'd go out and make a picture. First one was *An Awful Skate*. Anderson simply putting skates on Ben and paying bystanders two dollars to let Ben skate down the street and get into a series of collisions with innocent pedestrians … for two years we made nothing but comedies with Ben as our star. He made $50 a week."[9]

In 1909, Turpin recalled the perilous nature of acting in Anderson's early stunt comedies: "I had many a good fall, and many a good bump, and I think I have broken about twenty barrels of dishes, upset stoves, and also broken up many sets of beautiful furniture, had my eyes blackened, both ankles sprained and many bruises, and I am still on the go."[10]

An Awful Skate, which still exists today as a lengthy fragment, shows that Gilbert Anderson, as a director, understood the value of negative space in composing an image; he also understood the importance of pacing in slapstick comedy. Each shot features a different set of characters on a city sidewalk that Turpin's hobo comes crashing into. By the end of the film, a lot of the humor stems from the viewer's anticipation of the hobo's calamitous arrival in the frame.

Ironically, while George Spoor had had no problem infringing on copyrighted material by illegally duplicating the films of others as an exhibitor, he publicly complained as soon as he and Anderson, as producers, became victims of similar practices. Newspaper ads for the first Peerless movie were run with the following disclaimer:

> P.S. 'An Awful Skate' has been copied by a rival concern who employed spies to follow our camera. Our picture is the original and best value for your money. Don't let anyone convince you otherwise.[11]

The "rival concern" referred to in the Peerless Film advertisement was none other than the Selig Polyscope Company. While *An Awful Skate*

---

* One version of *The Roller Skate Craze*, preserved by the Library of Congress and widely available to view online, has been re-edited into a rapid-fire, Soviet-style montage lasting about ten seconds. Selig may have created this version only with the intention of having something to deposit with the Library of Congress for copyright purposes. It is extremely unlikely that whoever cut it together intended it to be seen that way by audiences in 1907. The full-length version of *The Roller Skate Craze*, several minutes longer and featuring a moderate tempo, can be seen only by visiting the George Eastman House International Museum of Photography and Film in Rochester, New York.

premiered in theaters on July 31, Selig's imitation film, titled *The Roller Skate Craze*, was released as soon as three days later. The only substantial difference between the two movies is that, in contrast to the Peerless hobo, the lead character of Selig's film is a middle-class father and husband who, in the opening scene, puts on his skates at home. Other than that minor change, the concept is essentially the same: a man skates through the streets, constantly crashing into other people and falling down.* A crucial difference, though, is that Selig's actor seems to be a better skater than the "hobo on rollers;" in a scene where he falls down a flight of stairs, one gets the impression that the man is an accomplished pratfaller who probably worked in vaudeville doing slapstick. The stunts in *The Roller Skate Craze* seem far more technically accomplished, though (perhaps illustrating a difference between theater and film) they are not quite as funny to watch as the *real* hapless antics of Turpin in *An Awful Skate*.

In the years ahead it would become commonplace for Spoor/Anderson and Selig Polyscope to release competing films on the same subject at the same time (e.g., dueling adaptations of John Greenleaf Whittier's poem "Maud Muller"), a practice that still exists between rival Hollywood movie studios to this day.

Produced for only a couple of hundred dollars, *An Awful Skate*, it is estimated, made between $5,000 and $10,000 in profits in spite of the challenge posed by Selig's knockoff. Hot on the heels of directing this first Peerless film, Gilbert Anderson personally embarked on a cross-country tour to establish contacts with regional film exchanges to which he and Spoor could sell prints of *An Awful Skate*. On July 22, 1907, Anderson wrote Spoor from the Hotel Henry in Pittsburgh. The letter indicates that distribution concerns like Pittsburgh's Calcium Light & Film Company recognized that Spoor and Anderson's inaugural film was a higher-quality production than what was coming out of most of the other "big" studios at the time. "Dear Spoor," Anderson wrote, "Arrived in Pittsburgh O.K., but as you know by this time, without our film, as Hamilton failed to bring it to the hotel before train time. Consequently, I will be detained in the 'Smoky City' another day. Nevertheless, I have visited the Pittsburgh Calcium Light people, and judging from their detrimental remarks about Edison, Selig and Vitagraph films, our stuff will find a ready market. I will show our film to various buyers and think we will sell as many to them as any other concern outside of Pathé. I feel absolutely certain that we will get rid of 40 or 50 copies. If there is room on your advertising circular, make a mention of our steady photography and brightness of lighting. G.M."[12]

The profits from *An Awful Skate* brought an influx of cash that allowed the Peerless Manufacturing Company to change its name and move into larger headquarters on the city's far North Side. Rechristened the Essanay Film Manufacturing Company ("Essanay" being the phonetic pronunciation of the first letters of the last names of Spoor and Anderson: "S an' A"), the company's new studio address was 1333 W. Argyle Street, which was soon expanded to also include 1345 W. Argyle Street, in Chicago's Uptown neighborhood. (St. Augustine College now owns this complex of buildings, which still stands relatively unchanged today.) For the company logo, Spoor and Anderson chose the insignia of an Indian head wearing a feather bonnet that was designed by Spoor's sister Mary. The logo reflected the studio heads' mutual love of the western genre.

Spoor and Anderson, however, were otherwise a study in contrasts: Anderson had movie star good looks and an affable personality, while Spoor was a heavyset, business-like man who has been described as "unsmiling."[13] When Charlie Chaplin went to work for Essanay in 1915, he found that the two men frequently engaged him in a sort of "good cop, bad cop" routine. Somehow, though, their partnership worked. It would span a full ten years, and the production of approximately two thousand movies, an eternity in the tumultuous, rapidly evolving era of the early American film industry.

To announce the formation of their new company, Spoor and Anderson proudly sent a joint letter to *The Moving Picture World* in 1908: "Dear Sir – The Essanay Film Manufacturing Company announce to dealers, renters and exhibitors of moving picture films the completion of their new film making plant in Chicago and especially request your attention to their new and original film subjects, which will be ready for the market at an early date, subsequent notice of which you will receive. Respectfully, George K. Spoor. Gilbert M. Anderson."[14]

With both Selig Polyscope and Essanay now firmly established as local powerhouses, the rivalry of the two major Chicago studios was about to begin in earnest.

- CHAPTER SEVEN -

The Edison Trust

George Spoor and Gilbert Anderson were getting their company underway during a particularly tumultuous time in the motion-picture industry. There were so many lawsuits and countersuits filed during 1907 and 1908 that the entire movie business was plunged into chaos. The American film industry in the northeastern United States was already stunted by the many patent lawsuits Thomas Edison had filed; he had been suing people and companies going back to the 1890s. The most important studio, apart from Edison Manufacturing and Vitagraph, operating in the New York/New Jersey area in the late nineteenth and early twentieth centuries, was W.K.L. Dickson's American Mutoscope and Biograph Company. Dickson, a thorn in Edison's side ever since he had defected from his former employer years earlier, had gotten around Edison's patents by using 68mm film, nearly twice the size of Edison's 35mm film, and his cameras used "friction feed" instead of Edison's patented "sprocket feed" to run the film past the aperture.

Although the Chicago filmmakers had fared better than their northeastern counterparts because geographically they were farther away from the "Wizard of Menlo Park," Edison's litigation with them, which had been

Thomas Edison in Chicago in 1912, one year before the Motion Picture Patents Corporation was sued by the United States Justice Deparment for violating anti-trust laws, *Chicago Daily News*. (Photo courtesy of the Chicago History Museum)

relentless since 1902, was beginning to take its toll. Soon, Selig Polyscope, Essanay and the Kalem Company (a new company co-founded by distribution giant George Kleine), along with a couple of the other major studios (Pathé Frères and Vitagraph) approached Edison about devising a licensing system that would end the litigation permanently and satisfactorily for all parties involved. The legal wrangling dragged on for months as various plans were bandied about, including one for a system whereby motion-picture manufacturers would make royalty payments to Edison of five dollars per week. Thomas Armat had initially proposed this plan, then balked when he realized that Edison wanted more money. During these discussions, the Méliès Manufacturing Company and the Lubin Manufacturing Company were also invited to join the potential merger. Siegmund Lubin, reportedly the most notorious of all when it came to piracy, was asked to "enter and behave himself" by Edison's lawyers.[1]

The licensing system was first legally put into place at the beginning of 1908. According to a *Chicago Daily Tribune* article from February 11: "In addition to the manufacturing and show places, the combination will control what is termed 100 rental places, where films are leased. A complete understanding has been reached and in lieu of the settlement of the legal battles in which he has indulged with the manufacturers, Mr. Edison will receive from the combination $200,000 a year royalty in return for which he is to permit no other concerns to use any of his patents without which films cannot be made."[2]

The phrase "no other concerns" must have sounded intimidating to aspiring independent motion-picture producers or those that were already established, like Biograph, which were not named in the agreement. Indeed, the licensing system had also been an overt attempt on Edison's part to freeze his chief rivals at Biograph out of the market by not naming them as licensees. Biograph responded by purchasing, at an auction held by the Anthony Scoville Company, the patent to the "Latham Film Loop." This loop was a device that, ironically, W.K.L. Dickson had co-invented in 1895 and that was now a standard feature on all motion-picture cameras and projectors. Biograph then served injunctions against all of the Edison-affiliated companies for violating *their* patent. Edison, predictably, countersued in an attempt to gain control of a patent that he claimed should be rightfully his. For once, a federal court ruled against him.[3]

Edison also sued George Kleine, his old on-again/off-again nemesis, in May 1908. Although Kleine had just co-founded Kalem (like Essanay, the company was named after the first initials of the last names of founders Kleine, Samuel Long and Frank J. Marion), he actually sold his shares in the company at a significant profit before it entered into the Edison agreement. Kleine, as an importer/distributor of European films, had rejected Edison's offer of a license: earlier, Kleine did negotiate with Edison's lawyers, but he was put off by their insistence that no new applicants would be granted licenses. Kleine then joined Thomas Armat and Biograph in waging a public relations war by placing advertisements about the dangers of an Edison trust in numerous motion-picture magazines and in the *Chicago Daily Tribune* (though, eventually, Kleine, Armat and Biograph would all reluctantly join such a trust).

When the *Daily Tribune* covered the Edison/Kleine suit, it reflected popular opinion in overstating Edison's role in "inventing" motion pictures and thereby also implied that his lawsuits were well-founded and that countering them was futile: "The art of reproducing motion by photography was invented and to a large extent made commercially possible by Edison. Patents were granted to him covering, first, the camera used for getting the pictures; and, second, the motion picture film as a new product. These patents expire in August, 1914. The present suit is based on infringements."[4]

With a federal court upholding Biograph's patent on the Latham Loop, Edison was now left with no recourse but to negotiate with his rival studio about including it in a new licensing agreement. This new organization, officially founded in December 1908, would be known as the Motion Picture Patents Company (also known as the MPPC or, informally, as the "Edison Trust"). In addition to controlling the production of motion pictures, the MPPC also attempted to corner the market on the production of the film stock on which motion pictures were shot. Eastman Kodak, the dominant manufacturer of raw 35mm stock, joined the Trust by agreeing to sell its product only to licensed studios. Because of these policies, the MPPC would rule the American film industry with an iron fist for the next seven years, during which time Chicago solidified its standing as the country's movie capital.

The merger between Biograph and Edison's interests was based on a four-page document drafted by both parties at a closed-door meeting in May 1908, a meeting that they would deny took place at future anti-trust trials. Titled "A Plan to Reorganize the Motion Picture Business of the United States," this document outlines how ruthless the MPPC, referred to in the document as "Corporation 'X,'" intended to be in attempting to rigorously control every aspect of the movie business (production, distribution, and exhibition):

> Manufacturers will pay to the Edison and Biograph interests ½ cent per foot royalty on all films marketed in the United States. Exhibitors will pay to the same interests a royalty running from $1.00 to $5.00 weekly for each motion-picture projecting machine in use by them, the amount to be based upon the seating capacity of the exhibitor's theatre.
>
> A corporation is to be formed which we will call 'X,' it's [sic] capital stock 'Y.'
>
> The business of Corporation 'X' will be the renting of films, sale of machines and other items usual in the trade.
>
> Manufacturers will sell exclusively to Corporation 'X.'
>
> Corporation 'X' will buy films from the manufacturers only.
>
> Corporation 'X' will rent films and is not to sell them.
>
> Corporation 'X' will not buy films from any manufacturer who does not maintain the conditions agreed to.

The Board of Directors of Corporation 'X' is to be composed of one representative of each manufacturer.

The Board of Directors will determine upon the cities of the United States which have been active in the film rental business and select from existing rental exchanges in each city one to three which are to receive an offer of purchase as hereinafter provided, these to be thereafter maintained as rental offices to Corporation 'X.'

The total number of agencies so selected is not to exceed fifty in the United States.

No fixed rental prices are to be established.

No theatre will be forced to pay a sum for film rental which is oppressive, the elastic scale acting in favor of those that need consideration.

Theatre owners engaged in evil practices can be disciplined.

Films can be withdrawn from the market when their condition becomes bad.[5]

A notice then appeared in the January 23, 1909 edition of *Moving Picture World* that formally announced the formation of the MPPC. It was an open letter addressed "To the Exhibitors of Motion Pictures":

The Motion Picture Patents Company has acquired the Edison, Biograph, Armat and Vitagraph Patents, which patents, we are assured by counsel, cover all modern moving picture films and all existing commercial types of projecting machines. The Patents Company has licensed the following Manufacturers and Importers whose present output is 18 reels per week:
  American Mutoscope & Biograph Company,
  Edison Manufacturing Company,
  Essanay Film Manufacturing Company,
  Kalem Company,
  George Kleine,
  Lubin Manufacturing Co.,
  Pathé Frères,
  Selig Polyscope Co.,
  Vitagraph Company of America.

The letter went on to name all of the currently licensed film exchanges across the United States and urged exhibitors to apply for a license before February 1. It also stated that any motion picture-manufacturer other than the nine named were operating in violation of MPPC patents and that any exhibitor or exchange that handled "infringing films" would be liable to suit for injunction and damages.[6]

Enforcement in Chicago of Trust policies was swift. Immediately after the notice appeared in *Moving Picture World*, "license officers" from every police precinct visited all of the city's nickelodeons to determine whether or not they had complied with the law requiring theater operators to be officially licensed by Edison. At the same time, the MPPC sent out a circular to all of Chicago's film exchanges demanding that they sign a new agreement refusing to distribute to these theaters any films that had not been officially licensed under Edison's patents. Max Lewis, president of the Chicago Film Exchange, one of the largest and earliest local distributors, refused to comply and publicly complained that the MPPC was acting in violation of the Sherman Antitrust Act.[7] (Unfortunately for the independents, Lewis's resistance was short-lived: the Chicago Film Exchange's license was cancelled after Lewis became embroiled in an unrelated business scandal later in 1909.) The Edison Trust also allegedly resorted to hiring thugs with mob connections, the notorious "Goon Squad," to enforce MPPC policy.[8] According to Chicago filmmaker and writer William Grisham, "Goon tactics were employed to break the backs of competition. Equipment and films were destroyed, property wrecked, lives threatened."[9]

The Trust also exerted pressure on its own licensed studios, which were required to meet a production quota (two one-reel films per week for the bigger companies and a single one-reeler per week for the smaller ones) to ensure that a steady supply of product would reach licensed theaters. While the Chicago studios saw an explosion of growth in 1908 and had no trouble meeting their quotas, New York-based Biograph, by contrast, initially struggled. Biograph had only a single director, Wallace McCutcheon, under contract. When McCutcheon became seriously ill in mid-1908, D.W. Griffith, then an undistinguished actor and playwright, replaced him. Griffith would be the sole Biograph director through 1910, during which time he would hone his impressive talents directing literally hundreds of pictures, almost single-handedly turning around his employer's fortunes in the process.

While touring Europe in 1909, Colonel Selig granted an interview to a British movie magazine, in which he defended the Trust (by essentially denying that it was a trust) while simultaneously denigrating the shoddy production methods of its independent American rivals. "Well," Selig said, "the independents can't stand up against the Patents Company, who have made enormous strides, and are now doing better than ever, because they have command of the best films. The fact is the independents are financed by the International Projecting Company, who may know something about finance, but nothing about films. The Patents Company was never a trust, and never meant to be. It was simply a business measure of protection and self-help to uphold their patents."[10]

The finance company to which Selig refers was actually named the International Projecting and Producing Company (also known as the IPPC), and it was a Chicago-based coalition of independents that announced its formation with an impressive capital of two million dollars in the February 6, 1909 edition of *Show World*. The mastermind behind this operation was J.J. Murdoch, the general manager of the Western Vaudeville Managers Association. The founding of this coalition inaugurated a bitter war between independents and the Trust that would last for years.

Although the United States Justice Department would eventually force the Edison Trust to dissolve for the very violations cited by Max Lewis, some of the MPPC's policies were in fact highly innovative and beneficial to the film industry: prior to 1908, foreign films dominated the American market. Once American manufacturers were licensed, they dramatically increased their pace of production in a period of intense competition both with each other and with foreign manufacturers. This dramatic increase in product led directly to a "golden age" for studios such as Essanay and Selig Polyscope. More important, the MPPC established a uniform rental rate for all licensed motion pictures. This fixed tariff meant that no studio could undercut any other by offering lower-priced films to distributors. Going forward, what would differentiate the movies of the big studios would no longer be cost but quality. In turn, the major studios each forged a distinctive "house style" (e.g., Essanay became known primarily for comedies and westerns, Selig Polyscope for period pieces and "jungle adventure" films, etc.). Finally, the MPPC provided fire and accident insurance for all of its licensed theaters, a progressive move that was considered "remarkable" in 1909.[11]

The Trust's policies also helped to change the way motion pictures were perceived in the broader culture. The MPPC's replacement of the sale of films with a strictly enforced rental policy, which still exists to this day, brought an end to the exhibition of old and damaged prints. This innovation guaranteed audiences a higher quality movie-going experience than that to which they had been accustomed. To help transform the reputation of movies from that of a low-class novelty to a respectable leisure-time activity, the MPPC also instituted a policy of systematically renovating all of its licensed theaters to "end the day of the dingy motion picture room."[12] Additionally, the MPPC joined forces with the newly formed National Board of Censorship and agreed to produce pictures that were "educational, moral [and] cleanly amusing."[13] The rehabilitation of the image of motion pictures was now nearly complete.

This newly respectable image of the movies, coupled with the increased rate of production, meant that the U.S. motion-picture industry began to grow dramatically. In a span of just four years, the number of movie theaters across the country more than doubled (from approximately 6,500 theaters in 1909 to more than 15,000 theaters in 1913).[14] Unfortunately for the MPPC, unlicensed independent theaters, which accounted for the majority of the movie houses in the country beginning in 1911, still managed to get hold of and exhibit licensed films. This flaw in its plan led the Edison Trust to form a new company, the General Film Company (also known as the GFC), the purpose of which was to purchase film exchanges in an attempt to "cut out the middlemen" and control distribution for themselves.

As with the MPPC, the formation of the General Film Company was outlined in a three-page document almost ominously entitled "Details of a Plan under Which Licensed Manufacturers and Importers Will Take Over the Licensed Rental Business of the United States." This blueprint was first presented to MPPC leadership at another closed-door meeting, and the General Film Company was first officially announced in mid-April 1910. Just as Thomas Edison was not single-handedly responsible for most of the inventions credited to him, however, neither was he the sole force behind the MPPC or the GFC. The "Edison Trust" was the brainchild of many individual minds; the president of the General Film Company, for instance, was Frank Dyer, who began his career as an Edison patent attorney in the 1890s but whose responsibilities had exponentially increased over the years.

Although all of the members of the MPPC appeared to be publicly loyal, its individual members sometimes drastically differed in their attitudes. George Spoor and Gilbert Anderson had eagerly joined the Trust and its affiliates, while George Kleine and William Selig, pronouncements in interviews to the contrary, had been more reluctant. Some film people felt that while the MPPC had initially spurred a healthy sense of competition among the studios, membership made them increasingly complacent as time went by. (Charlie Chaplin, for instance, thought that Essanay's membership in the Trust gave it a false sense of security and eventually led to a lack of concern about the quality of its output.) Selig, on the other hand, had become increasingly interested in innovation, as evidenced by his production of cliffhanger serials, longer-format films and experiments with sound and extensive color tinting. Privately, the Colonel was frustrated by the Trust's regulation of the form and content of the pictures it distributed, in particular by its initial, inflexible rule of distributing only one-reelers (i.e., movies that ran no more than seventeen minutes in length).[15]

By merging its production and distribution companies, a merger that would provide the model for the Hollywood "studio system" of the 1920s through the 1950s, the MPPC had successfully increased its monopoly over the industry. Although many film historians have, with some justification, negatively portrayed the Edison Trust as a repressive institution, its achievements in both stabilizing and helping the fledgling movie industry grow should also be acknowledged. The Motion Picture Patents Company and the General Film Company invented the template that would eventually be explicitly followed by the next generation of studio moguls in Hollywood's beloved golden age. The moguls of MGM, Paramount, Twentieth Century Fox, Warner Bros. and RKO would go even further with *their* monopoly by also vertically integrating exhibition when they established their own movie theater chains.

- PART THREE -

THE GOLDEN AGE OF CHICAGO FILM PRODUCTION

CHAPTER EIGHT

The Golden Age of Essanay

Following its first big success with *An Awful Skate* in July 1907, Essanay Studios produced more than a dozen additional shorts before the end of that year. Of these films, all of which are now lost, the catalog descriptions and the titles themselves (e.g., *Mr. Inquisitive, Where Is My Hair?* and the regrettably titled *The Dancing Nig*) suggest that most were comedies that were directed by Gilbert M. Anderson. The exceptions were the matter-of-factly named documentary *The Unveiling Ceremonies of the McKinley Memorial, Canton, Ohio, September 30, 1907*, which was released less than two weeks after it was shot (and which was also likely the only Essanay film of its time made outside of the city of Chicago) and the penultimate Essanay production of the year, the poignant drama *A Christmas Adoption*, which was released on December 20. (Releasing Christmas-themed films shortly before the holidays would soon become an Essanay tradition.)

For 1908, Essanay impressively managed to manufacture and release no less than seventy-two films. The production values of these movies increased drastically from the 1907 shorts: nearly all of them were shot in Essanay's new studio facilities in Chicago's Uptown neighborhood. No

Exterior of original Essanay
Studios building entrance,
erected in 1908, one year after
the company's formation.
(Photo: Michael Glover
Smith)

longer a two-man operation, Spoor and Anderson brought more diverse
and ambitious subject matter before Essanay cameras after naming Henry
McRae Webster as head of production, and hiring new writers, directors,
technicians, and actors. This new initiative included the making of prestigious "period piece" films because the Uptown studio space allowed for the
creation of elaborate sets and costumes. Several of these 1908 productions
would become landmarks: *The James Boys in Missouri*, the first movie about
the famous outlaw brothers, was released in April to much controversy; *The
Life of Abraham Lincoln*, released in October, was likely the first biopic of a
U.S. President; and the December release of *A Christmas Carol* would be
the very first of countless American film adaptations of Charles Dickens'
timeless novella. (For this film, Essanay imported an authentic English
stage actor, Tom Ricketts, to play the iconic role of Ebenezer Scrooge.)

The most significant extant Essanay movie following *An Awful Skate*,
however, is probably the 1909 production of *Mr. Flip*. Directed by Anderson,
Mr. Flip is an important and influential slapstick comedy (it is the earliest
such film included in Kino Video's 2002 "Slapstick Encyclopedia" DVD
boxed set) and also a good showcase for the comedic acting of Ben Turpin,

who had come a long way as a performer since his motion-picture debut in *An Awful Skate* less than two years earlier. Turpin plays the title character as a lascivious cad who repeatedly pops up in various establishments to sexually harass the female employees. In each instance, the women turn the tables on "Mr. Flip" by inflicting physical pain on him and/or humiliating him, causing him to flee the premises.

The film is similar to *An Awful Skate* in that almost every scene features a gag that plays out in a single unedited shot before cutting to a new location and also a new camera setup. The difference is that in *Mr. Flip* each location features an elaborate, impressively designed set; Mr. Flip is shown attempting to caress or kiss the cheeks of various women (in order: a store clerk, a manicurist, a telephone operator, a barber, a bartender, and a waitress) in each of their places of work. In succession, he finds himself unceremoniously escorted out of the store on a dolly cart, stabbed in the rear with a pair of scissors, shocked with electricity, smothered with shaving cream, sprayed with seltzer water, and attacked with a pie.

Aside from the intriguing way the plot opens itself up to a feminist reading (not only because the female victims flip the script on their harasser but also because an ensemble cast of women are portrayed as working diverse jobs eleven years before they had the right to vote), this movie is probably most noteworthy today for its final scene, in which a woman working behind the counter of a diner responds to Mr. Flip's advances by smashing a pie in his face. This scene is believed to be the first time the famous "pie in the face" gag was depicted in a film comedy.

In 1909, the language of cinema had not yet evolved to the point where directors were routinely cutting to close-ups of actors' faces during the emotional high points of a scene. D.W. Griffith's innovative use of extensive close-ups in *The Lonedale Operator* was still two years away. The one close-up in *Mr. Flip* is an insert shot of a woman sticking a tiny pair of scissors through the bottom of a wicker chair, a detail that would have gone unnoticed in the longer shots that otherwise characterize the movie. Still, in spite of the dearth of close-ups, which makes it impossible to clearly see Ben Turpin's famously crossed eyes, the comedian's performance nonetheless manages to be effective. Though the movie is lighthearted, Mr. Flip's nervous, jittery energy and his inability to keep his hands off of the female characters make him truly annoying and thus fully deserving of the comeuppance he receives at the end of every scene.

Interestingly, Mr. Flip's costume contains elements that would become part of the iconic looks of future screen comedians: his thick, obviously

Mr. Flip, 1909. Directed by
Gilbert Anderson.

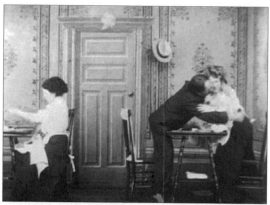

fake mustache predates Groucho Marx's famous greasepaint mustache by
many years (though both mustaches can be said to have a common root
in vaudeville), and his flat-topped straw hat is uncannily similar to the one
that would become forever identified with Buster Keaton in the 1920s.

In spite of the success of films like *Mr. Flip*, however, the still-new
motion-picture medium was neither lucrative nor respectable circa 1909,

especially in comparison to a prestigious, ages-old art form such as live theater. Anyone who worked for Essanay in the early years, in front of or behind the camera, would have to perform multiple jobs for the company. Ben Turpin, for instance, may have graduated from janitor to leading man, and become Essanay's first "star" in the process, but he still had to do double-duty as the company's props manager in order to make ends meet.

George Spoor would later tell a story about spying on Turpin as he took a bouquet of flowers from a film set at the end of a day's shoot and stole out with it across the back lot of the Argyle Street studio. Initially suspicious of the comedian/property manager's behavior, Spoor became deeply moved as he witnessed Turpin crawl beneath the barbed wire fence of the cemetery adjacent to the studio and place the flowers on a grave.

Spoor confronted the comedian at the back door of the studio: "Ben, I just saw you do a beautiful thing, a thing that moved me more than I can say. From now on, whenever we have any flowers left over from the scenes, I want you to put them on a grave."

"Gee, boss," Turpin allegedly replied, "that's where I got 'em from."[1]

In June 1909, less than a month after the release of *Mr. Flip*, *Moving Picture World* declared Essanay to be the "House of Comedy Hits." In spite of his success with comedy, however, Gilbert Anderson, as both director and actor, would soon shift his attentions to the western genre almost exclusively. Anderson's first Essanay western, *The James Boys in Missouri*, shot in Chicago and Scottdale, Michigan, created a firestorm of controversy for being sympathetic to the title outlaws (and thus inaugurating a debate that still rages to this day about whether or not movies "glorify" the exploits of criminals). It received mostly positive critical notices and was a big box office success for Essanay in 1908, while simultaneously it was also banned in several U.S. cities, including, ironically, Chicago.[2]

The experience of making *The James Boys in Missouri* whetted Anderson's appetite for making more westerns, however, which he began shooting on location regularly throughout the southwestern United States (e.g., Texas, Colorado, and California) in late 1909 and into 1910. During one such trip, Anderson created his "Broncho Billy" persona, a cowboy character he would embody as an actor in literally hundreds of films over the next several years. Although Anderson had long advocated the importance of location shooting for westerns, including during his short stint for Selig Polyscope a few years earlier, his very first "Broncho Billy" movie, 1910's *Broncho Billy's Redemption*, was still partially shot in Chicago (with additional location work being done in El Paso, Texas).

It has been estimated that an astonishing 21% of American films in 1910 were westerns.[3] Essanay, like Selig Polyscope, was therefore justifiably proud of the authenticity of its "horse operas," especially in an era when shooting on location in the southwest meant transporting cast, crew, and equipment over great distances in order to obtain convincing results. (Westerns shot in locations as far away as New Jersey or Paris were increasingly attacked by film critics of the time for their *inauthentic* scenery.) *The Essanay Guide*, the studio's official bimonthly publication, used vivid language to extol the virtues of the cinematography of its ace lensman Jesse Robbins: "Every one familiar with the Essanay Company's splendid Western films has noted the clear almost stereoscopic photography, which makes the figures apparently stand out from the screen in such a splendid perspective that it is hard to realize that one is not actually looking upon the scene of the picture itself. This is due chiefly to the absolute purity of the atmosphere, which seems to carry not a particle of dust, smoke or hazy fog. Clearly outlined to very minute detail objects several miles distant can be photographed with all the clearness and correctness as when seen with the naked eye."[4]

Although Essanay's Anderson-led "western company" was successful in 1910, George Spoor's home office unexpectedly ran into trouble when a new independently owned rival studio, the American Film Manufacturing Company, set up shop in Chicago in the fall of that year. American Manufacturing (also known as Flying "A" Studios) was based in Chicago for only a brief while (like everyone else, they soon relocated to southern California), but in that short span of time they nonetheless managed to lure away a lot of Essanay's top talent by offering higher salaries. Among the defectors were Essanay's most important leading man, J. Warren Kerrigan, and screenwriter Allan Dwan (who had started off his Essanay career as an electrician but had since worked his way up to become the head of their scenario department). Essanay rebounded by hiring a whole new roster of talent such as screenwriter Louella Parsons, who soon replaced Dwan, director Theodore Wharton, and prototypical movie stars such as Beverly Bayne, Francis X. Bushman, Ruth Stonehouse, Henry B. Walthall (the future star of D.W. Griffith's *The Birth of a Nation*), and Bryant Washburn. Rather than crumple, Essanay responded to this new challenge by rebuilding itself and rising to even greater heights.

In this era, many of Essanay's actors were initially given bit parts. Then, only after they had gradually proven themselves, they were allowed to play the more substantial roles (becoming part of Essanay's "first company") that led to stardom. Once popular, a "star persona" would coalesce in the public imagination, helped along by Essanay's public relations and advertising departments, and the actor would then typically play similar roles in many similar kinds of films. Most of these actors appeared in dozens or even hundreds of Essanay films in the second decade of the twentieth century.

A typical success story was that of Ruth Stonehouse, a former dancer who began her career at Essanay as an extra and eventually became one of the company's most prominent leading ladies. As she told *Photoplay* magazine: "So one day I went over to the Essanay studio, and asked for work. I got it, but only bits. I didn't seem to get ahead, and I began to feel that I was a failure. One day I was standing watching a scene. I was heartsick and discouraged, and really on the brink of giving up. Suddenly the girl playing the lead was taken ill, and had to leave. The director looked frantically around. He saw me. It was the beginning of the picture, and he was behind in his work; so he popped me into the picture.

"It was one of these weepy stories, and I guess the director thought I was the most forlorn thing he had ever seen. I was supposed to emote, and I did. I emoted enough for seven Sarah Bernhardts. I cried all over the place — and became the official sob-sister of the studio. I died in every way there was to die, I think, and had more children dead and alive than any woman that ever lived. Niobe was a dry-eyed, marble-hearted dame compared to me. So one day I wrote a comedy for myself. It was accepted, worked over a bit, and that's where I escaped the thrall of tears."[5]

More atypical was the story of Francis X. Bushman, who had a much quicker route to Essanay movie stardom. Bushman was a bodybuilder-turned-theatrical actor from the east whom Essanay had put under contract in early 1911. According to his biographers Lon and Debra Davis, Bushman made his first appearance in an Essanay film within an hour of his first arrival in Chicago. Bushman was approaching Essanay Studios to report for work when he saw a large group of people filming a scene in front of a house across the street. Bushman noticed that one of his old stage directors, Richard Foster "Daddy" Baker, was directing the movie. Baker beckoned over his former protégé, insisting that he appear in the scene. Baker wanted to be able to say that he "was the first" to put Bushman before a motion-picture camera.[6]

Baker's instinct about Bushman proved correct. Tall, muscular, and strikingly handsome, especially when seen in profile, the young actor would soon be Essanay's top draw, easily eclipsing the popularity of J. Warren

Kerrigan. Bushman's "classic profile and wavy locks literally drove the girls into a frenzy," Louella Parsons later recalled.[7] Although Bushman rarely had anything good to say in hindsight about his experience at Essanay, often claiming he could not remember the movies he made there, it was Essanay that first propelled the actor to superstardom, which led to more lucrative contracts with Metro and Vitagraph and, eventually, a prominent role in the epic 1925 version of *Ben-Hur*, the most expensive movie of the entire silent era. Bushman's animosity towards Essanay apparently stemmed from what he believed were the company's slipshod production methods, although it is also possible that the theatrically trained actor's education in the differences between stage acting and film acting came as a series of rude shocks that left a permanent bad taste in his mouth.

Bushman later recalled that while he was chatting with George Spoor in the Essanay offices on his first day of work, Henry McRae Webster, who had been assigned to direct the actor's first movie, arrived and immediately began barking orders. "Be on the floor ready to work at nine sharp tomorrow morning," McRae told Bushman. "You'll play an artist who falls in love with his model. Here, I'll jot down the address of a costume house, and you ride downtown and get yourself a velvet coat and beret."

Bushman found the experience of being on a film set appalling: "Just imagine a madhouse with all the inmates turned loose. Add to that a boiler factory going full swing. Plus a temperature of at least 120 degrees from the blinding lights. Well, my God, I was accustomed to the courtesy and quiet of the theater — I'd never seen or heard anything like it!" Bushman was also offended by Webster's direction, which he later remembered as occasionally being yelled from off camera while scenes were being shot. "I gritted my teeth and swore I'd remember what to do in the next scene," the actor recalled. "But then in the middle of everything, Webster starts improvising ideas and screams them at me. He screamed until his voice gave out and then stamped on the floor and hurled his megaphone."[8]*

Bushman later claimed to have been so horrified upon viewing his first one-reeler, *His Friend's Wife*, that he offered Spoor money to burn the negative. Spoor's incredulous reply was allegedly, "Burn it? Why that's the

---

* These improvisational directorial methods, however, were not unique to Webster: E. Mason "Lightning" Hopper was a comedy director at Essanay who earned his nickname in his vaudeville days, when he would create comedy sketches from scratch right in front of a live audience. Also nicknamed "the Nebraska Cyclone," Hopper would scream himself hoarse trying to get people to be funny, hollering, "Kick him! Sit on his head!" as a group of extras piled on top of a star.[9]

Undated publicity photo
of Francis X. Bushman.
(Courtesy of the Chicago
History Museum)

best picture Essanay has ever made." Bushman was relieved when Spoor
assigned "Daddy" Baker to direct the actor's next film.[10] In all, Bushman
appeared in more than a hundred Essanay movies between 1911 and 1915,
almost always playing the romantic leading man. Although Bushman was
already married and the father of five children at the time he appeared
in *His Friend's Wife*, Essanay's public relations department kept this information under wraps for years, fearing that it would hurt the star's image.
As Louella Parsons wrote in her 1944 memoir *The Gay Illiterate*, "Spoor
nearly went out of his mind keeping the fact from the palpitating fans
that his Adonis had 'begat' five offspring, and it was a hush-hush job that
required a bit of doing, believe me."[11]

Spoor's ploy worked, perhaps too well. Bushman received thousands of
marriage proposals from adoring female fans. The star's fan mail became
so voluminous that Essanay eventually hired three secretaries to forge
flirtatious responses. According to legend, one young woman was so
determined to marry Bushman that she showed up at the Argyle Street
studio in a wedding dress.

At the dawn of the film industry's "star system," Francis X. Bushman
became the silver screen's first true matinee idol. He also played the off-
screen role of "movie star" to the hilt, driving around Chicago's North

Beverly Bayne in a still from
an unidentified film.
(Courtesy of the Chicago
History Museum)

Side at night in a purple limousine with a special light on the dashboard that made it easier for him to be seen. He even had his name embossed in gold lettering on the car's exterior. The press dubbed him "King of the Movies." Bushman would eventually find himself at the center of a nationwide scandal when his extra-marital affair with his frequent Essanay co-star (and future wife) Beverly Bayne became public in 1918.

Bayne, famed for her big, saucer-like brown eyes, received her big break at the age of sixteen when she responded to an Essanay casting call seeking extras who could show up wearing "white gloves and pretty clothing" for ballroom scenes. After dropping off her photo at the Argyle Street studio, Bayne waited a week and then received a call from Henry McRae Webster's secretary asking her to report for work the next morning. Because she was still in high school at the time, Bayne's mother let her return to the studio only under the supervision of her aunt. "The next morning we were at the studio," Bayne recalled, "and Mr. Webster came bustling in, and he said: 'Here. Here's a script. You read the part of Marian. Go out and have your lunch and come back, and I'll take you thru [sic] a scene.' O, how my heart was palpitating."

While reading through the script, Bayne was astonished to find that "Marian" was the lead role in the picture. After walking through a scene with her one time, Webster seemed satisfied. "Now, little lady," he asked her, "what do you think an actress should be paid? You have to be in the studio every morning at nine. You'll work until late in the afternoon. And we work from nine until one on Saturdays. We never work on Sundays."

Bayne timidly negotiated a starting salary of $25 a week for her first four weeks at the studio, during which time she was under Webster's personal direction. Then, she went into the "regular stock" and began working with other directors. Six months later, her salary jumped to $75 a week and then $350 a week. Eventually, she would star in more than four hundred Essanay productions and become known as the "Queen of the Movies."[12]

In 1912, Essanay's increased output of western films led Spoor and Anderson to establish a second base in Niles, California, a small town forty miles south of San Francisco. After that, Niles was naturally where "Broncho Billy" spent most of his time living and working, as he continued to churn out westerns, while Spoor and Henry McRae Webster oversaw the productions of "parlor comedies" and dramatic movies back in Chicago. The most important surviving Chicago-shot Essanay film of this time, and arguably the masterpiece of all of its extant movies, is *From the Submerged*, a drama released in November 1912 that was written and directed by Theodore Wharton and starred the beautiful Ruth Stonehouse.

Theodore Wharton had begun his career as a director for Pathé Frères in 1910 and had the reputation of being something of an innovator. He was one of the new directors that Essanay had hired following the exodus of their talent to the American Film Manufacturing Company. Wharton's 1912 Essanay production of *Sunshine*, now lost, made a big impression on critics for its creative use of superimpositions: one scene featured a character making a confession to a priest while the story of his confession appeared as an image within the *same frame* as the shot of the man telling the story.[13] A similarly visually flamboyant device also serves as the emotional climax to *From the Submerged*, a movie that more than lives up to its evocative and poetic title.

From the Submerged tells the story of a young, homeless man, Charlie (E.H. Calvert), who is prevented from committing suicide in a public park by a complete stranger, a young woman (Stonehouse) who reminds him, by pointing to the heavens, that God still loves him. In a melodramatic plot twist, Charlie soon inherits a fortune and, flash forwarding to two years

From the Submerged, 1912.
Directed by Theodore
Wharton.

later, becomes engaged to a wealthy socialite. With several of their afflu-
ent friends, the couple attends a "slumming party" where they visit a bread
line that offers handouts to the homeless. Feeling guilty, Charlie confesses
his destitute past to his fiancée, who laughs and says, "How funny" (the
only line of dialogue in the film represented by a title card). Realizing her
shallowness, Charlie decides to break off the engagement. Remembering

the woman who saved his life, he then dons his former shabby attire and returns to the public park where he had almost killed himself two years earlier. There, Charlie encounters the same woman from the beginning of the film and reminds her of their previous encounter. After a quickie wedding, he takes her to his lavish home where she realizes, for the first time, that her husband is actually a wealthy man.

Although the plot of *From the Submerged* is similar to that of the contrived Victorian-style melodramas common to the era (a lot of narrative twists and turns are crammed into a running time of less than ten minutes), the film is nevertheless sensitively directed and extremely well acted. It also offers more psychological and emotional complexity than what one typically finds in a movie from 1912. One impressive scene, for instance, has Charlie ripping up a photograph of his fiancée, a way to indicate the end of their engagement through purely visual means. Although this may be, in and of itself, a familiar film image, what really impresses about the moment is the way that Calvert slowly and sadly shakes his head while tearing up the picture, a subtle and exquisite piece of movie acting. It is immediately followed by an even more impressive moment: Charlie slowly starts to nod as he remembers his encounter with the young woman in the park, a flashback shot of which is superimposed above his head (*à la Sunshine*) to illustrate his thought process.

The film's social criticism, the ironic juxtaposition of wealthy and poor characters, the bread-line scenes, the musical editing rhythms, and the use of an internally rhyming structure (e.g., bookending the film with scenes in the same park) all show the obvious influence of D.W. Griffith's groundbreaking *A Corner in Wheat* from 1909. In turn, the opening scene of *From the Submerged* may have influenced the Estonian-born French director Dmitri Kirsanoff, whose avant-garde masterpiece *Ménilmontant* from 1926 features a nearly identical sequence in which a character is prevented from committing suicide by a stranger in a public park. Perhaps the best way to gauge the film's effectiveness is to compare it to *Tempted By Necessity*, a Selig Polyscope movie from the same year that also attempts to address "social issues" (e.g., crime and unemployment). Selig's film, directed by one Lem B. Parker, is earnest and dull and possesses none of the visual inventiveness of *From the Submerged*.

The following year, 1913, was when Essanay began to decisively shift the bulk of its motion-picture production from Chicago towards its new property in Niles. The Selig Polyscope Company had been the first studio to establish a permanent base in southern California, in the Edendale district of Los Angeles, in 1909, and many other established studios and independents soon also tried their luck out west; it was easier there for the independents to get away with using equipment for which they did not possess the necessary Edison licenses and, perhaps more important, the climate and geography were considered more ideal than Chicago for film production. The warm and sunny weather was conducive to year-round shooting, unlike in Chicago where the brutal winters made exterior shooting difficult for a significant portion of the year, and the geographical terrain was diverse enough to easily accommodate the use of different kinds of exterior locations. In southern California, mountains, the ocean, desert, forests, and urban areas were all within close proximity to each other.

Because westerns were Essanay's specialty and because "Broncho Billy" Anderson had substantial experience shooting out west, it was only a matter of time before the studio would establish its own permanent facilities in California. (The base Essanay had established in Niles in 1912, which included using a railroad car as a laboratory and a barn as a makeshift studio stage, had been only temporary.) In July 1913, Spoor and Anderson invested $50,000 in a Niles studio that included indoor and outdoor stages, dressing rooms, a carpentry shop, a props room, and a wardrobe room. Additionally, ten cottages at a far end of the property were used as housing for the "talent" during production.[14]

Meanwhile, Essanay production in Chicago continued throughout 1913 and 1914. New performers, including future stars Gloria Swanson and Wallace Beery, signed contracts and made their first films at the Chicago studio. (Improbably, the hulking Beery began his career at Essanay playing a character named "Sweedie," a female Swedish maid, in a series of cross-dressing comedies.) Overall, though, production in Chicago was on the wane as production in Niles increased. In 1914, however, Essanay scored a major coup by luring young Charles Chaplin, already the top comedian in motion pictures, away from his employers at Keystone Studios. Chaplin's Essanay contract included, in addition to a lucrative salary, the alluring prospect of having his own production unit and thus achieving greater artistic freedom. The plan was for Chaplin to report to work at Essanay's Chicago studio at the beginning of the 1915 season where he would start work on a series of comedy shorts over which he would have complete creative control. A series of Chaplin comedy smashes would have conceivably established both Essanay's Niles and Chicago plants as film production powerhouses.

Things did not go according to plan.

CHAPTER NINE

The Golden Age of Selig Polyscope

Even before Colonel Selig had established his enormous new motion-picture plant in Chicago in 1907, he had begun looking at southern California as a place to do location shooting. As Essanay had done, Selig Polyscope immediately upgraded the production values of its films by taking full advantage of its new studio facilities and creating historical epics with impressively designed costumes and sets. One of the most ambitious Selig productions after opening the new Chicago studio was an adaptation of Alexandre Dumas' *The Count of Monte Cristo* (also known as *Monte Cristo*), which combined interior scenes shot in Chicago with exteriors from southern California. Although actualities had been made in southern California as early as the late nineteenth century, *The Count of Monte Cristo* was the first picture to effectively illustrate the superiority of southern California's exterior locations; it was, essentially, the "big bang" of Hollywood filmmaking.

Francis Boggs, a prominent Selig Polyscope director, made *The Count of Monte Cristo* in collaboration with cinematographer Thomas Persons. Hobart Bosworth, an acclaimed theatrical actor, was cast in the lead role of Edmond Dantes. (Bosworth would eventually appear in more than

Selig Polyscope movie set of an interior of a house, *Chicago Daily News*, 1914.
(Courtesy of the Chicago History Museum)

250 films and become known as "the Dean of Hollywood.") The Chicago scenes were finished in late 1907, and Boggs and his crew then departed for California where the movie was completed in late 1907 or early 1908. The decision to shoot in California was entirely practical: it was the dead of winter in Chicago and Lake Michigan would not have been conducive at the time to shooting the dramatic scene in which Dantes rises from the sea after escaping from prison. The scene was ultimately shot in the coastal California town of Laguna Beach, where the majestic, rocky cliffs could provide an appropriately dynamic setting.

The Count of Monte Cristo was released to favorable reviews and considerable box office success at the end of January 1908 (some theaters charged extra money for admission merely on the grounds that it was a high-quality production). Perhaps more important, Colonel Selig was so pleased with the Laguna Beach footage that he immediately began plans to expand his empire by establishing a second film studio in California. In 1909, Selig Polyscope's *The Heart of a Race Tout* would be the first film shot entirely in Los Angeles County (although the subsequently filmed *In the Sultan's Power* would actually be released a month earlier).

The Count of Monte Cristo, 1908. Directed by Francis Boggs and Thomas Persons.

Back in Chicago, Colonel Selig had begun a massive publicity campaign in an attempt to make motion pictures a more acceptable form of entertainment for people other than just the working class. As of 1907, the *Daily Tribune* was still vociferously against movies, fearing that they would lead children down a path to degradation. "There is no voice raised to defend the great majority of the five cent theatres," one *Daily Tribune* staffer opined, "because they cannot be defended. They are hopelessly bad."[1]

Selig eventually fired back with a five-page advertisement in the *Chicago Daily News Almanac*, "What Moving Pictures Are Giving the World: A Moral and Educational Tonic for the Young and Old Alike," in which he spoke in a voice like that of Professor Harold Hill to tout the educational virtues of movies: "The decision of the Supreme Court affirming the right of the mayor to censor the films and pictures exhibited in the cheaper as well as the more pretentious theaters," he wrote, "cannot fail to gratify those of us who belive that the five-cent moving-picture shows are possibilities for a great deal of good in the community. ... Hours unemployed are the devil's opportunity ... hours of relaxation are beset with perils. If not properly utilized, they are apt to breed and to encourage vicious indulgence. The moving picture show with immoral films eliminated is a valuable member of the company of modern devices to so direct the leisure hours of the young and old alike as to prevent their being wasted in frivolous and pernicious excitement of demoralizing entertainments ... the five- and ten-cent theater with its cinematographic plays is a most powerful rival of the saloon. ... Saloonkeepers have reported that their transient trade has fallen off in districts well supplied with these shows."

According to the ad, movies could even become the cure for society's ills: "they will develop into agencies of great value in the domain of education and culture." After all, most men could not afford to travel far or often, and movies could take them anywhere for a dime. Slide shows were already used in schools, but "even the lantern slide lacks the element of vitality which motion alone can supply."

Towards the end of the ad, Selig becomes nearly rapturous. "Soon a new president will be inaugurated. Yesterday King George paid a visit to Emperor William. Soon our fleet will sail through the great Panama Canal on its voyage around the world. Sicily devastated by earthquake calls for sympathy. These and many more happenings will fill the columns of the newspapers. Their descriptions convey information, but for all that they are deprived of the breath of life. The cinematograph has mastered the secret of power. It invites us to cheer the pageant or to shudder at the catastrophe as though we had been standing in the very street over which the procession passed or which the disaster overturned. It supplements the newspaper. It vivifies it … it brings history and geography within the very door of the house in which we live." He concludes with a third-person reference, as though people had forgotten that the five-page ad was written by him (with his logo appearing multiple times per page; no author was credited, but it was almost certainly written by Selig himself): "With these great and glorious objects in view … the great redoubtable Selig stands as a beacon from whom radiates, in fountains of knowledge, the greatest educational factor ever given the world."[2]

As was often the case, the Selig of this ad seemed to be able to see into the future. Few others imagined the vast educational or artistic powers of the movies as vividly as he did; indeed, 1908 marked the beginning of an era of extraordinary innovation at Selig Polyscope. That was the year they produced the first "two-reeler," *Damon and Pythias*, the longest American motion picture ever made.

Also unique was Selig's collaboration with L. Frank Baum, the renowned author of *The Wonderful Wizard of Oz* and a photography enthusiast. Baum made a deal with Selig to produce the first of the *Wizard of Oz* films, which were shot at the Selig Polyscope studio in Chicago and then color-tinted by hand. Baum toured the country with them in a remarkable-sounding live show, *The Fairylogue and Radio Plays*, which involved the author's interacting with the images on the screen.

"Fairylogue" was a play on Burton Holmes's term "travelogue," which Baum's shows in many ways resembled, and his use of the phrase "Radio Plays" is fascinating. "Radio play" would not come into its more modern usage, to describe an aural dramatization, for another decade or so. The word "radio" was virtually unknown in 1908. Baum once explained that the films had been color-tinted in France by a man named "Michael Radio," but that name seems to be just as much a fictional creation of Baum's as Dorothy and the Wizard. It is sometimes said that "radio" was a buzzword for anything "high tech" at the time (the way that "cyber" would be used in the 1990s), but the term hardly appears in print at all circa 1908 except in reference to radioactivity. The term "Radio Play" does not appear at all; perhaps, as Selig sometimes had, Baum (whose imagination was greatly excited by the "White City" at the Chicago World's Fair) had caught a glimpse of the future.

The show consisted of different filmed segments that have been credited to Selig's top directors, Francis Boggs and Otis Turner. In addition to the films, the two-hour extravaganza also featured live actors, a choir, rear projection, and slide shows. Baum himself narrated, appearing in a white suit with tails. *The Fairylogue and Radio Plays* rolled into Chicago to play at Orchestra Hall in October 1908. Although the innovative multimedia nature of this show was years, even decades, ahead of its time, newspaper reviews tended to brush off the whole enterprise as nothing more than an amusing novelty.

As the *Daily Tribune* reviewer put it: "The Scarecrow, Tin Woodsman, and a number of other pleasant characters returned to Chicago Thursday evening under interesting circumstances. In the first place, they brought with them their creator, L. Frank Baum, who wore a lovely white frock coat and won the affections of a good-sized audience of children and grownups. In the second place, they added two perfectly good new words — 'fairy-logue' and 'radio-play' — to the vocabulary of our already overworked press agents. ... A fairylogue is a travelogue that takes you to Oz instead of China. A radio-play is a fairylogue with an orchestra ... in a radio play there is the added advantage of having a cast of characters before you and knowing just who impersonate the people on the stereopticon screen. The idea is a new one, and with Mr. Baum's charming whimsicalities as its basis proved to be well worth while."[3]

Baum himself had supervised the casting of the show and selected eight-year-old Romola Remus as Dorothy. In 1977, when she was living in Uptown "with a menagerie that includes several cats, a parrot, and 35-year-old Pete the Turtle," she remembered the experience in an interview with the *Chicago Tribune*. "I was very young," she said, "but remember my mother taking me to the studio that day and saying 'It's just another movie.' I never would have dreamed that it would have amounted to anything more." When asked if she regretted not moving to Hollywood with the rest of the movie industry a few years later, she said she did not. "What if I had made it as a star? It probably would have meant endless cocktail parties, which I think are boring because of all the phonies."[4]

A couple of years earlier, Remus spoke about working with Baum and Selig: "The privilege of knowing Mr. Baum well was a happy and rewarding experience for me. I, also, portrayed the role of Dorothy in the first 'Wizard of Oz' movie. I believe it was the very first colored moving picture. It was produced by Selig's company. I remember Mr. Baum was always on hand offering encouragement or constructive criticism to all his workers. When the film was shown at various theaters, he would lecture about his various books. I recall some proud and joyous moments standing beside this tall, gentle, dignified gentleman on-stage after each matinee. The little children would clamor for his autograph, with cheers of joy!"[5]

Many historians writing about *The Fairylogue and Radio Plays* have fallen down a rabbit hole while researching the fascinating Romola Remus (later Romola Dunlap). Her father, George, became a bootlegger, ended up murdering a lover, and is sometimes said to be the inspiration for F. Scott Fitzgerald's *The Great Gatsby*. In her later years, Remus often reminisced in newspapers about turn-of-the-century Chicago, once writing about meeting Robert Todd Lincoln, with her father, on Michigan Avenue.

Unfortunately, *The Fairylogue and Radio Plays* film footage does not appear to survive today. Some say that it was incorporated into another Wizard of Oz movie that Selig made later, after Baum went bankrupt touring with the show, but this explanation is most likely apocryphal. As with 99% of the Selig Polyscope movies, it is probably a lost artifact. Although the *Fairylogue and Radio Plays* shows were well attended, they were ultimately too expensive to produce to turn a profit (even though tickets cost from 25 cents to one dollar). After losing money on his grand experiment, Baum granted the movie rights to three of his Oz books to Selig in order to cover his debts. This arrangement resulted in Selig's producing another Oz adaptation, the still extant *The Wonderful Wizard of Oz*, also directed by Otis Turner, in 1910.

Selig next turned his attention to a series of increasingly ambitious projects, including a return to the pseudo-documentary form that had brought him success a decade earlier. In 1908, Theodore Roosevelt had decided not to run for a third term as President. Instead, after his second term ended, he planned to go on a year-long safari in Africa. Selig boldly asked for permission to film the sojourn, and Roosevelt readily agreed. Selig's plan was to train Roosevelt's son, Kermit, to operate a Selig

The Wonderful Wizard of Oz,
1910. Directed by Otis Turner.

Polyscope movie camera. The ex-President soon informed Selig, however, that he had changed his mind and that he did not want anyone filming the safari. Selig was then outraged to learn that Roosevelt had enlisted Cherry Kearton, an acclaimed wildlife photographer-turned-filmmaker, to document the journey. Selig then resolved, without ever leaving Chicago, to make a film of "Roosevelt" hunting lions in Africa. In 1909, this pseu-do-documentary became a smash hit.

Hunting Big Game in Africa (also known as *Roosevelt in Africa*) was shot entirely on the interior and exterior Selig Polyscope stages in Chicago, using a Roosevelt lookalike, "native drummers" found on South State Street, bamboo fish poles, and artificial leaves. Anecdotal evidence, however, indicates that many viewers thought it was genuine footage of the adventurous former President, and many theaters probably exhibited it under exactly that delusion.

Though Selig did not discourage anyone from thinking the film was real, he also made no secret of its being a fake; the filming of the movie was extensively documented, and a handful of feature articles about it were published, including one in the *Daily Tribune*, that went into great detail for the benefit of a public that was still mostly in the dark as to how movies were made. Selig often had lions in the stable on his vast Northwest Side lot (according to legend, one of them went on to become the iconic lion in the MGM logo), but he brought in a new one just to be killed on camera for the movie.

The film's jungle set was constructed in a 60 x 20 foot cage on the lot, to the exacting specifications of the producer. "You've got to have the real color in a moving picture," he said. "We come as near to doing the real thing here as it can be done. Get ready for the hunt!"[6] In addition to the lion, the film also boasted a "cast" that included tigers, elephants, a baboon, and even a little lamb, all of which, according to Selig, "were trained and posed to act their parts."[7]

According to most accounts, "King Leo," the lion, was terrified of the set. He was bred in captivity and had never been anywhere near a jungle. He spent much of his time hiding in the artificial bushes, but his tracks gave him away. As the *Daily Tribune* reporter put it, the man playing Roosevelt "got down to examine the tracks, made sure it was a lion, then … waved his arms in frantic delight. His (false) teeth gleamed some more, and the native-tracker and ex-president shook hands and Teddy said right out loud 'Dee-lighted!'"

By all accounts, "Roosevelt" spent much of the film shaking hands, smiling, and saying "dee-lighted" while everyone did a lot of frantic waving around. Between shots, the lead actor would take out the false teeth and remark that they were a pain to wear. "It must be fierce to have 'em growing on you," he said.

The poor lion, for his part, spent most of his time hiding, while the crew did its best to scare him into looking fierce for the three movie cameras. When the first shot (fired by an off-camera marksman) hit him in the jaw, the lion let loose a mighty roar and proceeded to scare the daylights out of the crew by jumping for the platform where the cameramen were stationed. The platform was twelve feet above the ground but it seemed sufficiently likely that the lion would make the jump that the crew jumped down on the opposite side and ran. King Leo, however, hit the bars at about the eight-foot mark and fell to the ground. The cameramen then re-took their positions and continued filming as the off-screen marksman fired two more shots that brought the lion down. (Obviously, no title card would be claiming that no animals were hurt in the making of this motion picture.) The film ended with the lion's carcass being skinned on camera, while "Roosevelt" grinned, shook hands, and said "dee-lighted."[8]

The lion had cost Selig $300. *Hunting Big Game in Africa* made the company about $15,000 in profits. Meanwhile, Pathé Frères released the Cherry Kearton movie consisting of actual footage of the Roosevelt safari, but it was not nearly as popular as Selig's film. Footage of the Roosevelt party crossing a river just was not as exciting as a lion hunt, real or otherwise. The enormous financial success of *Hunting Big Game in Africa* led directly to Selig's purchase of an entire zoo for his Edendale studio and the production of a new spate of jungle adventure films featuring live animals.

Hunting Big Game in Africa has been credited variously to both of Selig's most important directors, Otis Turner and Francis Boggs. Unfortunately, Boggs was murdered at the Edendale studio not long afterwards. Although Essanay had made a star out of its janitor, Ben Turpin, Selig Polyscope did not have as much luck with theirs: Frank Minematsu, a Selig janitor, shot and killed Boggs in an attack that also involved a gunshot wound to Selig's right arm. According to the *Los Angeles Times*, "[Minematsu] is thought to have nourished a trifling grudge against Boggs and to have shot Selig because the latter attempted to avert the tragedy."[9]

In the century since this episode occurred, it has been widely reported that the Japanese Minematsu was drunk and/or mentally deranged at the time and that he subsequently offered no motive for the murder to police other than that he believed Boggs to be a "bad man." For his Selig biography, Andrew Erish undertook excellent detective work in determining that the incident may have been retaliation for an episode in which Boggs, known for hurling racial epithets, physically attacked Minematsu after he had allegedly made a pass at Boggs's wife. Whatever the truth may be, Boggs had been the specific target of Minematsu's attack, and Selig himself just happened to be in the wrong place at the wrong time. Minematsu died in Folsom Prison in the mid-1930s. The Colonel made a full recovery.[10]

Tom Mix, Selig Polyscope's most important discovery, swinging a Lasso in Chicago's Soldier Field, *Chicago Daily News*, circa 1928. (Courtesy of the Chicago History Museum)

The greatest movie star ever discovered by William Selig was undoubtedly rodeo-rider-turned-actor Tom Mix, who made his first onscreen appearance in the Chicago-shot Selig Polyscope western, *The Cowboy Millionaire* (also known as *Fell Heir to a Million Dollars* and *The Millionaire Cowboy*), in 1909.[11] (This is not to be confused with the 1913 Selig Polyscope film of the same title, which also starred Mix.) Incredibly, Mix spent the early years of his film career alternating between acting in movies for Selig Polyscope and serving as a real-life U.S. Marshall in the town of Dewey, Oklahoma. Mix was one of the very few screen cowboys with practical cowboy experience, and his impressive ability to do his own stunts, as well as his charismatic personality, eventually made him the most famous western star of the entire silent film era. In an illustration of a maxim attributed to David Bowie that "It doesn't matter who did it first, what matters is who did it second," it was not long before Mix's popularity easily eclipsed that of the original cowboy star, "Broncho Billy" Anderson.

Selig, like his rivals at Essanay, prided himself on the authenticity of his westerns, and in fact he had been the first motion-picture producer to make films of that genre in actual western locations. Even back in Chicago, real Native Americans were frequently employed to populate Selig Polyscope's horse operas. On one memorable occasion, Sioux Indians under their "Chief Whirlwind" visited the Chicago plant to appear in the 1909 production of *On the Little Big Horn; or, Custer's Last Stand.* According to a magazine article from the time, this cast included three "old timers" who had actually participated in the Battle of Little Big Horn over thirty years earlier. Selig employees interrogated them extensively about the fight, but, according to superintendent Tom Nash, "The most we could get from them was that the fight was over so quick that they could remember little about it. This was about all any of the Indians who were known to have been in the fight had to say. They showed us a good many details about the management of horses that we didn't know before, however."[12]

An incredible Selig Polyscope document from around this time that survives today is titled "Pointers on Picture Acting." Meant as a handy guide of "dos and don'ts" for thespians in Selig's employ, it offers a fascinating window into how movies were made in Chicago circa 1910. Among the interesting tidbits in the document: actors in Selig Polyscope films were often required to create their own costumes and make-up ("In the making of beards one cannot be too careful"); the morality of the actors' off-screen behavior was frequently dictated by the studio ("Let the gentleman exercise care when in the presence of ladies and children to use no profanity"); and whoever composed the list of "Pointers" clearly had a wonderful sense of humor: "Do not play too many parts with your sleeves rolled up. Cowboys and miners use the sleeves of their shirts for what they were intended. If you are playing tennis, or courting a girl at the seaside, you may display your manly beauty to your heart's content." (See Appendix A for the complete text of "Pointers on Picture Acting.")

Despite the limited commercial success of *The Fairylogue and Radio Plays,* William Selig continued to experiment with color, extended running times, and even sound. In 1912, taking advantage of relaxed General Film Company laws, he embarked on production of a "feature-length" film (i.e., one running more than forty minutes in length) about Christopher Columbus. *The Coming of Columbus* utilized replicas of Columbus's ships that had been built for the World's Fair in 1893, which Selig had purchased and restored. Shot entirely in Chicago and northern Indiana, with the banks of Lake Michigan standing in for the "New World," this ambitious, color-tinted feature was released to great acclaim in May of 1912. After a private Vatican screening, Pope Piux X even awarded the non-Catholic Colonel a medal for his efforts in "providing the film industry an artistic, moral model of production." Needless to say, this gesture effectively ended the Catholic Church's previous ban on motion pictures. Selig's efforts to convince people that motion pictures could be a force for good, and that he was a "beacon of light," were clearly meeting with remarkable success. The Pope was a most important convert.

In February of 1914, Selig teamed up with theatrical agent William Morris to make a series of short "singing and talking" films with synchronized soundtracks that starred the Scottish comedian and singer Harry Lauder, a William Morris client who had recently finished a phenomenally successful U.S. tour. While Lauder was passing through Chicago in February 1914, he went to the Selig plant and recorded seventeen short films, as well as a 300-footer featuring Lauder and Selig himself (though this one does not seem to have been released). The "talkers" showed Lauder singing Scottish tunes, such as "I Love a Lassie," "When I Get Back to Bonnie Scotland," and "Roamin' in the Gloamin." Selig and Lauder both seemed pleased with the results. Selig wrote: "I have seen the positives of all the Lauder films, part of these were projected in accompaniment with the records. The synchronism was perfect and Mr. Lauder himself was greatly elated because of the success."[13]

These "talkers" also enjoyed commercial and critical success in the spring of 1914, at least for a while. The program was highly touted in the trade papers, including *Variety*, in which the reviewer wrote: "The Harry Lauder Singing and Talking Pictures appear to have well nigh reached perfection in lingual and optical synchronisation [sic]. In the Lauder 'talkers' the art of the famous Scottish comedian is reproduced in marvelously real fashion."[14]

Unfortunately, a complex combination of technical and financial problems, as well as legal disputes between Selig and Morris, soon brought the theatrical run of the Lauder films to an end. For once, Colonel Selig was perhaps too far ahead of his time. It would not be for another thirteen years that audiences would be able to regularly enjoy talking pictures. Selig did, however, arguably achieve his greatest successes around this time with two other series of films: *The Adventures of Kathlyn*, the first American cliffhanger serial, and the *Hearst-Selig News Pictorial*, a landmark newsreel.

On December 29, 1913, Selig Polyscope debuted the first episode of *The Adventures of Kathlyn*, a thirteen-part serial starring its most popular leading lady, Kathlyn Williams. (Directly inspired by the Biograph Company's promotion of Florence Lawrence, Selig Polyscope promoted the golden-haired Williams, originally discovered by D.W. Griffith, as "The Selig Girl.") *The*

Adventures of Kathlyn detailed the adventures of the eponymous heroine, a young woman who, in order to save her father's life, becomes an unlikely Indian queen, menaced by both wild animals and a villain played by Charles Clary. The series, boasting the tagline "a wild animal melodrama," won instant popularity, and subsequent episodes were released on a bi-monthly basis over the next half-year. Although other American studios had made earlier serials, Selig's was the first to feature suspenseful, "open" endings in an attempt to lure viewers back to the theater week after week to see future installments. Selig had borrowed the basic cliffhanger conceit from master filmmaker Louis Feuillade, whose pioneering *Fantômas* serial had premiered in France the previous April and received distribution in the United States by Gaumont in the summer of 1913. *The Adventures of Kathlyn* was itself soon widely imitated: it was the template for *The Perils of Pauline* and countless other American cliffhangers to follow.

It is hard to overstate how phenomenally popular motion pictures were in 1914. In an era before the advent of television and commercial radio (not to mention long before the internet and video games), there was simply no other form of audio-visual entertainment with which the movies had to compete. Movies were actually more popular then than they are today in terms of the number of tickets sold, and Kathlyn Williams was as popular as any movie star of the era. *Moving Picture World* wrote of fans waiting in line for hours, even in the notoriously bad Chicago winter weather, to attend the latest Kathlyn serial. The *Daily Tribune* office had to answer hundreds of inquiries every day regarding where "Kathlyn" would be screening on certain days because "thousands who missed the first installments are anxious to learn where they may see the first part of the interesting subject."[15]

The Adventures of Kathlyn made Williams so famous that there were soon a clothing line, a cocktail, and even a dance (the "Kathlyn Waltz") named for her. The down-to-earth Williams never let the success go to her head, however. In contrast to, say, Francis X. Bushman, she made it clear in an interview that she personally read her own fan mail: "I appreciate so much the letters I get, particularly those from children, because it means so much effort when a child is enough interested to take the trouble to write, and then I like the suggesting letters which are really very helpful. I have had some on gowns and different things that have been of great assistance to me."

Williams also noted that she saw an opportunity for films to improve, just as theatrical producers were now, she said, being forced to put on better plays in order to compete with motion pictures. She even announced, in the course of talking up her film *Ne'er Do Well* to Chicago newspapers, that what she really wanted to do was direct, making her one of the first movie stars to utter the now-iconic phrase, "I really want to direct." That it was Kathlyn Williams making the statement was notable, as female directors were, in the phrase of *Daily Tribune* reviewer Kitty Kelly, "an undiscovered species."

"Women can direct just as well as men," Williams said. "And in the matter of much of the planning they would be more successful because they often have a keener artistic sense and more of an eye for detail — and so often it is just one tiny thing, five feet of film maybe, that quite spoils a picture, for it is always the little bit of unpleasantness that one remembers … women have shown that they can do a great many things men can — of course, there are some (things) they can't, but then they don't want to — but they have had to work hard for all they have achieved."[16]

What that remarkable interview leaves out is that Kathlyn had *already* directed a two-reeler for Selig, *The Leopard's Foundling*, a jungle adventure that hit theaters two weeks after the last installment of *The Adventures of Kathlyn*. According to a long synopsis published in the papers, it tells the tale of a girl separated from her family on safari, then raised by leopards in the African veldt. Kathlyn played the "jungle girl" who winds up captured, bound, and tied to the back of an elephant by a man who falls in love with her in time for her to save him from being eaten by leopards. The happy couple then marries, and Kathlyn's character "Balu" performs several comedic scenes upon re-entering society.[17]

It was a lot of story to cram into a two-reeler. According to advertisements, Williams both wrote and directed it as well as starred in it. "Kathlyn Williams's genius," one ad proclaimed, "is not confined to acting. She takes rank today with the leading scenario writers and motion picture producers in the world. In *The Leopard's Foundling*, she has produced a play in jungle dangers and tense dramatic climaxes that rivals the most thrilling scenes in the entire *Adventures of Kathlyn* series."[18] The surviving stills show Kathlyn dressed as one would expect — in a tattered rag dress, stalking through dense brush. Some modern sources state that Francis J. Grandon co-directed the film, but his name is absent from any available contemporary notices. The banner of the ad says: "Kathlyn's Own Play," and the copyright information, dated June 11, 1914, notes that it was written and produced by Miss Williams. Many ads for the picture made a point of stating that Kathlyn directed it. Although female directors in Europe were not unheard of (one of whom, France's Alice Guy-Blaché, opened her own studio in the U.S. in 1910), Williams was one of the very first American-born women to direct.

The movie also seems to have been a success artistically. Though there are few reviews, *The Cleveland Plain Dealer* noted that, "It possesses originality and also possesses some amount of probability, which was not one of the strong points of the serial thriller." It also noted that the second reel contained "excellent comedy [as] she objects to corsets and is a bitter foe of shoes and stockings. Her adventures with a piano are highly amusing … both in the wild scenes of the jungle and in the later transformation, Miss Williams performs most convincingly. It is one of the best parts she has ever taken. When a tiny little girl, Baby Lillian Wade . . . lies down among [the leopards] and apparently goes to sleep, one fancies that the limit of cinematographic realism has been reached. In a production of much general excellence the only possible adverse criticism is that the photography of some scenes is not as clear as it might be."[19]

In 1915, when asked by *Photoplay* if women could direct, Williams spoke of having directed "two or three" photoplays. "One, in particular, *Balu, The Leopard's Foundling*, was a great success. I wrote the play, produced it, and took the lead — a wild girl brought up with leopards. There were some excellent effects in it, and a leopard ran at me and put its head on my shoulder at the right moment. Isn't that enough for you?" (The interviewer replied "Not quite. What are your likes and dislikes," and Williams responded with "I dislike being interviewed, for one, and housework for another.")[20]

By this time, Williams was certainly a sensation. The *Daily Tribune* often published an "Answers to Movie Fans" section that would include answers to letters, though not the letters themselves (the content of which could usually easily be guessed). The April 26, 1914 installment shows that letters about Kathlyn came in constantly; answers that day included "Miss Marion: No, Kathlyn is not married to Bruce in real real," "Vida: Yes, Kathyln Williams has lived in Chicago," and "C.P.: Aside from *The Adventures of Kathlyn*, Kathlyn williams has played in *The Young Mrs. Eames*, *The Coming of Columbus*, *The Leopard's Foundling*, and numerous other Selig productions."[21] (This column was printed nearly two months before *The Leopard's Foundling* was released; it had been in production for some time. The August 1913 issue of *Motion Picture Magazine* mentioned it in its "Green Room Jottings" column, stating that "Kathlyn Williams is probably the first actress to write, direct and play in a photoplay.")[22]

1914 was a good year for Colonel Selig, his last truly good year as a film producer. In 1912, he had finally won over the *Chicago Daily Tribune* by contracting with them to publish "Photoplay(s) in Story Form" (essentially, the *Daily Tribune* published the plots of Selig Polyscope's movies as short stories on an entire page of their Sunday edition). The *Daily Tribune* may have been won over less by Selig's preaching than by the boost in circulation they got, but it was clear that by 1912 they saw some literary merits in the stories told by motion pictures. In 1914, the serialized "novelization" of *The Adventures of Kathlyn* took this concept to a whole new level. The *Kathlyn* novelization not only catapulted the cliffhanger serial to new heights of popularity, but also greatly raised the *Daily Tribune's* circulation (by as much as an astonishing 10% according to some estimates). The *Daily Tribune's* embracing of movies, in turn, helped the motion-picture medium finally to become completely acceptable to the middle and upper classes.

Selig Polyscope's western studio was thriving at this time as well. The April 1914 release of the gold rush epic *The Spoilers*, also starring Kathlyn Williams but shot in Edendale and its surrounding environs, would prove to be Selig's biggest ever financial success. *The Spoilers* also has the distinction of being the first two-hour feature-length film produced in America, and it is the best (and almost only) surviving example of Kathlyn Williams' work.

Another collaboration with the fourth estate came in the form of the *Hearst-Selig News Pictorial*, the first weekly newsreel, which debuted in early 1914. The *Pictorial* covered a wide variety of news topics, from social problems to celebrity gossip, and even included one amusing episode in which Colonel Selig and partner William Randolph Hearst were seen talking on telephones in alternating shots, allegedly discussing their newsreel with each other. The *Pictorial* ultimately instituted many of the conventions that would become standard in filmed (and televised) news, such as using Hearst columnists as "on camera reporters." Millions of Americans were reading Hearst papers at this time, and the newspaper tycoon's name on a newsreel was, for many, a guarantee of both quality and authenticity. Indeed, many of the (non-Hearst owned) trade papers raved about the *Pictorial*. Typical was this gushing review from *Motography*: "No staging, no make-believe, no 'play acting' – just the actual drama of life with its heroes, unconscious of their audience, snapped in the great crises of the world's events and their every look, every gesture, every movement brought from the uttermost ends of the earth and flashed upon your theater screen."[23]

Although William Randolph Hearst's origins in dubious "yellow journalism" were legendary, and William Selig had made his share of faux "documentaries," *Motography*'s superlatives were somewhat justified. In the late summer of 1914, a Hearst-Selig camera crew traveled to Europe to document the war-ravaged city of Louvain, Belgium. This footage, screened in the United States in October, contained what may have been the earliest non-faked filmed images of World War I. Justifiably proud of this war coverage, Selig and Hearst soon took out epic advertisements extolling the visceral nature of their newsreels: "Get in there! Woman, child and man, get in line! There's your place. March in step with the soldiers in this bloodiest of wars. You want to know what war is like? Well, come and see it in all its grim realism. You will go through all the havoc — charge with the chargers, shoot with the shooters. The cannon will yawn and spit at you. The shot will drop at your feet."[24]

Less than two years later, and for reasons never made public, Hearst switched allegiances, signing a new deal with American Vitagraph to produce a new newsreel, the *Hearst-Vitagraph Daily Pictorial*. The rift with William Randolph Hearst ultimately wounded Colonel Selig more than Frank Minematsu's bullet. Although Selig later claimed that he had instigated the dissolution of his partnership with Hearst, existing records indicate that the opposite was actually true.[25] Along with the U.S. Justice Department's litigation of the Motion Picture Patents Company, this rift signaled the beginning of an irreversible decline in Selig's movie empire.

CHAPTER TEN

Essanay Signs Charlie Chaplin

In 1914, the Essanay Film Manufacturing Company was poised to become the most powerful movie studio in the world. Despite being financially strapped at the end of the previous calendar year, it still had in its employ many of the top draws in America's nascent film industry. A series of high-quality, popular movies on the cutting edge of the new medium might have saved the studio.

George Spoor, however, had lost the power that had brought him this far in the first place: his ability to see the future. Unlike his cross-town rival William Selig, Spoor believed that short films would continue to dominate the movies. Spoor had also stopped caring much about quality; by now he cared mostly about product. Essanay star Gloria Swanson thought the movies in which she acted were so stupid that she allegedly never even agreed to spend the twenty-odd minutes it would have taken to see one of them in its entirety.

Essanay seemed to have recognized some sort of star quality in Swanson, although they never used her as anything but an extra. She noted in her autobiography that although some girls fretted over their parts, she did not. "I couldn't tell the good parts from the bad ones," she

His New Job, 1915. Directed by Charlie Chaplin.

wrote. "Every picture started out new and different and ended up just like the last one." She did not like working at Essanay much at all, and often wished she had listened to people who told her to stay away from the movies on the grounds that they were "vulgar." Certainly there were some "vulgar" goings on; she could hear Francis X. Bushman and Beverly Bayne carrying on an affair in the latter's dressing room. At one point, in a wordless exchange towards the end of her tenure, Bushman put a hand on Swanson's knee, and she responded by slapping him in the face.[1]

In 1914, Essanay made a bold move that could have ensured both its ongoing success and Chicago's place as the film capital of the world: it signed Charles Chaplin, the man who would soon become the most popular single actor in motion-picture history, to start working for Essanay for its 1915 season. As it had done when it turned down the $45 a week salary demand of Mary Pickford, the studio blew the Chaplin connection; and 1915 would be the year the company began to fall apart.

The British-born Chaplin had first been to Chicago in 1910 on his initial trip to America with the Karno Company, a vaudeville troupe, with which he was best known for playing a funny, elderly drunk in sketches (though he himself was only twenty years old at the time). That year, the Karno troupe had played an engagement at the American Music Hall at 8th Street and Wabash Avenue during a cold stint in February, and Chaplin had found the city to be stimulating, if not necessarily pretty.

Chicago was, he later wrote, "attractive in its ugliness, grim and begrimed, a city that still had the spirit of the frontier days, a thriving, heroic metropolis. ... The vast plains approaching it are, I imagine, similar to the Russian Steppes. It had a fierce pioneer gaiety that enlivened the senses, yet underlying it throbbed masculine loneliness."[2]

Chaplin was back in town with Karno in 1911 and 1912, but the life of a traveling vaudeville player was hardly glamorous, even though the $75 per week he earned was good money at the time. The hotel on Wabash Avenue where the troupe stayed was a seedy joint where quarters were shared with burlesque dancers. 'L' trains clattered constantly past the window and, Chaplin later recalled, "flickered on my bedroom wall like an old-fashioned bioscope." He also noted, perhaps with a hint of regret, that nothing ever happened between him and the dancers.[3] Of course, if he were seeking such an encounter, he would not have had to look far. Chicago at the time was still well known for its red-light districts with which most vaudevillians, certainly including the Karno Company, were well acquainted. In smaller towns, the Karno Company would sometimes even rent out entire bordellos for the night.

Had they walked a mere block west from the American Music Hall to State Street, they would have been right in the middle of an area known as Satan's Mile, which extended from Whiskey Row, a few blocks north, to the levy district four blocks south. There, a man of means could attend the Everleigh Club, which offered its own orchestras, a library (which one patron famously said was educating the wrong end of the girls), and a client list that included royalty. A man who could not afford such luxury could walk another block and find himself at places with names like Bed Bug Row and the Bucket of Blood, with several middle-class options in between. In his autobiography, Chaplin particularly remembered a place called the House of All Nations, though he avoided saying that he had actually been there. (In all likelihood, he probably had not. The brothel he described was actually not the House of All Nations, but the Everleigh Club, where the $50 per night minimum was far beyond his means at the time. The actual House of All Nations was a somewhat seedier joint with two entrances, one for two-dollar girls and one for five-dollar girls, with the dim lighting scheme preventing patrons from realizing that the same girls were behind both doors).

The child of English music hall performers, Chaplin had spent much of his childhood in poverty. His father had been a performer in the days when performers were expected to drink with patrons after every show, and his alcoholism killed him at the age of 37, when Charles was only twelve years old. His mother lost her voice, killing her theatrical career, and then lost her mind. She was sent to an insane asylum, and the young Charles was sent to a Dickensian workhouse. Having dealt with hunger and uncertainty, he never became complacent in success. "The saddest thing I can imagine," he wrote, "is to get used to luxury."[4]

Comedy was a means to an end for Chaplin, the best way he knew to keep his rent paid and his stomach full. During his first tour of America with Karno, he and a fellow performer, a trapeze artist, very nearly gave up showbiz to buy a thousand acres of land in Arkansas on which to start a hog farm. Cinema might have lost the performer and director that would come to be known as the first true genius of silent comedy had he not picked up a book on the science of hog farming and been horrified to learn that, as a farmer, he would have to castrate hogs. Given a choice between continuing to play a drunk onstage for an uncertain paycheck and gambling on a more respectable future that involved cutting off pig testicles, he stuck with the stage.

It did not take long for film companies to notice Chaplin's talent on the vaudeville stage. Around the time Karno played Chicago for a third time in the fall of 1912, he caught the eye of two companies: Essanay and Los Angeles-based Keystone.

Gilbert Anderson sought out Chaplin to offer him a contract with Essanay. With films still widely regarded as a novelty and the engagement with Karno steady, Chaplin was hesitant. Anderson was unable to work out with Spoor the exact details of the contract and, while Anderson and Spoor delayed, Chaplin signed first with Mack Sennett of Keystone and headed to L.A.[5] The delay was the first of many mistakes Essanay would make with regard to Chaplin over the next few years.

Of course, no one knew at the time that the funny young comedian who played a drunk in a vaudeville show would turn out to be a genius, and Chaplin himself was not optimistic about the whole business of motion pictures. He had seen a handful of Keystone comedies and did not think much of their rough-and-tumble style, which generally featured as many cops as possible falling over one another in scenarios that invariably ended with a chase.

Chaplin knew, however, what a great vehicle for publicity the movies could be. If he could survive a stint at Keystone, he could soon return to vaudeville as a major star. And Sennett was offering $150 per week, twice what he made with Karno.

At the Keystone studio, three pictures were generally made side by side. The awestruck Chaplin likened it to something one would have seen at the World's Fair. There was seldom anything like a script. Sennett would simply get an idea and a location and then let things develop into a chase scene.

Chaplin had been engaged, he felt, to fill the shoes of Ford Sterling, a popular star of the day, who was leaving to join Universal Pictures. Many, Chaplin included, felt that Sennett may have made a mistake. Screenwriter Elmer Ellsworth, in particular, was openly skeptical.

"Well," Ellsworth said to Chaplin, "you'd better be funny."

"If I'm half as funny as you look," Charlie quipped, "I'll do all right."[6]

Ellsworth bought him a drink.

Instead of simply imitating Sterling, Chaplin, in need of a different costume, created the now-familiar character of the Little Tramp, the wandering romantic with mustache, in baggy pants, a tiny jacket, and bowler hat. As soon as he put on the costume for the first time, Chaplin immediately understood the character completely and ran to Sennett to introduce him to what would be his new star.

"You know," he told Sennett, "this fellow is many sided: a tramp, a gentleman, a poet, a dreamer, a lonely fellow, always hopeful of romance and adventure. He would have you believe he is a scientist, a musician, a duke, a polo player. However, he is not above picking up cigarette butts or robbing a baby of its candy. And of course, if the situation warrants it, he will kick a lady in the rear — but only in extreme anger."[7]

Or, anyway, that is how Chaplin later remembered his conception of the character. His early Keystone shorts did not show the Tramp to be nearly as multi-faceted as this description.

Chaplin would, however, come to change the way people think about getting kicked in the rear. In just a few short years, Chaplin would become the most famous comedian in the history of the world and the first international motion-picture superstar. Lacking dialogue, his comedies were just as popular with the waves of immigrants who were landing on American shores and did not speak a word of English as they were with native English speakers. One did not need to understand any particular language to find the Little Tramp funny.

The medium of the film comedy was still a brand new one, and that situation gave Chaplin a certain confidence. "No one was positive or sure of himself," he wrote, "[so] I concluded that I knew as much as the other fellow. ... Thus grew a belief in myself that I was creative and could write my own stories."[8]

Soon, this creativity put him at odds with the Keystone method. "Any three-dollar-a-day extra can do what you want me to do," he roared to one director. "I want to do something with merit, not just be bounced around and fall off of street cars."[9]

As Chaplin became more assured, he began to tailor his performances more and more to the medium. In particular, he performed in such ways that the "butchers" in the editing room could not change his routines. He was always distressed when the editors cut out his favorite bits, so he started working gags into his entrances and exits that he knew they would never be able to excise without confusing what little story there was.

In time, as his comedies grew more successful, Chaplin was able to talk Sennett into letting him direct his own pictures (though Sennett made him put up some of his own money), giving him the chance to experiment with such things as how the placement of a camera could enhance or subtract from the effectiveness of a gag. He began to introduce a certain subtlety into the medium, which had always relied on very broad panto-mime for comedy.

The use of subtlety in Chaplin comedies made them a stark contrast to nearly every other movie on the market, and, unlike the many short-sighted pioneers before him, Chaplin immediately realized that he was onto something big. He likened himself to "a geologist ... I was entering a rich, unexplored field ... on the verge of something wonderful."[10]

The 25-year-old Chaplin was, in fact, turning a slapstick medium into a sort of art, and the public loved it. The studio heads were slow to realize it, but it was this kind of vision, not just plain business sense, that they needed to stay on top in the long run.

Soon, with a bonus of $25 for each picture he directed, Chaplin was earning $200 a week, a considerable sum at the time. Chaplin lived "in sumptuous style" with expenses of only $75 a week. Still, the films he made were grossing tens of thousands, if not more, and Chaplin was no fool: he knew that fame was a passing fancy, and that he needed to take advantage of what could be a very narrow window of opportunity.

When the time came to renew his contract, he told Sennett he wanted $1,000 per week.

"I don't make that!" Sennett exclaimed.

"I know," said Chaplin, "but the public doesn't line up outside the box office when *your* name appears."

Sennett pointed out that it was only the Keystone organization that made the pictures successful, and Chaplin knew that he had a point. Ford Sterling's career had floundered since he left. Chaplin, however, stood his ground. "All I need to make a comedy," he said," is a park, a policeman, and a pretty girl."[11] (D.W. Griffith would later tweak this formula by saying that all *he* needed to make a film was "a girl and a gun."[12])

Sennett eventually offered Chaplin a three-year contract at $500 a week the first year, $700 the second, and $1,500 the third, which would average out to around $1,000 a week. Chaplin, fully aware that he might be out of fashion, and not be worth $1,500 a week in two years' time, offered to sign if the rates were reversed. Sennett was dumbfounded.

Meanwhile, Essanay was on the lookout for a comedian. The studio already had a few in their employ, such as Ben Turpin and Wallace Beery, but none were true superstars of the comedy genre. They had a romantic idol in Francis X. Bushman and a cowboy hero in Anderson. Adding a great comedian to their roster would make the studio a more formidable force than ever.

One day, Jesse Robbins, who had graduated from cinematographer to producer/director at Essanay (and who would later direct the first Laurel and Hardy film), put in a call to Chaplin at Keystone. "I understand," he said "that you want a $10,000 bonus before signing a contract and $1,250 a week."

Chaplin, who was nearing the end of his contract with Keystone, and secretly nervous that no one else would want him, invited Robbins to dinner, where Robbins said that $1,250 per week was certainly doable, but that he did not know if he could arrange the bonus.

"That seems to be a hitch with so many of (the studios)," said Chaplin. "They're all full of big offers, but they don't put up any cash!"[13]

In fact, it had never occurred to Chaplin to ask for a cash bonus before he got the call from Robbins. His best other offer was from Universal, which had offered twelve cents per foot of film but no actual salary.

No better offer had actually come in, but Chaplin played the conversation like a poker hand, letting Robbins do all the talking and implying that he was getting many more offers than he was. At the end of the meal, Robbins put in a call to Gilbert Anderson, who was filming a new horse opera in San Francisco, then came back to the table to tell Chaplin that the deal was on, and the bonus had been approved. Chaplin fulfilled his contract with Keystone over the next two weeks, then left for Chicago.

Essanay now had, arguably, the greatest cowboy, the greatest romantic idol, and the greatest comedian all working in its Chicago studio. George Spoor, however, thought that Anderson had lost his mind. He had never even heard of Charles Chaplin, and he sent a wire to Anderson asking if he had, in fact, gone mad. Most of the comedians Spoor employed were making far less than a tenth of what Chaplin would be making, and their pictures barely broke even.

Spoor, naturally, did not always remember the events quite like that. In 1943, he told the *Chicago Daily News*, "I heard of a new comedian in New York, a little man with a mustache, a cane, tall hat, baggy pants and big shoes. I wired my brother to find out about him and sign him up. He answered that it must be an extra named Charlie Chaplin that I meant, and $50 a week would be enough to pay him. Then it started, one wire after another. From $50, Charlie demanded $100, then $200, then $500, finally $1000 a week. Each wire would find my brother more indignant and me hopping mad that he didn't give Chaplin whatever he asked and get his signature on a contract."[14]

This is surely an instance of Spoor's trying to clean up his own image in his twilight years; by all accounts he was furious over the initial contract. When Spoor was overcome with people congratulating him on the big coup of signing Charlie, however, he began to become more optimistic. As an experiment, while dining at a hotel, he gave a boy a quarter to run through the lobby announcing a call for Mr. Charles Chaplin, which led crowds of people to stir about excitedly, hoping for a glimpse of the famous comic. This experiment lifted Spoor's spirits, but he took a leave of absence from Chicago to avoid having to cut the check for Chaplin's bonus.

For the trip to Chicago from California, Chaplin traveled in considerably more style than he had on his Chicago trips with Karno. Anderson himself accompanied him on a train ride, which they shared with a sheriff, a policeman, and a convict on his way to be hanged who, in exchange for behaving himself, was being treated to a ride in first-class comfort. Chaplin wished him luck.

The two arrived in Chicago shortly before Christmas 1914, and were greeted at the station by Molly, Anderson's wife. It was, Molly later remembered, "bitterly cold. I met G.M. ... There was the little fellow with him. He had no luggage, no handbag ... no overcoat, and there was a severe wind. Well, we all rode back to my Chicago apartment. When I could get

G.M. alone, I asked him 'who is this little chap?'"

Though he surely would not have admitted it to Spoor, it seems that Anderson knew little of Chaplin's work and had signed him solely on Robbins's recommendation. He did, however, tell his wife that he saw great potential in the young man. "I find him clever and amusing," Anderson told her. "I think he could be a great comedian. He's being wasted in Los Angeles."

The trio proceeded to Anderson's luxurious high-rise apartment on the city's North Side, at 1027 West Lawrence Avenue, where Chaplin was charmed by the homey atmosphere created by the Christmas tree and the presence of little Maxine, Anderson's baby daughter. "A Christmas tree, a baby. It's wonderful!" he said.

Though Molly was as charmed by him as he was by her home, she was still shocked at his artistic temperament and habits. "He slept late. Very late," she recalled in the 1960s. "And when he appeared, it was without a shirt collar. He had curly hair and never ran a comb through it. The maids kept his food waiting."

Gene Morgan of the *Chicago Daily News* became a friend of Chaplin's, and took him shopping in second-hand stores along State Street to find a new Little Tramp costume. Having cobbled his original one together from bits of clothing borrowed from his Keystone co-stars, Chaplin did not have a Tramp costume of his own. Finding oversized shoes proved a challenge. Morgan later noted snidely that Chicago was the "city of broad shoulders, not the city of big feet."

Chaplin settled in with the Andersons for a week; no work would be done at the studio until the new year. All the while, he waited restlessly for Spoor to arrive with the rest of his bonus. The Andersons' North Side neighborhood was bustling with well-to-do families and movie stars, a long way, if only a short ride on the "L," from the seedy Wabash Avenue hotels Chaplin had shared with burlesque dancers only two years before.

On New Year's Eve, the Andersons took Charlie to a five-dollar-per-plate dinner at the College Inn, a stylish nightclub in the basement of the Hotel Sherman at Clark and Randolph Streets where the modern jazz music was in sharp, one might say "Chaplin-esque," contrast to the Elizabethan-style décor.

Chaplin, a man who himself stood out by sheer contrast, did not exactly dress to the nines. "I had to find a good shirt for him," said Molly, "and cuff links and a suit. We wanted him to be presentable ... but I never thought of a muffler." Still, when the trio got into the car to be taken downtown, she noticed he was wearing a scarf. "On closer inspection," she recalled, "I discovered that he was wearing his pajama bottoms around his neck. I suppose that was an indication of his ability to improvise, but it just wouldn't do at the College Inn!"

In the crowd that night were many well-known stage actors, including Henrietta Crossman, Maclyn Arbuckle, and Mabel Taliaferro. The local papers the next day also mentioned that one star was there to represent the film world: comedian John Bunny, who appeared with a red paper clown's hat on his head. Bunny was, at the time, arguably more recognizable than Chaplin, particularly when Chaplin was not in his comedy makeup (reporters often mentioned that they had no idea what Chaplin looked like offstage, and most assumed he was middle-aged or older until they met him). Nonetheless, one of the Howard Brothers, a vaudeville troupe, recognized Chaplin at once. He grabbed him by the scruff of the neck and made him stand on a chair while he waved to the crowd of revelers to calm down. "Ladies and Gentlemen," Howard announced, "I want to introduce you to the funniest man in moving pictures — Charlie Chaplin!"

Publicity photo of Charlie Chaplin flanked by Francis X. Bushman (left) and "Broncho Billy" Anderson (right). (Courtesy of the Chicago History Museum)

A few minutes later, a furious man stormed the table where the Andersons and Chaplin were sitting, now accompanied by Howard. "Do you mean to tell me," the man growled, "that this *boy* is the funniest comedian in moving pictures? Do you know that John Bunny is in the audience tonight? And he has always been considered the funniest man in films!"

Howard scoffed. "Did John Bunny say that, or did you say that?"

"We both said that," said the man.

Howard glared. "Well," he said, "you go right on back to John Bunny and tell him *that* is the funniest line he ever handed me!"[15]

In fact, Bunny had already filmed what was to be his final picture. He died only a few months after his near-encounter with Chaplin.

On New Year's Day, Anderson returned to California, and Chaplin began work at the Essanay studio on West Argyle Street. To his chagrin, Spoor had still not arrived with his check.

Chaplin and Chicago were quickly turning out to be a bad fit. On his first day of work, the temperature was recorded as being one degree Fahrenheit, while the high barely scraped the low 20s. The wind-chill factor made it even colder, something Chaplin would have keenly felt when commuting from "Broncho Billy" Anderson's apartment near the lake to the Essanay building just a few blocks away. A publicity photo of Chaplin in Chicago, probably taken earlier, is revealing: the suave Francis X. Bushman and the more ruggedly handsome Anderson flank him on either side. Both men tower over the diminutive Chaplin, who is wearing an overcoat still buttoned to the very top button as well as what looks like a forced smile.

Chaplin in Chicago: His New Job

D espite his best attempts to put on a brave face, Charlie Chaplin was
miserable with Essanay by the time he commenced work for the studio on his first picture, fittingly titled *His New Job*. When he asked to see the rushes at the end of the day, Essanay screened the original camera negative to save itself the expense of making a print. Chaplin was mortified.

Chaplin traced most of the studio's troubles back to one source: Thomas Edison, who had attempted to monopolize the industry through his Motion Picture Patents Company. Essanay was, Chaplin wrote, "smug and self-satisfied. Having been one of the first to enter the film business, and being protected by patent rights that gave them a monopoly, their last consideration was the making of good pictures. And although other companies were challenging their patent rights and making better films, Essanay still went smugly on, dealing out scenarios like playing cards every Monday morning."[1]

Chaplin was distressed by the inner workings of the studio, which he found to be grim and business-like, a far cry from the happy atmosphere

His New Job, 1915. Directed by Charlie Chaplin.

Louella Parsons would later describe. He said that the staff were "stuffy and went around like bank clerks. ... The business end of it was very impressive, but not their films. ... The different departments were partitioned like tellers' cages — it was anything but conducive to creative work." Certainly it was quite a change from the genial Keystone, which Joyce Milton described as having the atmosphere of a slightly disreputable summer camp.

The grim atmosphere Chaplin found may have been simply a reaction against the company's recent discovery that its business was in trouble, largely because it had not been careful *enough* in the previous years. The Essanay at which Chaplin arrived was trying to get its act together. When he arrived, he was directed to the front desk, so that Louella Parsons could give him a script. This instruction was merely an example of the studio trying to be responsible, but Chaplin was furious. "I don't use other people's scripts, I write my own," Chaplin said, curtly.[2]

Parsons, in fact, was a bit distressed by the signing of Chaplin, knowing full well that Essanay could not really afford him, and that, as the head of the scenario department, she had taken the brunt of responsibility for the dire financial state of the company. Indeed, the same month Chaplin arrived, Parsons left, robbing the studio of its most esteemed screenwriter.

Chaplin wandered about the studio all day, miserably wondering what he should be doing and why nothing was being done for him after all the trouble they had gone to bring him there in the first place. He also wondered where his bonus check was.

The next morning, Chaplin requested a cast and was given one, including Ben Turpin, who Chaplin liked instantly. When looking for a leading lady, Chaplin immediately picked out a young Gloria Swanson. In *Tramp*, her Chaplin biography, Joyce Milton suggests that this was not a case of Chaplin's recognizing star quality in Swanson, but Chaplin trying to ingratiate himself with his hostess, Molly Anderson, who employed Gloria's cigarette-smoking Aunt Inga as a nanny. Chaplin was, however, by no means concerned with ingratiating himself to anyone at Essanay; he was clearly concerned with making the best picture he could. It is doubtful that he would have picked her had he *not* seen a leading lady in Swanson.

Chaplin spent a full day working up routines with the future screen legend. In a still photo that survives today, Swanson looks less like the proverbial deer caught in headlights than like a deer that has actually been hit by a truck. "These [routines]," she recalled, "all involved kicking each other in the pants, running into things, and falling over each other. … He reminded me of a pixie from some other world altogether. … I felt like a cow trying to dance with a toy poodle."[3] She haughtily told Chaplin that she did not see what was funny about any of these routines. Her comment hurt him more than he let on.

When Chaplin finally began work on *His New Job*, a movie about a stagehand brought in to cover for an unpunctual star, Swanson was downgraded to a bit part as a stenographer; another actress was given the lead. The lesson did Swanson some good however: she would do a Chaplin impersonation in *Manhandled* in 1923 and again in her famous role in *Sunset Boulevard* in 1950.

Francis X. Bushman was not terribly amused by *His New Job* either. He felt that the "unpunctual star" was a caricature of him. Still, seeing that Chaplin was unhappy with Essanay, Bushman tried to reassure him. "Whatever you think of the studio," he said, "it is just the antithesis." "I don't like the studio," Chaplin said, "And I don't like the word 'antithesis.'"[4]

He had barely been in the studio for three days when a reporter for *Picture-Play Weekly* arrived. Chaplin was not yet used to reporters. Few of them had made the journey out to Los Angeles. "I'm afraid," he told her, when she said she had enjoyed his vaudeville appearances in Chicago, "you are trying to put me in good humor for the interview … and really you haven't a chance to succeed."

As he said this, someone who thought the room was too warm opened a window to the January air. Chaplin immediately "did one of those funny little turn-the-nose-up-and-look-to-the-side tricks," then moved his chair closer to the steam pipe. He had already decided that he would not be in Chicago for long. "And to think I was in California last week!" he moaned, eliciting a laugh. "Broncho Billy did this. [If it wasn't for him] I wouldn't be freezing! I'll have to stand it a while longer. Then it's back West for mine!"[5]

The reporter quickly noted that this performance was all for laughs, not based on any real anger at Anderson. Everyone present had a good chuckle (though it was not, in fact, entirely a joke), and Chaplin, perhaps still smarting from Swanson's critique, went on to tell the reporter that he really aspired to more dramatic roles.

If Chaplin's appearance at the College Inn had failed to warrant a mention in the *Chicago Daily Tribune*, his presence at Essanay did the trick. He had been there for barely a week when the *Daily Tribune's* pseudonymously — and splendidly — named movie writer Mae Tinee ("matinee") came to conduct an interview.

By this time, Chaplin was already hiding out, making himself scarce and waiting for Spoor to arrive. The guide who met Tinee at the front desk had no idea where he was. "You may not believe him," he said, "but he is scared to death of publicity, and I had my hands full, I can tell you, to pry permission out of him for this interview." They looked all over the studio without success before trying the projection room, where Tinee hoped that even if Chaplin was not there, maybe she could meet Anderson or Bushman.

The projection room consisted of two rows of schoolroom-style seats, with desks attached, facing the screen. There, they found Bushman seated at one desk and Anderson, freshly back from California, in another. His over-sized cowboy physique dwarfed the tiny chair. A handful of other people, clerks, and crew, sat at other desks. Over in the corner sat Chaplin. The guide sat Tinee down and told her to sit there until the picture (Anderson's newest, *When Love and Honor Called*) was over. "I'll guard the door," he said, "and see that Mr. Chaplin doesn't get out."

Tinee assured her readers that Anderson was all that they dreamed he would be. "Believe me, girls," she wrote, "Mr. Anderson in the flesh is some winner!" All through the screening, though, Anderson looked, she wrote, as if he wished he were any place but there. Chaplin, too, clearly was not in the mood to be interviewed. He was still dismayed at the way things were going, and only the brusque arm of Tinee's guide stopped him from bolting from the room the minute the screening ended.

"Mr. Chaplin?" said Tinee. "I guess there's no use denying it," he said. "Glad to meet you."

As the guide led them upstairs to an office, Tinee asked why he did not like to be interviewed. "Don't you know it's good for you?" she asked.

"I doubt it," said Chaplin. "You see, people aren't strong for celebrities that are already made. When a man's been boosted to the skies, they're apt to sit back in their seats and say 'I don't see anything so wonderful about that chap ... he's over-rated.' But if the man is not made, they take joy and pride in discovering him."

By this time, Chaplin had been writing and directing his own films for nine months, an eternity in the film business. "I think I'm going to like it here," he said, politely. "Nice people, nice studio. I'll miss California and the old Keystone bunch, though." "Your audience will follow you," Tinee said, as Chaplin sighed. "That will delight your soul, and your correspondents will write to you!"

Now Chaplin grinned. "You bet they will," he said, and his smile broke into a laugh as he told Tinee about the first fan letter he had ever received, from a boy who used the word "favrit" "about six times," and who ended his letter by saying "You was certainly grand, Mr. Chaplin, all threw [sic] the pixter [sic], but the way you squirted watter [sic] out of your mouth was classic!"

Though Tinee noted that Chaplin seemed relieved to be pulled back to work, she was duly charmed by him, or at least claimed to be. "He's a nice as well as a funny Charlie Chaplin," she wrote. "25 and unmarried, girls!"[6]

To *Motion Picture Magazine*, he granted a somewhat lengthier interview, expounding about his life story, which he embellished a bit, and his method of work. Chaplin created the impression that, goofy as he was on camera, he had become very serious about his craft in a way that few other motion-picture actors had been. "Motion picture comedy is still in its infancy," he said. "In the next few years I expect to see so many improvements that you could then scarcely recognize the comedy of the present day."[7]

He did not say that he was pretty sure that those improvements would not be coming from Essanay, but he was. He had already decided that *His New Job* would be his only Chicago movie. Chaplin seems never to have bothered to find a permanent address in the city. While rumors persist that he lived in a penthouse in the Brewster Apartments in Lincoln Park (a building that still stands at 2800 N. Pine Grove Avenue today), this is likely nothing more than an urban legend. The books that claim Chaplin resided there fail to cite sources, and the Brewster Apartments are located about three and a half miles north of the former Essanay complex (in contrast to Broncho Billy's apartment, which was mere blocks away). Given the short amount of time he was in Chicago, and his notorious thriftiness, it is more probable that Chaplin bunked with the Andersons for the entirety of his three-week stay.

Though he wrote of living in "sumptuous style" while working for Keystone, those who knew him in Chicago saw no evidence of it. Hazel Buddemeyer, who worked as a negative cutter, later remembered that she and her co-workers thought that their own salary, eighteen dollars per week, was fantastic. The studio employees, actors, and crew alike, would take turns taking spins in one another's cars and dine in high fashion at the stylish Green Mill. "We all took turns buying drinks, except Charlie," Buddmeyer recalled. "When his turn came, he would hide down at the end of the bar. He was the stingiest man I ever saw!"[8]

In 1969, William Grisham asked Molly Anderson, "Broncho Billy"'s widow, on what in the world Chaplin spent his money, and she also remembered him as a skinflint. "Well," she laughed, "he didn't exactly throw [his money] away! Charlie has the first nickel he ever earned. I'm certain of that."[9]

Orson Welles, who was born in Wisconsin during Chaplin's tenure at Essanay, and would later provide the story idea for Chaplin's *Monsieur Verdoux* (1947), referred to Chaplin as the "cheapest man who ever lived."[10] Indeed, when it eventually came time for Chaplin to build his own house in Hollywood, he saved money by using studio carpenters. These men were used to building temporary sets. Visitors to Chaplin's house were stunned to find doorknobs and railings coming off in their hands.

Chaplin himself was already joking about his stinginess in 1915. He told *Motion Picture Magazine* that when he first got off the train in Chicago, a newsboy had seen him and shouted to his friend, "What do you think of that hamfat? $100,000 a year, and he looks like a tramp!"[11]

Chaplin was almost finished with *His New Job* when, after two weeks, Spoor finally arrived. Chaplin wasted no time in confronting him about the promised bonus. Spoor hemmed and hawed, saying it was not really his department and that he had not seen the contract, but he was sure that the front desk would take care of it all. Chaplin was positively enraged. "What are you scared of?" he asked. "You can still get out of your contract if you wish — in fact, I think you've already broken it!" "We'll take care of the matter right now," Spoor said, softly.[12]

Naturally, when he retold the story, Spoor told it differently, and made a crack of his own about Chaplin's legendary cheapness. "Came the day I was to meet the man whom I was paying $1,250 a week," he told the *Daily*

News, "and there stood a little chap in the Chicago winter cold without an overcoat. I gave him his first week's pay and a bonus of one week's pay, which he demanded for signing. He tucked $2,500 into his pocket, and I sent him downtown with an advertising man to buy a coat. I couldn't believe it when I saw it, an over-sized, ragged coat with no belt and just one button that kind of camped over Charlie; it was the most misfit coat I ever saw. So I called in the advertising man and asked him if Charlie was pulling a gag on me. The answer was no. 'I took him to Willoughby & Hill, Mr. Spoor,' said the man, 'but every coat was too expensive. He bought a coat at a second-hand place on Clark Street for two dollars.' That was Charlie Chaplin."[13]

Spoor did see to it that the check was cut, and did whatever he could to make Chaplin happy, but the two never quite warmed up to one another. Chaplin was not adjusting to Chicago; he missed California. Spoor offered to send him to the Western studio in Niles, where Anderson was still doing most of his work. Anderson had told Chaplin that the Chicago studio was better suited to comedy, but Chaplin had just told the *Daily Tribune* that "with conditions favorable a man can do so much better work, you know." He also liked Anderson better than Spoor.

Hence, Chaplin left Chicago for Niles as soon as *His New Job* was completed. Essanay's public relations department, as well as the *Los Angeles Times*, said that Chaplin blamed the cold. In fact, though he certainly was not enthusiastic about Chicago's weather, he blamed Spoor. Chaplin's entire Chicago residency lasted just twenty-three days. When *His New Job* was released on February 1, 1915, he was already in Niles, never to look back.

It is extremely impressive that the 25-year-old Chaplin could write, direct, and star in a film, even a two-reeler, in less than two weeks' time, using Chicago facilities and collaborators with whom he had previously been completely unfamiliar. One of the reasons Chaplin was able to work so quickly and efficiently in Chicago was his ingenious idea to make *His New Job* a "meta film": the movie begins with Chaplin's familiar Little Tramp character showing up to audition for a part in a movie at "Lodestone Studios" (an obvious reference to former employer Keystone). The interior stages, as well as the employees of Essanay, essentially play themselves as Lodestone, which saved Essanay the expense of having to design and construct new sets and costumes but also had the benefit of giving audiences a fascinating, documentary-like peek into the process of movie-making in 1915.

The slim plot of *His New Job* centers on the Tramp getting a job first as a production assistant, then as a carpenter, and finally as an extra in what appears to be a prestigious "period" film set in nineteenth-century Russia. Of course, he wreaks havoc on the set, and the entire production soon devolves into a state of slapstick anarchy.

Interestingly, advertisements for *His New Job* played up the film's self-reflexive aspect. Although the title obviously alluded to the beginning of a new phase in Chaplin's career, the ads also billed Chaplin and co-star Ben Turpin as playing "themselves." *His New Job* opened to positive reviews both locally and across the nation, some of which attempted to contextualize it within Chaplin's budding filmography. In her *Daily Tribune* review, Kitty Kelly noted that Chaplin's persona seemed a "little nicer" than he had been in his Keystone films while also claiming, "It is hard to conceive of his being any funnier."[14]

If *His New Job* remains one of the high points of Chaplin's Essanay output, that is likely because it was made before his problems with Spoor and Anderson had become irreversible. Although Chaplin never truly felt at home at Essanay, he also admitted that Spoor and Anderson initially gave him "*carte blanche*" to do what he wanted. This freedom allowed Chaplin to try new things, in particular the blending of comedy and pathos that would become the hallmark of his mature masterpieces of the 1920s and 1930s. Various sources claim Chaplin co-wrote *His New Job* with Louella Parsons but, as with Chaplin's Keystone comedies, the film was most likely improvised, as the inclusion of a behind-the-scenes game of dice between the Tramp and a member of the crew suggests.

The dice game was apparently inspired by the real-life dice games played by Essanay cast and crew members while taking lunch breaks at Al Sternberg's bar and restaurant on the corner of Broadway and Argyle Streets, just a few blocks away. This was an old Essanay custom that had apparently not fallen by the wayside, even given the company's financial woes. Since the loser had to pay the bill, one can only assume the notoriously thrifty Chaplin excelled at dice.

Indeed, he wrote in his autobiography that he had had ample time to practice this skill in his vaudeville days. "In those days, the Middle West had charm," he wrote. "The atmosphere was romantic; every drugstore and saloon had a dice-throwing desk in the entrance where one gambled for whatever products they sold. On Sunday Morning, Main Street was a continual hollow sound of rattling dice, which was pleasant and friendly; and many a time I won a dollar's worth of goods for ten cents."[15]

Although *His New Job* is still quite funny by modern standards, its most interesting aspect today is probably the dramatic moment in the film-within-the-film when the Tramp tearfully pleads for the leading lady not to leave him before accidentally ripping her dress and using the torn garment to dry his eyes. From here, the masterful tonal shifts between tear-jerking melodrama and uproarious physical comedy displayed in Chaplin's feature films, beginning with *The Kid* in 1921, are just a few artistic steps away.

Once in Niles, Chaplin actually lived in Anderson's own bungalow, which stood in stark contrast to the fancy apartment in Chicago. It was drab, scarcely lit, barely furnished, and offered no working appliances.

His New Job, 1915. Directed by Charlie Chaplin.

"The bathroom was unspeakable," Chaplin recalled. "One had to take a jug and fill it from the bath tap and empty it down the flush to make the toilet work. This was the home of G.M. Anderson, the multi-millionaire cowboy."[16] In fact, Anderson spent most nights in a suite at the Saint Francis Hotel, commuting back to the Bay. Chaplin may have found that living in relative squalor was helpful to him, creatively. Years later, visitors were shocked to see his tiny dressing rooms. "If I had a room like [Douglas Fairbanks Sr.'s] dressing room, I couldn't possibly portray the Little Tramp," he said. "I need a room that looks like him."[17] Of course, that could have also simply been an excuse for his thriftiness.

For his part, Chaplin, the rich young comedian, arrived in Niles carrying nothing but a small handbag containing "a spare shirt, a few dingy changes of underwear and a frayed toothbrush."[18] Though the weather could only have been more agreeable, Chaplin was even less happy in the rustic Niles, where cows seemed to outnumber people and none of the other bathrooms were any nicer than the one in Anderson's bungalow, than he had been in Chicago, where at least he felt as at home as a London boy would in another large city.

Around the world, the motion-picture business was changing. D.W. Griffith's three-hour epic, *The Birth of a Nation*, which forever codified the "language" of movies, premiered exactly one week after *His New Job*. Chaplin went to see it at least once a week and became seized with the notion that he, too, could make feature-length movies, applying the same "language" to comedy that Griffith did to drama.[19]

More and more creativity was being seen in the film world: directors were now being regarded as artists, and movies had clearly turned a corner in the journey from short snippets of Fred Ott sneezing to modern epics that would characterize the golden age of Hollywood cinema. The opportunities for longer-form movies were almost nil at Essanay, however, where Spoor was still stuck in the old days.

Much of Chaplin's post-*His New Job* Essanay work was simply recycled from earlier material. The plots for his hastily made movies tended, wrote Joyce Milton, to start strongly and go nowhere. On the plus side, the pictures were made much more carefully, and with less simple rough-and-tumble humor, than his Keystone work, and the artistic isolation he had been able to make for himself allowed him to refine, even improve upon, the character of the Tramp. Chaplin, a perfectionist, knew that he could make better movies.

He also knew that Essanay was not the atmosphere in which he could do so and that things were about to get worse. Already fearing that the smugness of being part of the old guard lorded over by Edison and his patents kept Spoor from caring much about quality, Chaplin resolved to go elsewhere.

When 1915 drew to a close and his contract with Essanay was running out, Chaplin's star was clearly on the rise. His Little Tramp persona had made him one of the most recognizable faces in the world, and Chaplin knew that he was more than earning his large salary. He also knew that movies were changing and that if he wanted to be a part of this growth and change, as he deserved to be, he would be better off at a studio that had not been made complacent by its membership in the Edison Trust.

Even before he started with Keystone, Chaplin had known, he later said, that "nothing transcends personality" in movies. Like Edison, his real victory was largely the result of his personality, not necessarily his considerable talent. There have been other silent comedians and directors who historians have held in higher esteem (Buster Keaton's movies today are generally regarded as more "modern"), but it was Chaplin who was most successful at winning the hearts of audiences, just as Edison became the father of electricity despite his own actual accomplishments being overshadowed by those of Tesla.

Essanay seems to have understood the value of Chaplin's personality. It was that studio that first credited him as "Charlie," not "Charles" (to his chagrin), and it was Essanay that launched the marketing campaigns that infected the public with "Chaplinitis" in 1915. Also, like Edison, Essanay failed to understand the importance of keeping hold of the top personalities in the field, even while understanding the value of personality. Just as Edison had lost W.K.L. Dickson to Biograph, and all of his esteemed vocal talent to the Victor Talking Machine Company, Essanay too lost its own stars. Over the course of 1915, it had already lost Bushman to Metro, and Louella Parsons had left the studio to pioneer the gossip column for the *Chicago Record-Herald* around the same time Chaplin left the city.

Ben Turpin, too, was now gone. He had left with Chaplin for Niles, but found that Chaplin was not about to let him steal any scenes, and he made only one movie there before relocating to Los Angeles. Even Gloria Swanson, with her mother, had moved away. She would soon land at Keystone, where she found the "disreputable summer camp" atmosphere and the improvised style of making movies delightful.

Essanay, however, was not dead yet. George Spoor traveled to California to make Chaplin an offer for another year at a handsome raise: he was prepared to offer him $350,000, plus production expenses, for one two-reel picture per month for the next year.

"On signing any contract," Chaplin said, "I want $150,000 bonus plunked down first."[20]

This offer meant that Chaplin would be earning a half-million dollars' pay for the year, a huge increase over the previous year (not to mention the $700 per week he would have been earning in the second year of the contract Sennett had offered). When Spoor balked, Chaplin made up his mind once and for all that he was through with Essanay.

Chaplin dispatched his brother, Syd, to New York to field offers from other studios in January 1916. This time, there were plenty. Over the course of the year, Essanay's publicity machine had helped catapult Charlie to unheard-of stardom. Trinkets bearing his likeness were sold everywhere (though the honor of being the first to market Chaplin statues belonged to a Chicago man who sold them in catalogs). Stan Laurel, who had once been Chaplin's roommate in his vaudeville days, was still on the stage circuit, performing as a Chaplin impersonator.

Chaplin knew that his movies were making tremendous amounts of money, but it seems that in his comparative isolation in California, he had no idea exactly how popular he had become across the country. When he boarded a slow train to New York to meet with his brother and negotiate offers with other companies, he still felt that no one would recognize him when he was not wearing his comedy makeup. After all, he had not even made the finals at a recent Charlie Chaplin lookalike contest in San Francisco.

He was shocked when huge crowds gathered at every stop, even dragging him out of the car in his dressing gown to accept a key to the city of Amarillo, Texas, when the train stopped there. This kind of event — mobs waiting at every train stop in an age when the lack of airports and interstates made it impossible for stars to travel privately and in secret — would horrify a number of stars. When it happened to her in 1925, Gloria Swanson would say that she felt like the half-dead whale that people had lined up to see when P.T. Barnum had moved it across the country in a seaweed-lined train car years before.

At the end of 1914, only Molly Anderson had been present to greet Chaplin when he arrived in Chicago, despite the fact that he was traveling with her husband, the famous "Broncho Billy." Now, barely more than a year later, when Chaplin's train pulled into Union Station, cheering crowds mobbed him as a waiting limousine took him to stay a night as a guest at the Blackstone Hotel. The Blackstone was an opulent palace right around the corner from the American Music Hall, where he had quietly made his Chicago debut less than six years earlier.

Though he managed to avoid them in Chicago, Spoor and Anderson traveled to New York onboard the *Twentieth Century Limited*, the same train Chaplin took, eager to renew the contract despite the earlier breakdown in negotiations.

By this time, Essanay had lost nearly its entire stable of stars, and Spoor was not eager to lose his last great comedian. He was not far from losing his last great cowboy star, and partner, either. Spoor and Anderson were not on the best of terms by this time. Anderson, who Chaplin had found to be something of a charming eccentric, infuriated Spoor with his antics. Like Edison, Spoor simply did not seem to understand that movies were to be a business driven by creativity and talent, and that if he did not treat the most important talent like royalty, they would simply find a studio that would. Despite his being a partner in the business, Spoor does not seem to have treated Anderson very well at this time.

Any attempt they made to retain Chaplin's services fell on deaf ears. Chaplin was eventually signed by the Mutual Film Corporation at a rate of $10,000 per week, plus the $150,000 bonus Spoor had refused to pay him.

Many commentators and historians have since pointed to the loss of Chaplin as the single greatest mistake Essanay ever made. It would prove to be not just a nail in the company's coffin but also a signal of the end of the days when Chicago was a major film center. None of the stars who left Essanay stayed in Chicago. They all headed for Los Angeles. Less than two months after Chaplin signed with Mutual, Spoor sent a cable to Niles announcing that the Niles studio was to be shut down. Only weeks later, *Harper's Weekly* became the first major publication to seriously put forth the proposition that Chaplin was no mere comedian, but a genius of the highest order.

Nearly all of the actors had left by now. Swanson was gone before Essanay could make her into a star. Bushman was gone. Beery, for one, seemed to leave behind a trail of bad memories. More than twenty years later, when most of the backstage people from Selig and Essanay were working as stagehands in Chicago theaters, the *Daily Tribune* wrote that, "The stagehands of Chicago almost to a man have very little to say in honor of Wallace Beery. They remember an experience they had with him when he was leaving Essanay in Argyle Street for the lush celluloid pastures of California. They determined to touch off a party in honor of his trek west. They took up a collection so that they could send a taxicab for Beery at his lodgings. He refused to ride in it, allegedly demanding a limousine. So he didn't show up at the party, and the stagehands have never forgotten it."[21] Michael Figliulo, a stuntman, may be the only one who remembered him well, describing him in 1989 as "the kind of guy who would take in a stray dog or cat." (Figliulo did, however, also note that Chaplin was "a real son of a bitch ... cheap as hell.")[22]

Essanay had lost most of its leading lights, most of the talent that could have kept them on top of the film world. The company, and the Chicago film scene, was hanging on to life by a thread.

- PART FOUR -

IT ALL CAME
CRASHING DOWN

CHAPTER TWELVE

The Decline of the Chicago Studios

As of 1915, Chicago technically remained a hub for filmmaking. There were still certain advantages that the Windy City could provide that the lush celluloid pastures of Los Angeles could not, such as the opportunity of capturing urban street shots. In 1915, Mack Sennett of Keystone hired Michael Figliulo to perform motorcycle stunts in Chicago city streets. Figliulo later remembered filming a scene in which he rode off the roof of a twenty-story building downtown. "They sent me off of the building into a big steel net that was suspended from the window a floor below," he said. He got steady work doing stunts for Sennett in Chicago throughout 1915.[1] The studios there were already in decline, however, and by the time Figliulo's career was halted by an injury in 1916, there was not much film work left in Chicago.

The story of the decline of the major Chicago studios is inextricably tied to that of the decline of the Motion Picture Patents Company. The MPPC first ran into serious trouble in February 1911 when Eastman Kodak, exploiting a loophole in its contract, began selling film stock to unlicensed independent companies. By this time, the independents had started to fight back in earnest against the Trust by organizing themselves into something called the Motion Picture Distribution and Sales Company. The budding studio heads who ran this outfit, William Fox, Carl Laemmle, and Adolph Zukor, established relationships with independent film exchanges, and themselves began producing feature-length films in an attempt to provide an alternative product to the Trust-sanctioned one- and two-reelers. (Foreign-produced features had already been around for years.) Shortly thereafter, the Trust reluctantly changed its policies to allow for the production and distribution of longer-format movies that could compete with these foreign and independent films. (William Selig, virtually alone among MPPC members, relished this change.) This change of policy established a pattern that still exists to this day: foreign and independent filmmakers have often defined themselves as alternatives to Hollywood, only to see Hollywood respond by co-opting their alternative strategies.

The next blow to the Trust came in August 1912 when the Supreme Court reversed its decision to uphold the Biograph Company's patent on the Latham film loop.[2] This ruling meant that the independents were now free to use cameras and equipment that had previously been available only to members of the MPPC. As a result, the technical quality of independent films immediately improved. D.W. Griffith, sensing which way the wind was blowing, soon left Biograph to form his own independent company, Reliance-Majestic Studios, and began producing features almost exclusively.

The Trust became increasingly embattled as more lawsuits were filed against it, first by William Fox (soon to be the namesake of the Fox Film Corporation), who charged "restraint of trade," then by the United States Justice Department on the same grounds. "On or about April 1910," the Justice Department's filing read, "defendants set out to monopolize the business of all rental exchanges in the United States, their purpose being to drive out of business all persons so engaged and to absorb to themselves the profits theretofore made therein."[3] This suit was filed at the beginning of 1913. By the time the case was decided once and for all five years later, a sea change had already occurred in the industry that saw virtually all of the MPPC-licensed studios go out of business while the former independents they had tried to squeeze out had established a new order in Hollywood.

In hindsight, the fatal flaw of the MPPC's plan to rule the American film industry lay in Thomas Edison's stubborn decision not to allow any newcomers to join the Trust after its formation. Edison was shortsighted in not anticipating the long-term resistance that the independents would offer. He believed he could simply keep them shut out indefinitely through subpoenas and lawsuits. In this respect, George Kleine was correct to fight Edison over the issue in 1908; had the MPPC been more generous in the granting of its licenses, it probably could have prolonged its reign for many more years.

Internal struggles within the Trust became increasingly contentious in 1913 and also contributed to its decline. The MPPC's escalating legal costs, for instance, had to be split equally among all of its members, even though the vast majority of their profits were going only to Edison and Biograph. As a result, George Spoor and George Kleine threatened to sue Edison for damages. In addition to the troubles the Trust faced as a result of the lawsuits, they also saw the expiration, in 1913, of the last of the patents relating to motion-picture cameras and projectors that Edison had filed in the mid-1890s. Going forward, the Trust could rely only on revenues generated through the distribution of movies by the General Film Company. Suddenly, membership in the Edison Trust seemed to be more trouble than it was worth.

In 1914, the outbreak of World War I caused further damage to the Trust. Because the GFC was responsible for importing more European films than its independent rivals, the halt in the flow of European imports meant a sharp decline in business. Conversely, the Trust also exported more of its own films to Europe than did the independents, a source of lucrative income that now also sharply declined. (This change was significant: in 1913, the number of movies Vitagraph distributed abroad was double the amount it distributed domestically.[4]) George Kleine, ever the voice of reason, begged Edison and Biograph to let the GFC distribute feature films regularly, especially after he had made a killing by distributing ten-reel European epics such as *Quo Vadis?* (1913) and *The Last Days of Pompeii* (1913) in limited release. The myopic MPPC brass declined the request by saying that the future of motion pictures would be "the old regular program with film not longer than three reels."[5]

Even more damning than the MPPC's failure to recognize the staying power and widespread appeal of the feature film, however, was its insistence on relying solely upon internal financing while its independent rivals turned to Wall Street. In 1914, maverick distributor-turned-producer Adolph Zucker founded Paramount Pictures in Hollywood; he promptly listed it on the New York Stock Exchange. This action would be the beginning of a long financial partnership between Wall Street and the

American motion-picture industry. The MPPC, as it had in so many other ways, made a poor decision not to open itself up to outside investors. The access to Wall Street funds sent the financial profile of the independents surging ahead of those of Edison and the old guard.

The final nail in the coffin came on October 1, 1915 when a federal court decided that the Motion Picture Patents Company had operated in violation of the Sherman Antitrust Act in going "far beyond what was necessary to protect the use of patents or the monopoly which went with them."[6] Although the MPPC was not officially terminated for another three years, when all of its legal appeals had finally been rejected, its members had by that time long ceased to be major players in the American motion-picture industry.

Most of Essanay's acting talent left the company in 1915. After inheriting a large sum of money, Gloria Swanson and her mother determined to go on vacation in Manila, with no intention of ever returning to Essanay. Swanson gave her notice. When she first arrived in California en route to Manila, Swanson was met by Wallace Beery in Los Angeles, which then primarily still consisted of rickety houses, with the occasional cow wandering around. When they drove towards the city she began to see signs that read "FOR RENT: DOGS AND ACTORS NOT WANTED." "This is it," said Beery with a laugh. "This is Hollywood. Look at some of these freaks. No wonder homeowners won't put them up. They'll do anything to attract attention to themselves and get into movies."

Swanson could clearly see that Hollywood was becoming the city of movies. "The men, women, children and animals all looked absurd," she wrote in her autobiography. "I had never seen such weird costumes — loud suits, ruffled dresses, fur jackets, cowboy boots and crazy hats." "They're desperate," Beery explained. "Everyone wants to get into pictures ... when I finish the series of pictures I'm making in Niles, I'm coming down here too. It's *the* place, no question."[7]

Swanson had intended only to stop briefly in Hollywood, but was snapped up by Keystone at a rate of $100 a week. "Maybe pictures weren't so bad, after all," she thought to herself.[8] Soon, she would be arguably the most famous, and well paid, woman in the world.

Chicago's time as a prototype Hollywood was clearly coming to a close. Decades later, in 1969, Chicagoan Andrew Sullivan remembered the atmosphere in Uptown: "We school kids of the neighborhood used to hang around the studio and got to know most of the actors, directors and cameramen. They would sometimes tell us to come in a gang on a certain day to appear as a bunch of kids in a picture taken in the neighborhood. We would get 50 cents a piece … We got to know by sight Francis X. Bushman, Beverly Bayne, Ruth Stonehouse, Ben Turpin, Charlie Chaplin, Wally Reid and Wallace Beery. They acted in outside scenes and tore around the neighborhood in a low-slung yellow Mercer racing car. Also we knew George Spoor … he used to hire us boys sometimes to do odd jobs around his home."[9]

Such a friendly, mid-western atmosphere never could have existed then in Los Angeles, which was already referring to itself as "Studio City." Chicago, after all, already had an identity. In Hollywood, a whole city could grow up around the nascent industry. Those who talk about why motion-picture production moved on from Chicago usually cite the weather and the Edison Trust as primary factors, but another reason may simply be that the industry was outgrowing the confines of an already-busy city, and needed a place of its own.

In the wake of the 1915 court decision to dissolve the MPPC, and the migration of acting talent westward, the now-floundering Chicago studios employed new strategies in an attempt to resuscitate business. Essanay tried its hand at producing animated films, which were then still in their infancy. They hired the St. Louis-born animator Wallace A. Carlson to create animated shorts featuring recurring characters, the most popular of which was the "Dreamy Dud" series of 1915/16. These black-and-white hand-drawn animations were minimalist in style but funny, charming, and inventive as storytelling. A good example is *Dreamy Dud: He Resolves Not to Smoke* (1915), in which the title character, an imaginative little boy, gets into mischief when he steals a pipe, smokes it obsessively, and is whisked away by a spirit that emerges from his smoke rings. This "spirit of smoke" takes Dud to the moon and leaves him there in order to teach him a lesson. Dud falls off the edge of the moon and then, waking up in his bed to realize that it was all a dream, resolves never to smoke again. By 1917 Wallace Carlson was working for Paramount.

1915 was also the year that the Trust finally relented on its decision not to produce and distribute feature films. Essanay combined with the most powerful remaining MPPC studios to form a new distribution company, V-L-S-E (Vitagraph-Lubin-Selig-Essanay), and later K.E.S.E (Kleine-Edison-Selig-Essanay), the aim of which was to release features exclusively. Its timing was, of course, too late. Although the Essanay-produced feature *Graustark* (1915) was a smash hit, stars Francis X. Bushman and Beverly Bayne soon defected to Metro in Hollywood. A sequel, *The Prince of Graustark* (1916) was devoid of big-name stars and subsequently did not fare as well.

Francis X. Bushman in a publicity still from Graustark, 1915. (Courtesy of the Chicago History Museum)

During this time, the relationship between George Spoor and Gilbert Anderson, which had grown increasingly uneasy throughout Charlie Chaplin's Essanay tenure of 1915, reached a breaking point. The final straw between the two, as recalled by Bill Cato, Anderson's stunt man, came when Spoor installed a time clock at the Niles studio, which was still cranking out a new horse opera every week (or, in some cases, seven in one week, after which Anderson would take six weeks off). Furious, Anderson smashed the time clock with an axe and had it sent back to Spoor.[10] Spoor bought out Anderson's share of Essanay in early 1916, which was around the same time that the Niles studio was shuttered.

The most significant Chicago-shot Essanay films of this era were *The Raven*, an Edgar Allan Poe biopic directed with imaginative flair by Charles Brabin and starring the great Henry B. Walthall, and *Sherlock Holmes*, a seven-reel feature directed by Arthur Berthelet. The latter was the first feature-length Sherlock Holmes movie as well as the first film in which the famed detective was portrayed wearing his soon-to-be-iconic deerstalker cap. William Gillette, an acclaimed theatrical actor who had originated this look onstage, reprised his role for Essanay's screen version. Gillette had originally worked with Arthur Conan Doyle on a theatrical script about

Holmes in 1899, and had spent the previous decade and a half traveling the world starring in it. In her *Chicago Daily Tribune* review, Kitty Kelly wrote, "It is a production to which Essanay may point with pride and may file away in the strong box for future and again future revival." Unfortunately, the Essanay "strong box" was almost not strong enough: *Sherlock Holmes* was lost for almost a century until it turned up at the Cinémathèque Française in 2014.* *The Raven*, on the other hand, has always been in circulation and has always been one of the easiest Essanay films to see.

The Raven begins with an exceptionally bizarre prologue that traces Edgar Allan Poe's ancestors all the way back to Ireland in the eighteenth century. This scene has absolutely nothing to do with the story that will follow but it does introduce some interesting trivia, such as the fact that Poe's biological parents were theatrical actors. Brabin then shows a still photograph of the actual Poe, which dissolves into a close-up of lead actor Henry B. Walthall. The moment is startlingly effective because Walthall bears a striking resemblance to Poe — albeit if Poe had possessed movie star good looks. (Walthall's casting may also have been the result of his having starred in D.W. Griffith's Poe-inspired *The Avenging Conscience* a year earlier.) This dramatic introductory scene was also fitting for a star of Walthall's caliber: *The Raven* was the eleventh of twelve films he would appear in that were released in 1915. (The second was Griffith's *The Birth of a Nation*, in which he played the lead role of the "little Colonel.") *The Raven*'s narrative proper begins with Poe as a young man living in Virginia as the adopted son of the wealthy Allan family. He courts his cousin Virginia (the first of several women in the movie, real or imagined, to be portrayed by Essanay contract player Warda Howard). One of the most interesting sequences in the film is from this section: Poe sees a slave being beaten by his owner and, though he cannot really afford it, arranges to buy the slave's freedom. The shocking progressiveness of this scene as written is somewhat tempered, however, by the fact that the slave is played with broad comedic flourishes by a white actor in blackface make-up.

The death of Poe's beloved bride is seen as precipitating his descent into madness, which provides *The Raven*'s dramatic high point: a reenactment of the title poem with Poe in the role of the narrator, alone in

---

* At the time this book went to press, *Sherlock Holmes* was undergoing a digital restoration through the joint efforts of the Cinémathèque Française and the San Francisco Silent Film Festival, with theatrical "re-premieres" planned for both France and the United States in 2015.

Henry B. Walthall as Edgar Allan Poe in a still from *The Raven*, 1916. (Courtesy of the Chicago History Museum)

his study, taunted by a real raven and haunted by the ghost of his "lost Lenore" (Howard). In this scene, Walthall's tortured and highly emotive performance is effectively matched by director Brabin's use of proto-Expressionist high-contrast lighting and an impressive and creative use of Theodore Wharton-style superimpositions (e.g., a human skull appears as an eerie vision before Poe). The Gothic atmosphere of this climactic scene — and Poe's "wine"-induced hallucinations — was certainly ahead of its time: the horror genre would not really catch on in America until the late silent era, after which time it had already fully blossomed in Germany.

The Raven would prove to be the highlight of Walthall's tenure at Essanay, although he would continue to appear in productions for the studio on and off through 1917 before returning to Hollywood for good. Among the scrapbooks that belonged to "Major" Marvin Spoor (brother of Essanay-founder George Spoor and one of Essanay's top directors of photography) that are now in the archives of the Chicago History Museum, one is devoted entirely to photographs of *The Raven*, an indication of just how important the studio thought the movie was at the time. Charles Brabin would go on to a fairly distinguished Hollywood career, directing, among many other films, the Boris Karloff vehicle *The Mask of Fu Manchu* in 1932. He may be best known today, however, for being the answer to a trivia question: he was also the husband of notorious stage and screen star

Max Linder and Martha Mansfield in a publicity still for *Max Comes Across*, 1917.
(Courtesy of the Chicago History Museum)

Theda Bara. Their long and, unusual for Hollywood, successful marriage lasted from 1921 until her death in 1955.

George Spoor's final big gamble as a studio boss was to sign a contract with French comedian Max Linder in 1916. Linder had starred in and directed a series of hits for Pathé, and Spoor felt that he could turn Linder into the "next Charlie Chaplin." Spoor paid Linder $260,000 for a one year contract.[11] Unfortunately, the American Linder films were mostly poorly received, critically and commercially, though some critics and historians have since positively reappraised them. This failure was probably just as well for Linder, who, like Chaplin, despised the Chicago weather and returned to France in 1917.* In one of Essanay's last official acts, a desperate Spoor unsuccessfully attempted to sue Charlie Chaplin for breach of contract. Production at the Argyle Street studio ceased for good in 1918.

---

* Linder's first two Essanay films, *Max Comes Across* and *Max Wants a Divorce*, were shot in Chicago in the dead of winter but the third, *Max in a Taxi* (the only one to enjoy moderate success at the time), was made in Los Angeles. Newspaper reports made much of the fact that the stress of traveling to the U.S. had exacerbated Linder's World War I injuries. It was likely a combination of ill health and Essanay's financial woes that led to the premature cancellation of Linder's ocntract.

Selig Polyscope, meanwhile, had responded to the MPPC crisis by again turning its focus to the newsreel format. Because the novelization of *The Adventures of Kathlyn* had been successful for both parties involved, William Selig formed a partnership with the *Chicago Daily Tribune* to produce a new weekly newsreel in 1916. The Colonel called this new endeavor the *Selig-Tribune*, and advertised it as "The World's Greatest News Film" (a riff on the *Daily Tribune*'s motto of "The World's Greatest Newspaper"). Selig granted an interview with the *Moving Picture World* to coincide with the newsreel's launch. He claimed, disingenuously, that he had severed ties with William Randolph Hearst because he thought the public was demanding something "interesting" and "different," implying that these were qualities that Hearst was lacking but that the *Selig-Tribune* would now be able to provide.

"In my opinion the *Selig-Tribune* will meet a want long felt by distributors of motion pictures," Selig said. "These exhibitors desire a news film that is strictly up to date, interesting and entertaining. The patrons of the various motion-picture theaters have felt there was something lacking in the news pictorial films and have not hesitated so to express themselves not only to the exhibitors of motion pictures, but to the film manufacturers. It has been my ambition to supply that something.

"When I concluded to sever our connection with the *Hearst-Selig News Pictorial* and to manufacture and release a news film that would be something 'different,' I was naturally pleased to cooperate with the *Chicago Daily and Sunday Tribune*, as the reputation of that publicity medium for universal pictorial and news service is flattering. I am sure that the picture-play public will be more than satisfied with the Selig-Tribune. No time, money or thought will be spared to make this news film everything it ought to be."[12]

While the Selig Polyscope studio in Edendale continued to focus on producing fictional narratives, the Chicago plant began to focus more and more on the newsreel. Admittedly, the *Selig-Tribune* was a big operation but Colonel Selig had not constructed a man-made lake and giant outdoor stages for what was rapidly turning into a mere post-production facility. In addition to the war correspondents it had stationed all over the world, there were seventy-five Selig Polyscope employees in Chicago who worked solely on the creation of the *Selig-Tribune*, prints of which were shipped out twice weekly to hundreds of theaters across the United States. The newsreel, however, was not financially successful enough to justify the enormous expense involved in its creation and distribution. Production of the *Selig-Tribune* stopped at the end of 1916.

William Selig had first ordered a halt to the production of fictional narratives at the Chicago plant in mid-1914, but would then periodically re-open for the production of special projects over the next couple of years.[13] One prominent example was 1916's *The Crisis*, an ambitious attempt to make a *Birth of a Nation*-style Civil War epic. *The Crisis* was successful, but not enough to reverse Selig Polyscope's declining fortunes. Selig would never, in fact, recover from the financial troubles he encountered in 1916. The rate of production of his jungle adventure films had dropped from one per week in 1915 to just one per month the following year. Another blow came when Kathlyn Williams, his top star for several years running, became married to Paramount Pictures executive Charles Eyton and signed a new contract with his studio. (In an interview not long before Williams's departure, Selig had ironically boasted of his star's loyalty while criticizing other studios for not treating their top talent as well as he had: "I've seen some of them [movie stars] looking pretty unhappy," said Selig. "They ought to remember that their company spent a lot of money in making them … Miss Williams, for instance, owes a great deal to us, but she is loyal to us, and so are we to her. We will always keep her, even when she doesn't play much anymore."[14]) To help compensate for these financial losses, Selig leased out his Edendale studio to William Fox.

A zebra belonging to the ill-fated "Selig Zoo", *Chicago Daily News* (Courtesy of the Chicago History Museum)

The Colonel was, however, in Chicago as of 1917, apparently still working with an eye to the future. In that year, newspapers carried a photograph of him kissing one of four chimpanzees he owned at the Lincoln Park Zoo, where the chimps — Mike, Mary, Betty, and Bill — were being trained for a career in movies. Mary had learned to smoke cigarettes, unlock locks, and "expectorate like a coal heaver." Even so, when their training was complete, the chimps were ultimately sent to California to launch their acting careers.[15]

The most press Selig seems to have received at this time was not for a movie at all but for a bizarre publicity stunt: he sued Chicago millionaire George Fabyan on the grounds that Fabyan's claims that Francis Bacon had written William Shakespeare's plays would hurt the ticket sales of future Selig Shakespeare adaptations. Even Selig's friends at the *Daily Tribune* could barely disguise their mirth at the disingenuous nature of this stunt: they pointed out that Fabyan and Selig were friends and that some "experts" had estimated Selig would receive "10,000,000 columns of free advertising" as a result of the suit. Like Essanay, Selig stopped production altogether in 1918.[16]

The ultimate irony in this saga is that Thomas Edison, who had been directly responsible for the decline of the MPPC-affiliated studios, was relatively unaffected. There was good reason: in the second decade of the twentieth century, Edison's scientific and business concerns were so widespread that he had begun focusing increasingly on audio-recording technology while leaving his motion-picture concerns mostly to business associates. For men like George Spoor, Gilbert Anderson, and William Selig, however, the decline of their movie empires also meant the decline of their personal fortunes. The only Chicago motion-picture mogul to remain relatively unscathed by the unceremonious end of this era was George Kleine who, because his interests had always been in distribution rather than production, retired a wealthy man in 1928.

By the end of the 1910s, the total number of films being produced each year in Chicago was a mere fraction of what it had been just a few years earlier. Most of the movies being made at this time were independent productions, including "race films" (movies created by, about, and for African-American audiences) such as the landmark *The Slacker* (1917) by Peter P. Jones, and gimmicky stunt films such as *Cousin Jim and the Lost Fraternity Pin* (1916). Members of the high-society Casino Club financed the latter, the production of which was amusingly documented by the Daily Tribune.

Cousin Jim and the Lost Fraternity Pin told the story of a country boy who comes to the big city, and it was to climax with a stunt in which two characters plunged from "Suicide Bridge," the high bridge over the Lincoln Park lagoon (a location that had also been central to *From the Submerged* four years earlier). A professional swimmer was brought in as a stunt performer and offered $250 (a lot of money in 1916) to take the jump, but he determined that it was impossible since the water was only about ten feet deep. The two actors, however, figured they could just do it themselves, and ran up to the top of the bridge. A squirrel set up shop nearby, leading an onlooker below to remark, "That's a wise squirrel. Coupla nuts up there." The two men made the drop and calmly swam to shore, one of them remarking, "Where in [beep] is my hat?"[17]

The fact that the local media covered such a story so comprehensively in 1916, when Essanay and Selig Polyscope were still ostensibly in operation, was one more indication that the true golden age of film production in Chicago had come to an end.

CHAPTER THIRTEEN

Major M.L.C. Funkhouser and the Chicago Censorship Code

Besides its pioneering roles in the production, distribution, and exhibition of motion pictures in America, Chicago has the dubious distinction of pioneering movie censorship laws and ratings boards as well. Chicago's stringent early censorship code almost certainly hurt the local filmmaking industry and probably contributed at least in small part to its decline. Ironically, the censorship laws seemed to hurt local filmmakers the most between 1908 and 1912, when the Chicago studios were at their strongest; after that, the censors laid off the local industry just as it began to decline, and became more vigilant about going after the MPPC's independent rivals as they were growing increasingly powerful. Indeed, the story of the birth and evolution of film censorship laws in Chicago has curious parallels to the rise and fall of the major Chicago studios in general.

Beginning in 1907, the Second City became one of the first cities in the United States to censor movies at the time, when George Spoor and Gilbert Anderson were in the process of founding the Peerless Manufacturing Company and when Colonel Selig's production fortunes were taking a drastic turn for the better. This is also the year in which Chicago's city hall first gave George Shippy, the Chief of Police, the authority to grant exhibition permits to theater owners on a film-by-film basis.[1] A movie without the proper permit could face being re-cut to meet the local censorship code or else risk being banned outright. Because of the sheer volume of new films that were being exhibited in Chicago's hundreds of theaters every week, it was impossible for each one to be screened in advance at police headquarters. Chief Shippy therefore assigned ten police officers to the task of patrolling nickelodeons to watch out for pictures depicting "blood and thunder" violence or behavior that might be deemed salacious. Theater owners who allegedly violated this code were subject to having their licenses revoked.[2] Essanay's *The James Boys in Missouri*, from 1908, in spite of being a local production that had proven popular elsewhere across the country, was deemed so immoral in its overall tone that no amount of editing could have resulted in its being granted a permit to play in Chicago.

Recognizing that the local censorship laws were bad for business, the Motion Picture Patents Company challenged them on legal grounds in 1909, but both the Illinois Supreme Court and the United States Supreme Court upheld the censorship code. Shortly afterwards, Chicago municipal law also decreed that a separate permit, pink in color, be issued for movies that were deemed fit only for "adult" audiences. The plan was to divide Chicago theaters into two categories, those for general audiences and those for adults only. Humorously, but perhaps unsurprisingly, this phenomenon was short-lived: it was quickly discovered that the "pink permit" actually functioned as the best possible form of advertising for the films to which it had been affixed.[3]

As the film industry became regulated and stabilized by the policies implemented by the Edison Trust, Chicago put in place in 1912 an official censorship board. The chief censor was the incredibly named Metellus Lucullus Cicero Funkhouser, a career military man and veteran of the Spanish–American War who had joined the Chicago police force and gradually risen to the rank of Second Deputy Superintendant. He was, in the grand Chicago fashion, fabulously corrupt, not only for allegedly taking bribes from motion-picture studios but also for reportedly breaking his own laws by holding private exhibitions of the naughty bits that he had ordered cut from the movies he had censored.[4]

Descriptions of censorship activity were also published in local newspapers every week. Kitty Kelly's "Flickerings from Film Land" column in the *Daily Tribune*, for instance, contained a popular sub-feature that

Major M.L.C. Funkhouser, far right, examines a couple standing in a dance pose, *Chicago Daily News* (Courtesy of the Chicago History Museum)

provided curt descriptions of banned films and excised scenes that had been provided to her by Funkhouser's board. This arrangement meant that Funkhouser's censorship work received favorable publicity in the *Daily Tribune* while, somewhat hypocritically, the paper simultaneously allowed its readers the thrill of experiencing banned movies or controversial movie scenes by at least being able to read about them.

A typical banned picture was an independently produced instructional film from 1913 on how to dance "the hesitation waltz, the turkey trot, and the tango," which the *Daily Tribune* colorfully described as "freak dances." (Presumably, these dances were more risqué than the waltz that was soon to be named for Kathlyn Williams.) In a *Daily Tribune* article, Major Funkhouser warned against the dangerous influence that such a movie would allegedly have on the youth of the day: "The objection is not based so much on these pictures in themselves, but upon the effect they would have on young people. After witnessing these professional performers go through these dances in a carefully regulated way, they will go to the public dance halls and try them. That is where the danger is. Most of these halls either sell liquor or are close to the places where it is sold. Think of a young girl or a young man with two or three drinks down trying these dances."[5]

In a speech given not long afterwards to the Evanston Women's Club, Funkhouser elaborated on what his standards were for what he considered to be moral pictures. In addition to showing zero tolerance for "scenes showing the degradation of women, the hero worship of criminals, the portrayal of crime or the ridiculing of those in authority," Funkhouser made it clear that all films exhibited in Chicago should be fit to play for audiences of all ages: "85 percent of those who attend moving picture shows," he said, "were women and children. Many of the latter are under 15 years of age, and nothing harmful to them should be shown."

Funkhouser then revisited the dance theme by declaring not only what he considered permissible in a dancing scene within a movie but also how Chicagoans should behave when dancing in public themselves: "Tango dancers must keep a six-inch space between them; they may touch hands and a man's arm may encircle a fair dancer's waist, but if a couple fails to observe the rule as to space it will mean a ride in a patrol wagon."

At the same meeting, Harriet Vittum, "superintendent of the Northwestern University settlement," stated that movie theaters should ideally provide "fairie stories" for children, before also complaining that the congested nickelodeons forced children to "breathe air laden with germs." Covering the meeting for *Moving Picture World*, James McQuade wrote with indignation, "Miss Vittum evidently would like to see theaters turned into nurseries, and Major Funkhouser in his zeal would assume divine rights to prescribe a code of morals." McQuade ended his notice with a sentence that would prove to be prophetic: "The moving picture will outlive all such narrow-minded restrictions, and in a few years one will look back in amazement at these Puritanical outbursts."[6]

In a 1915 column titled "Among the Missing," Kitty Kelly noted that the two "rejections" (i.e., banned films) for that week were Pathé's *It's a Long, Long Way to Tipperary* and the independently produced *The Great Mysteries of New York*. The former was rejected on grounds that it depicted "national factionalism, bellicose activities between nations engaged in the present European conflict, and has a tendency to violate the laws of neutrality and to disturb the public peace." The latter was refused a permit because it "shows operative methods of criminals, morbid scenes of violence, the bringing of a woman into a life of crime by drugged wine, and is not relieved by any adequate moral lesson." Significantly, neither film was produced by an MPPC-affiliated studio. Among the descriptions of scenes that had been censored for that week were "cutouts" from films produced by a host of independents as well as a few by Edison Manufacturing and

Vitagraph. These offending scenes ranged from a "defaulter making false entry in bank ledger" to that of someone "handing police officer tip," but no locally produced movies were censored that week.[7]

The board seems to have been willfully inconsistent. No cuts to *The Leopard's Foundling* were noted, and that film contained scenes of Kathlyn Williams scantily-clad in jungle rags, as well as in a corset, not to mention various scenes of her and her love interest in bondage. Similar kinds of scenes, meanwhile, were cut from many other non-Trust movies.

Chicago authorities did, however, censor at least one notable locally produced film around this time. On July 24, 1915, the SS *Eastland* capsized in the Chicago River; it had been loaded to its new capacity, 2,500, for the first time, and suffered from both mechanical failures and a few design flaws. The exact nature of what caused it to capsize is still in dispute, but the body count is generally agreed to be 844. While the disaster was still under way, cameramen from the *Chicago Daily Tribune* set up camp on the fire escape of the Reid Murdoch building, a grocery warehouse on the other side of the river from the disaster, and shot about a thousand feet of film. Other scenes consisted of footage shot at the two main buildings that functioned as morgues (the Reid Murdoch and the Second Regiment Armory on Washington Boulevard), as well as a few shots of survivors. By all accounts, the film, simply titled *The Eastland Disaster*, was "tasteful." Stretchers could be seen being carried out of the hull of the ship, but they were all covered. No actual corpses were seen.

The *Daily Tribune* promptly offered all profits from exhibitions to the funds that were established to provide for the families of the victims, and the footage was being shown in several regional theaters within three days of the disaster. A Flint, Michigan theater advertised that viewers could thrill to "the struggle for life in a river teeming with death" on a double-bill with *The Knockout* (1914), a Chaplin two-reeler from his Keystone days.

The Eastland Disaster was also on exhibit in suburban Forest Park, but Chicago proper would not see it. On July 28, a screening was held in city hall for a few local dignitaries. A spokesman for the *Daily Tribune* said that forty prints had been struck, and all of them were being used strictly to raise funds for the survivors, not to commercialize the disaster. "We feel there is nothing morbid in it," he said. "We feel that it properly may be shown as a graphic illustration of the disaster, carrying its clear lesson."

He made an interesting case. The dead were dead, and their survivors were in difficult financial straits. Still, charging admission to see a film of the disaster arguably skirted the bounds of good taste. The *Daily Tribune's* own description read, "There are no horrors of a repulsive nature. All figures on the stretchers are covered so there is no possibility of recognition of the dead. The distance of the camera prevented any close-up effects at all, except two girl survivors, safe and dry, who posed for the film."[8]

In the end, it was banned in Chicago, along with all other *Eastland*-related films. The one made by the *Daily Tribune* was not the only such film put before the municipal censor board. A series of slides made by one Harry Cohan was forbidden to be exhibited, as was *Eastland Disaster*, a "Hearst-Selig News Pictorial Extra." The nature of the Selig film of the disaster is wholly unknown; it may simply have been a series of still photos, actual footage of the disaster and morgues, or even a re-enactment filmed at Selig's studio. The same board meeting, for the record, ordered a subtitle removed from Selig's *Isle of Content* ("Go with your paramour, but I will take the child") and ordered Essanay to cut a scene showing a woman kicking a man from *Street Fakers* and a scene showing a woman's leg above the knee in *A Bunch of Keys*. These cuts give an interesting view of the kind of scenes to which the board objected.[9] (See Appendix C for a longer selection of censored scenes.)

The Eastland Disaster film by the *Daily Tribune* is now thought to be lost (along with any other film versions, of which there seem to have been several). The owner of a Toledo theater bought the rights in September, and it was said that the *Daily Tribune* destroyed its footage in 1926. Since the disaster led to numerous legal proceedings and hearings, it seems likely that a print must have been kept for evidence. With so many prints having been struck, it is far from impossible that one survives somewhere.

That the important *Eastland* footage was unavailable in Chicago, but easy to see elsewhere, was one of many factors that began to sour people on Funkhouser and the board. Under Funkhouser's reign as censor, it appears that foreign and independent pictures (i.e., non-Trust movies such as the *Daily Tribune's Eastland* film) were consistently banned more frequently; they came in for far harsher censorship than their MPPC counterparts. The Chicago censorship code was allegedly based on excising material deemed politically inflammatory or too violent or sexually explicit in nature, but it also appears that many films were censored or banned arbitrarily and that these fates were more likely to befall non-Trust pictures. This bias meant that, while the local papers may have portrayed Major Funkhouser favorably, he was spectacularly unpopular with the nationally distributed trade papers and magazines, especially as the independent studios were growing more powerful. *Moving Picture World*, for instance, denounced Funkhouser's "extreme and narrow view of film censorship" and compared his puritanical zeal to that of the persecutors in the Salem witch trials.[10]

Major Funkhouser's over-zealous attitude and unfair practices as censor ultimately hurt the local film culture not only because he denied Chicagoans the right to see important movies but also because, according to author Richard Koszarski, he "continually suppressed material that had been passed by the National Board in New York."[11] Because Chicago's standards were stricter than national standards, Funkhouser's continuous meddling repeatedly halted the regular flow of local distribution and exhibition. Inevitably, during his five-year tenure, Second Deputy Superintendent Funkhouser was himself continually litigated for his controversial practices.

Major Funkhouser was finally fired by Chicago Mayor William Hale "Big Bill" Thompson in 1918, just as the major Chicago studios were at the end of their own ropes. The ouster came about as the result of friction between Funkhouser's censorship board and the new Chief of Police John Alcock, who claimed that "the division which Funkhouser heads has not been properly cooperating" with him. The final straw appears to have been the bad publicity generated by Funkhouser's censoring of two war films from 1918: *Hearts of the World* by D.W. Griffith and *My Four Years in Germany* by William Nigh. These non-Trust films were both massive hits across the nation, and Funkhouser's interference came in for severe criticism in the media. Morris Gest, a theatrical producer who was responsible for distributing Griffith's film in Chicago, actually accused the censor of "pro-German sympathies," a serious charge that was widely quoted in the press.[12] Even Mae Tinee at the *Daily Tribune* accused Funkhouser of going too far and suggested that he should be "soundly spanked" towards the end of his career as censor.[13]

After Funkhouser was fired, it was schadenfreude time for the trade papers, some of which reported the story with barely concealed glee. The *Daily Tribune*, however, which had been aligned with the Selig Polyscope Company for years, praised Funkhouser for doing his job efficiently and defended him against charges of corruption. "We believe," a *Daily Tribune* staffer editorialized, "that Maj. Funkhouser, an aggravation as a censor of any kind of artistic expression, was doing able and effective work in an endeavor which almost defies any one to do successful work. The larger idea in the police management that led to the attempt to get rid of him has not been made apparent. A low-minded person might even suspect that the intent was to rid the force of an activity useful to the city but embarrassing to the police."[14]

If, as the anecdotal evidence suggests, the Edison Trust had Funkhouser in its pocket, this situation almost certainly played a role in the Chicago censorship chief's downfall. Historian Raymond J. Haberski notes that Funkhouser "failed to play favorites with the 'right' distributors and exhibitors and had alienated not only the moving picture industry but the police who had friends in the business."[15] If Major Funkhouser had indeed allied himself with the Edison Trust beginning around 1913, it would have seemed to be a wise decision at the time: the Motion Picture Patents Company was, after all, the mainstream center of the nation's film industry. Funkhouser could not have known then that its position would soon be usurped by the new Hollywood-based "independents," with which he was to make enemies, in a span of just five short years.

Epilogue

The later fortunes and careers of the major players in Chicago's original motion-picture scene varied wildly.

George Kleine, because his business had long depended upon importing European films, went into semi-retirement after the outbreak of World War I; he had already amassed his fortune by that time. Kleine would continue to dabble in production and distribution throughout the 1920s, mostly in the educational film market, but more as a hobby than out of necessity. He died in 1931, three years after officially retiring, at which time he was estimated to be about 67 years old.

A decade after closing up shop, George Spoor gave an interview in which he discussed the hectic final days of Essanay. He blamed other studios for essentially forcing him out of business and thus absolved himself of having made poor business decisions in the process. "The place was a madhouse," Spoor recalled. "I tried a number of general managers with no success. I found I was running a high-class school for directors and actors. I'd make stars out of them and other producers would offer them more money. I had to meet those offers or lose the stars. Had I met all the offers, I would have gone broke myself, constantly doubling salaries. So I locked up the place and took a good, long rest."[1]

Ironically, George Spoor showed more flair for innovation in his post-Essanay career as an inventor and independent producer than he ever had as a head of studio. In the early 1920s he invented, along with Dr. Paul John Berggren, an early 3-D process called "Natural Vision." This complicated process used a camera with two lenses that shot two images simultaneously. The images were then supposed to be projected onto two screens (one transparent and one opaque) to deliver a three-dimensional effect that did not require the use of 3-D glasses. By the time Natural Vision officially debuted years later, however, it had morphed into a 65mm widescreen process that gave an impressive *illusion* of depth but without any true stereoscopic effects. In addition to a few shorts and one never-released feature, RKO's well-regarded railroad adventure film *Danger Lights* was made with this process in 1930. The widescreen version was, however, only exhibited in two theaters, one in Chicago and one in New York. All of these experiments were ahead of their time: neither 3-D nor widescreen technology would enjoy widespread popularity with movie audiences until the 1950s.

Spoor estimated that he sunk more than four million dollars of his own money, the last of his personal fortune, into the Natural Vision process, an investment that he never recouped. He later described Hollywood's reaction to Natural Vision like this: "They were all my friends, but they didn't hesitate to murder me."[2] Still, if Spoor felt betrayed by the industry he had helped to create, he certainly did not let it crush his spirit. Even into his late seventies, the former mogul continued to tinker with inventions in his home laboratory on Argyle Street, just a few houses down from the original Essanay studio.

In 1948, Spoor was given an honorary Academy Award along with his old rival William Selig as well as Thomas Armat and Vitagraph's Albert E. Smith. The Academy of Motion Picture Arts and Sciences cited them as a "small group of pioneers whose belief in a new medium, and whose contributions to its development, blazed the trail along which the motion picture has progressed, in their lifetime, from obscurity to world-wide acclaim." To coincide with this honor, Spoor was interviewed by the *Chicago Sun*. "Movies?" Spoor replied when asked his opinion of the contemporary film scene. "No, young fellow, I don't go to the movies much anymore. You see, there are only about thirty stories in the world, and by this time I guess I know them all by heart."[3] George Kirke Spoor died in Chicago on November 24, 1953 at the age of eighty.

After ending his partnership with Spoor, Edward Amet relocated to California where he continued his own inventing ways with considerable success. He styled himself the "Wizard of the West" (in opposition to Edison's designation as the "Wizard of the East"), and he returned to dabbling in motion pictures, inventing both a 3-D projector and a sound process he called "Audo-Moto-Photo," which synchronized a phonograph with a film projector. In describing the latter, Amet suggested that it could be used to create what sound like prototypical music videos: "With a singer in a garden, photographed at a distance of a few feet, the possibilities of dramatic entertainment through the Audo-Moto-Photo are illustrated. The lips of the performer move in exact accord with the utterance of the phonograph." Among Amet's other important late inventions were a torpedo guidance system and a manned glider. Edward Hill Amet died in Redondo Beach, California, in 1948, at the age of 87.[4]

As both filmmaker and actor, Gilbert "Broncho Billy" Anderson retired many times and made just as many comebacks in the decades after he sold his Essanay shares to Spoor in 1916. First, he bought a theater in New York and tried his hand at producing plays. When that effort was not successful, he briefly returned to motion pictures, producing comedy shorts for Metro, including *The Lucky Dog* (1921), the first pairing of Stan Laurel and Oliver Hardy. As a former studio head however, Anderson was understandably unhappy working for others and again tried his luck as an independent. After a few unsuccessful films, Anderson retired again in 1923.

Anderson made news in 1943 when he sued Paramount Pictures for including a character named "Bronco Billy" in their musical film *Star-Spangled Rhythm*. Alleging defamation (the character was portrayed by Victor Moore as a "washed up and broken down actor"), Anderson asked for $900,000 in damages, but the outcome of this suit is not known.[5] In 1958, ten years after his former partner George Spoor had received a similar honor, Anderson too was given a special Academy Award "for his contributions to the development of motion pictures as entertainment." This award was followed two years later when he received a star on Hollywood's "Walk of Fame." In 1965, Anderson came out of retirement yet again at the ripe old age of 85 to play a cameo role in the western *The Bounty Killer*. In a career that included approximately 350 screen appearances, it was the one and only time his voice was ever heard on film.

Gilbert M. "Broncho Billy" Anderson died in South Pasadena, California, on January 20, 1971 at the age of ninety. Although some sources reported him to be two or three years younger, Anderson, like many movie stars, had long ago shaved a couple of years off his age. Pulaski County, Arkansas census records show that he had, in fact, been born in 1880.

Among Essanay's stable of stars, many went on to successful Hollywood careers. Charlie Chaplin went from strength to strength, becoming one of the world's most popular and, even today, instantly recognizable entertainers and filmmakers. His mature Hollywood masterpieces such as *The Gold Rush* (1925), *City Lights* (1931) and *Modern Times* (1936) have continually been revived, restored, and re-released, and they continue to win over legions of new admirers. St. Augustine College has named Essanay's old interior stage, where Chaplin made *His New Job*, and which still looks remarkably similar to its original, early-twentieth-century appearance, the "Charlie Chaplin Auditorium."

Ben Turpin left Essanay around the same time as Chaplin. He first made a series of comedic two-reelers for the Vogue Company before signing with Mack Sennett and achieving superstardom in 1917. As much a clown off-screen as on, Turpin took to introducing himself while simultaneously boasting of his salary with the phrase, "I'm Ben Turpin. $3,000 a week."[6] The beloved comedian retired at the end of the silent era, although he would continue to make guest cameos after that for a flat fee of $1,000 per film. When Turpin died of a heart attack in 1940, Charlie Chaplin sent a seven-foot spray of red roses, the single largest floral piece at the funeral.[7]

Upon leaving Essanay, and later Keystone, Gloria Swanson went on to successfully rebrand her image as a serious dramatic actress in a series of films with director Cecil B. DeMille before appearing in such important late silent movies as Raoul Walsh's *Sadie Thompson* (1928) and Erich Von Stroheim's *Queen Kelly* (1929). At the height of her fame, Swanson would earn $250,000 per picture (which, at 1927 prices, would have bought her five million "fresh from the brine" dill pickles at the Stop & Shop on Michigan Avenue.[8]) A victim of the transition from silent to talking pictures, Swanson's star then faded, but she would later resuscitate her career with her best-known role in Billy Wilder's *Sunset Boulevard*.

Unlike Gloria Swanson, her Essanay co-star Wallace Beery (with whom she also had a brief, unhappy marriage) found his biggest success in the early sound era. He played lead roles in important MGM films like *The Champ* (1931), for which he won a Best Actor Academy Award, and *Grand Hotel* (1932), before settling into a long career as a character actor.

After his star had waned at Metro, Francis X. Bushman made a surprising comeback in 1925 by playing the villain in Fred Niblo's *Ben-Hur*, a movie that guaranteed his screen immortality. As soon as he had returned, however, the actor seems to have disappeared just as mysteriously back into obscurity. Bushman later claimed that he had been blacklisted by

Wallace Beery, left, in a still as "Sweedie," the Essanay character that made him famous. (Courtesy of the Chicago History Museum)

MGM studio boss Louis B. Mayer, and he wound down his career doing guest spots on radio and television; his last appearance was as a silent film collector in an episode of the 1960s *Batman* television show. A gorilla named for Bushman is stuffed and preserved at Chicago's Field Museum.

Beverly Bayne left Essanay for Metro along with Bushman. The two starred there in a series of popular films between 1916 and 1919, which established them as the first superstar screen couple. She then took off four years from acting, following the birth of her and Bushman's son in 1919. When Bayne returned to the screen in 1923, she did not regain her former popularity and retired two years later, at which time she and Bushman also divorced. In 1948, Bayne came out of retirement for one last performance, a memorable cameo in the classic film noir *The Naked City* (1948). It was her one and only appearance in a sound movie.

The lovely and talented Ruth Stonehouse, although a forgotten figure today, left Essanay for Universal Studios where she not only acted but also wrote and directed a series of films. In spite of being treated poorly by the studio, she managed to direct ten well-regarded movies between 1917 and 1919, becoming one of Hollywood's very first female directors. Stonehouse continued acting until the end of the silent era, at which time she got married and retired.[9]

Essanay publicity photo of Ruth Stonehouse. (Courtesy of the Chicago History Museum)

Film historian and Gilbert Anderson biographer David Kiehn has esti-mated that Essanay's Chicago studio produced about 1,500 films (with another five hundred or so produced out west). Unfortunately, many of these films were destroyed in a studio vault fire in 1916. More were thrown away in 1932 when George Spoor sold the studio buildings on Argyle Street. More still have perished as a result of the ravages of time. That only approximately 10% of Essanay's total output survives today makes it difficult to evaluate the quality of its films. Essanay always had a reputation for a cha-otic, "anything goes" approach to production, and Spoor and Anderson, as studio heads, were known to be less interested in innovation than was their rival William Selig. It is perhaps curious then that Essanay's best known surviving movies (e.g., *Mr. Flip, From the Submerged, His New Job*, etc.) seem to hold up better than their surviving Selig Polyscope counterparts from an artistic as well as an entertainment point of view. Then again, it is also possible that the reason for this disparity lies in the fact that simply more Essanay films survive than do their Selig Polyscope counterparts. Extant Essanay films are certainly easier to see: they are more widely available on commercial home video releases today (see Appendix B).

William Selig, however, probably had the most fascinating career of all the former Chicago moguls following the end of the Second City's golden age of film production. In 1918, Selig permanently relocated to Los Angeles and pinned all of his hopes on his zoo. His plan was for what he dubbed "Selig Zoo Park" to become a major tourist attraction, and his ideas about amusement parks were as ahead of their time as his ideas about filmmaking had been: decades before Disneyland, Selig envisioned a theme park that would feature a hotel, mechanical rides, a "water park," restaurants, and theaters. In reality, Selig went bankrupt before Selig Zoo Park could be completed, in part as a result of slow business. He attempted to rebound from his losses by renting out space in the zoo to other Hollywood studios looking to shoot their own jungle adventure films. Eventually, the zoo became a mere animal rental company before permanently closing.

Selig did produce a few independent movies in the 1930s. He is sometimes named as an uncredited producer on D.W. Griffith's final film, the innovative early talkie *The Struggle* (1931), although this may be a misattribution: Selig had produced a movie with the same title a decade earlier. The last film on which Selig's name appears is the 1938 low-budget quickie *Convicts at Large*. None of his later movies, however, were financially successful, and Selig retired from production for good at the end of the decade. Selig remained spry and resilient to the last, though, switching careers yet again and reinventing himself as a literary agent; he continued to make a living by re-selling the rights to the stories that he had originally acquired during his glory days as a studio boss decades earlier.

William N. Selig died in Los Angeles on July 15, 1948, not long after accepting the honorary Academy Award he shared with George Spoor and the other early film pioneers. He was 84 years old. In 1960, he also posthumously received a star on Hollywood's "Walk of Fame." This was the same day on which his former employee Gilbert Anderson and his former uneasy ally Thomas Edison received their stars only a few blocks away.

William Selig's biggest discovery, Tom Mix, would eventually star in approximately 290 films, all but nine of which were made during the silent era, and he came to be known as the "King of the Cowboys." In the mid-1930s, Mix retired from screen acting and returned to rodeo riding and circus performing. He died in a car accident in Arizona in 1940 at the age of sixty. To this day, his Stetson-hatted visage remains the most recognizable of any screen cowboy from the pre-John Wayne era.

Selig Polyscope's biggest female star (and Tom Mix's occasional co-star), Kathlyn Williams, continued to be a star at Paramount Pictures where she made the transition from playing ingénues in the late 1910s to playing matronly character roles in the 1920s and 1930s. She retired from acting in 1935. For years there were rumors that Williams would come out of retirement and mount a screen comeback, rumors that were sadly quashed when the actress lost her right leg in a serious car accident in 1949. Many accounts of Williams' post-movie career describe her later life as a series of tragedies capped by the accident, at which time she allegedly became a shut-in. Historian Eve Golden disputes that story: she claims that Williams threw a party in 1951 to debut a new prosthetic leg and resumed a normal social life that even involved her re-learning her dancing skills. Kathlyn Williams died of a heart attack in her Hollywood home in 1960, at which time she is thought to have been 81 years old.[10]

Only one of the original buildings from the Selig Polyscope lot still stands today, the glass-roofed studio on the corner of Byron Street and Claremont Avenue. The building has been converted into upscale condominiums, although the once-famous "diamond S" logo is still visible above the front entrance. An unusually elaborate water works in the basement still testifies to the lagoon it originally had to service. Comparing the building today to early illustrations depicting its glass-roofed exterior, it is easy to see where the glass once was and the ways in which the original building has been changed.

Given their reputation for creativity and innovation, it is particularly regrettable that precious few of Selig Polyscope's Chicago-shot films survive today. Nonetheless, William Selig's contributions to and influence on the American film industry are incalculable. As David Kiehn has noted of the early Chicago filmmakers, "They built the foundation for an industry that didn't exist before and changed the world." Unfortunately, American film scholars have always tended to show an aversion to writing about "lost" movies, and so the official film histories are consequently incomplete and distorted, especially when it comes to the silent era. As Kiehn succinctly put it, "Unfortunately, 1907 to 1918, when [the Chicago studios] were all thriving, is a black hole in film history."[11]

After losing his job as censor, Major M.L.C. Funkhouser appealed to the courts, which ultimately ruled he had been "illegally ousted" and ordered his reinstatement as Second Deputy Superintendent of Police. By that time, "Big Bill" Thompson had abolished the post of Second Deputy Superintendent, but Funkhouser nonetheless successfully sued the city for $12,000 in back wages. Two Deputy Superintendent posts were then created by Thompson's successor, William Emmett Dever, and Funkhouser was technically reinstated, but he immediately resigned from the job. Forever dogged by corruption charges but officially vindicated in the courts, Funkhouser spent his final years working as an insurance broker. He died of a sudden heart attack while dining at Chicago's Atlantic Hotel in 1926. He was 62 years old.[12]

Thomas Edison's last known credit on any movie is as a producer of the 1914 film *The Patchwork Girl of Oz* (the script of which L. Frank Baum adapted from his own novel), although the Edison Manufacturing Company continued to release films until as late as 1918. Following his legal troubles with the Motion Picture Patents Company, Edison turned his back on movies altogether and focused instead on other areas of research, although in 1927 he was given an honorary membership in the Academy of Motion Picture Arts and Sciences during its inaugural year.

The inventor did, however, correspond at length with historian and author Terry Ramsaye who published a book in 1925 entitled *A Million and One Nights*, which was considered at the time to be the definitive account of the origins of the American cinema. In his pioneering history, Ramsaye hyperbolically called Edison the "inventor of the motion-picture film, the camera and the Kinetoscope — the technological foundation of the art of the motion picture."[13] Again, Edison was more than happy to take the credit. Subsequent historians would eventually come along, however, conduct more thorough research and give many of the other early movie pioneers their due. If anything, Edison has come to be vilified by more recent film historians for his monopolistic business practices, while his positive contributions to the medium have tended to be ignored.

For better or for worse, directly and indirectly, Edison caused both the rise and the fall of the Chicago motion-picture industry, which soon gave way to the American film industry's more permanent base in Hollywood. This was an evolution that he observed from a distance, Godlike and aloof, and for which he apparently felt neither pride nor regret. In spite of its enormous popularity, the medium itself had grown into something for which he did not much care or understand.

Thomas Alva Edison died on October 18, 1931 in West Orange, New Jersey, at the age of 84. His last words, spoken to his wife after slipping in and out of consciousness, were reportedly "It is very beautiful over there."[14] His description of this glimpse of paradise was uncannily similar to what many had said decades earlier when first peering into the wondrous Edison Kinetoscope.

Post-Script:
Oscar and Orson

Although William Selig shut down production at his Chicago studio for good in 1918, it would be another two years before he sold the complex of buildings to an automobile manufacturer. In the interim, he rented out his facilities to independent filmmakers looking to break into the market with low-budget productions. It must have seemed ignominious to many of Selig's army of former employees that the once-mighty studio was being used for cheap productions by inexperienced companies at the same time that all of the real talent was migrating to southern California. During this time, however, the Selig Polyscope lot would serve as the unlikely launching pad for the career of one more major figure of the silent-movie era.

One of the best-kept secrets of Chicago's secret film history is that the Second City was in fact first when it came to producing "race movies." William Foster, the African-American manager of Chicago's Pekin Theater, had founded the Foster Photoplay Company and directed what is believed to be the first film with an all-black cast, *The Railroad Porter*, in 1912. The success of that slapstick short film, reportedly inspired by the Keystone Cops, in turn inspired other African-Americans to try their

Within Our Gates, 1920.
Directed by Oscar Micheaux.

hand at film production, and black-owned independent film companies soon sprang up in major metropolitan areas across the U.S. The most significant and durable filmmaker to emerge from the race-film boom was Chicago-based Oscar Micheaux. His debut film was *The Homesteader*, an epic "super-production" running more than two-and-a-half hours that was released to critical and box-office acclaim in 1918. It would be the beginning of a remarkable movie career that spanned decades.

Micheaux was well known in Chicago even before he ventured into the movie business. As a young man he spent five years homesteading a farm he had purchased in Gregory, South Dakota. From there, he published articles in the *Chicago Defender*, one of the nation's most widely circulated African-American newspapers, urging black Americans to follow his example by moving west and purchasing land. Micheaux's experiences as a farmer served as the basis for the plot of his first novel, *The Conquest*, which he self-published in 1913. He followed up with *The Forged Note* in 1915 and *The Homesteader: A Novel* in 1917. Micheaux traveled around South Dakota, selling these novels door-to-door to his predominantly white neighbors.

Micheaux incorporated as the Micheaux Book and Film Company in 1918 and used the same door-to-door business model to sell shares in what would be his first film, an independently produced adaptation of his most recent novel. The resulting movie, shot entirely at the recently abandoned Selig Polyscope studio, was phenomenally successful with African-American audiences and critics. It is, sadly, a lost film today. The success Micheaux had with *The Homesteader* encouraged him to invest his profits back into his company: a follow-up film, *Within Our Gates*, was rushed into production and released the following year. This incredible movie, an incendiary and unflinching look at racism (also mostly shot in Chicago, this time at "Capital City Studios"), remains the earliest surviving feature made by a black director.

One of the most interesting aspects of *Within Our Gates*, especially from a twenty-first-century perspective, is that the film effectively functions as a response to Griffith's *The Birth of a Nation*. Griffith's movie, a technically astonishing piece of virtuoso filmmaking, galvanized audiences wherever it played. This result was in part due to Griffith's unparalleled skill with dynamic framing and cutting and in part due to the film's unfortunate racism, notably the climactic scene in which the Ku Klux Klan heroically ride to the rescue of the movie's white protagonists who are trapped in a cabin besieged by a black militia. This climax is a good example of Griffith's pioneering and greatly influential technique of using cross-cutting to create suspense during rescue scenes. The fact that *Within Our Gates* would appropriate Griffith's editing schemes (on a tiny fraction of the budget of *The Birth of a Nation* and in order to explicitly reverse the earlier film's ideology) has ensured that, ironically, Griffith and Micheaux are now jointly studied in film history classes in colleges throughout America.

Within Our Gates tells the melodramatic and somewhat convoluted tale of Sylvia Landry (played by the peerless Evelyn Preer), a young African-American woman who endeavors to raise money to save a school for black children in the rural south. Much like *The Birth of a Nation*, Micheaux's story alternates between scenes taking place in the north and scenes taking place in the south, and also cuts back and forth between action occurring in separate locations in order to generate a suspenseful climax.

The climactic scene in *Within Our Gates* is, however, rendered even more complex because it contains a lengthy flashback to Sylvia's youth (and thus involves cutting across time as well as space) and, specifically, the events that led to her adoptive black parents being lynched by an angry white mob. This lynching scene is intercut with an equally horrifying scene in which Mr. Gridlestone, a villainous middle-aged white man, attempts to rape the young Sylvia before recognizing a scar on her chest that identifies her as his own illegitimate daughter. This disturbing near-rape pointedly occurs beneath a portrait of America's Great Emancipator, Abraham Lincoln.

The Birth of a Nation justifies and even valorizes the actions of the Ku Klux Klan as necessary in order to combat the threat of potential assaults on white civilians (particularly white women) by supposedly dangerous black men. The complex and clever intercutting of the climax of *Within Our Gates* deconstructs this racist ideology by showing the historical reality of who did the lynching as well as who represented a more likely sexual menace.

Upon its initial release, *Within Our Gates* created its own *Birth of a Nation*-style controversy, which included a protracted two-month battle with Chicago's local censorship board (headed by Charles Frazier following the ouster of Major Funkhouser). This battle may have been more contentious than it otherwise would have been: the city was still reeling from a major race riot in the summer of 1919 that had killed dozens of people and injured hundreds more. The censorship controversy, extensively covered in the black press, virtually guaranteed that the film would play to packed houses when it eventually did open in early 1920.

Reviews in the black papers were extremely favorable. The *Chicago Defender* said: "It is the claim of the author and producer that, while it is a bit radical, it is the biggest protest against Race prejudice, lynching and concubinage that was ever written or filmed. ... There are more thrills and gripping, holding moments than was ever seen in any individual production. ... People interested in the welfare of the Race cannot afford to miss seeing this great production, and remember, it TELLS IT ALL."[1]

Like *The Homesteader*, *Within Our Gates* was thought to be a lost film until a single print was discovered in Spain (under the title *La Negra*) in the late 1970s. Restored by the Library of Congress in 1993, the movie is still only an approximation of Micheaux's original vision. Sadly, all fifteen of Micheaux's known surviving films exist today only in truncated form, typically a result of censorship boards excising material deemed inflammatory (although, as with Major Funkhouser, oftentimes such decisions were made arbitrarily).

Even more remarkable than the movie itself is the fact that *Within Our Gates* was merely one of the earliest events in a directorial career that lasted thirty years and comprised approximately forty-five feature films (by far the most prolific career of any black filmmaker in the first half of the twentieth century). Micheaux would go on to be the first director to cast the great Paul Robeson in a film (*Body and Soul*, 1925) the first to make an "all-talkie" race movie (*The Exile*, 1931) and, undaunted, he would continue to make films, even under the threat of looming bankruptcy and occasionally in the face of scathing criticism by the black press, until shortly before his death in 1951.

The Oscar Micheaux story deserves to be much more widely known, and his films deserve to be more widely seen. Throughout his career,

Micheaux's fortunes rose and fell, the quality of his output varied wildly, and his battles with local censorship boards were legendary. He was, however, always indefatigable and resilient. He had to be: Micheaux spent decades touring the country with his movies, which he self-distributed out of the trunk of his car, oftentimes while staying just one step ahead of his creditors. Impressively, he did it all during an age when independent film production was not considered a viable career path for anyone in America, much less a black man.

Today Micheaux is honored with a star on the Hollywood "Walk of Fame" and an annual film festival in Gregory, South Dakota. Unfortunately, there is nothing in Chicago to mark the addresses where he shot his first feature films. The Oscar Micheaux story is yet another too little known chapter in the remarkable history of early motion picture-production in Chicago.

***

> I warn you, Jedediah, you're not gonna like it in Chicago. The wind comes howling in off the lake and gosh only knows if they ever heard of lobster Newburg.
> – Orson Welles as Charles Foster Kane in *Citizen Kane*, 1941

By the mid-1920s, film production in Chicago had ground to a halt. Even Oscar Micheaux had left to try his luck in New York. In the ten years since the Edison Trust had dissolved, Chicago had gone from being the nation's film capital to a veritable cinematic ghost town. The arrival of "talkies" helped to consolidate the power of the major Hollywood studios and made location shooting (i.e., shooting on actual locations outside of sets constructed in the California studios) increasingly rare.

The Hearts of Age, 1934.
Directed by Orson Welles.

It would not be until after World War II that a gritty new documentary-style aesthetic would become popular in American movies, bringing Hollywood crews back to the Windy City for evocative crime films like *Call Northside 777* (1948), *Union Station* (1950), and *City That Never Sleeps* (1953). There was, however, one belated silent short made in the suburbs of Chicago that deserves a mention for marking the beginning of one of the all-time great filmmaking careers.

In 1934, seven years before he set the motion-picture world on fire with *Citizen Kane*, a nineteen-year-old Orson Welles made his directorial debut with *The Hearts of Age*, an experimental short film shot during downtime while he was studying at the Art Institute of Chicago. Ostensibly a parody of classic avant-garde movies he had seen while on trips to New York City (in particular Robert Wiene's *The Cabinet of Dr. Caligari* [*Das Cabinet des Dr. Caligari*, 1920], Luis Buñuel's *Un Chien Andalou* [1929] and Jean Cocteau's *The Blood of a Poet* [*Le sang d'un poète*, 1932]), the seeds of Welles' visionary genius are already evident in this formative work: it is one more example of a fascinating film, and the story of its making, that are both rooted in Chicago and unjustly unknown.

Young Mr. Welles shot *The Hearts of Age* entirely in suburban Woodstock, Illinois, on the campus of the Todd Seminary for Boys where he had graduated from high school three years earlier. At this time, Welles was already something of a local celebrity, having been featured in a 1933 *Daily Tribune* article titled "Eighteen Years Old, Scores Hit in Shakespeare" that touted him as a "Wonder Boy of Acting." According to the article, Welles had astonished "Chicago's first nighters" with his recent performance as Mercutio in a Milwaukee production of *Romeo and Juliet*.[2] Although a Chicago resident, Welles frequently returned to Woodstock to direct theatrical productions for the Todd School, an institution to which he felt a lifelong sense of loyalty. It was during one such trip that he made *The Hearts of Age* with a team of close friends, including producer/co-director/cinematographer William Vance and actors Paul Edgerton and Virginia Nicholson (Welles' future bride).

While the resulting eight-minute short film is unquestionably the work of an amateur, fans of Welles' feature films should find it especially interesting: the entire movie relies on rapid-fire montage editing, which Welles would eschew in his early features a few years later in favor of the deep-focus/long-take style so beloved by the French critic André Bazin. Intriguingly, Welles would return to this montage-based approach to filmmaking towards the end of his life, primarily out of necessity caused by budgetary constraints. From *The Hearts of Age* to *F for Fake* (1973) nearly forty years later, Welles, in his film career, truly came full circle.

The Hearts of Age begins with shots of a well-dressed woman (Nicholson) wearing old-age make-up and sitting atop a giant bell on the second story of an anonymous-looking building. On the first floor below her, a man in blackface and colonial dress (Edgerton) pulls a rope that rings the bell. At one point, the woman waves her umbrella at the man and seems to chide him into ringing it harder. The film boldly enters murky psychosexual (not to mention racial) territory by showing the woman pleasurably rocking back-and-forth astride the bell with what appears to be her black servant toiling under her. The ringing of the bell also seems to have an unintended consequence: it brings a series of strange-looking characters out of a door on the floor above the woman, all of whom acknowledge her as they walk past her on a nearby fire escape. One of these passers-by is a sinister-looking dandy (Welles), also wearing old-age make-up, who repeatedly passes by the woman and, in the process, politely tips his top hat to her each time.

Then things get really weird: the man in blackface hangs himself as Welles and Vance cut to shots of a gravestone with a beckoning hand superimposed over it, and shots of a human skull in negative (*à la* F.W. Murnau's *Nosferatu: A Symphony of Horror* [*Nosferatu, eine Symphonie des Grauens*, 1922]). The sinister-looking dandy then enters a room holding a candelabrum. He sits down at a piano and begins to play, only to find that one or more of the piano keys are not working properly. The old dandy, whom the viewer can now infer is Death, opens the piano to find the life-less body of the old woman inside. The film ends with Death holding up a series of gravestone-shaped title cards reading: "SLEEPING / AT REST / IN PEACE / WITH THE LORD / AMEN."

It is not known when or even if *The Hearts of Age* was screened in the years immediately following its production. It was certainly an "unknown film" for decades. In the late 1960s, film critic and future Orson Welles biographer Joseph McBride learned about a 16mm print in the William Vance collection of the Greenwich, Connecticut Public Library. McBride published an article in the Spring 1970 issue of *Film Quarterly* entitled "Welles Before Kane," which discussed both *The Hearts of Age* and another Welles short, the then-lost *Too Much Johnson*. In McBride's excellent biography *What Ever Happened to Orson Welles?*, he writes, "Welles seemed bemused and somewhat irritated by the discovery," before quoting Welles' long-time cinematographer Gary Graver: "Orson kept saying, 'Why did Joe have to discover that film?'"[3]

Orson Welles as "Death" in *The Hearts of Age.*

In the indispensable book-length interview *This is Orson Welles* (based on transcribed conversations between Welles and filmmaker Peter Bogdanovich, edited by Jonathan Rosenbaum), the great director claims that *The Hearts of Age* was nothing more than "Sunday afternoon fun out on the lawn" and "a send-up."[4] Of course, it is entirely possible that Welles did not originally intend the film to be a light-hearted parody of the avant-garde but rather an earnest attempt to work in a mode that he had seen and admired as a young man, and his later comments may have been made in defensive hindsight. If *The Hearts of Age* indeed embarrassed old Mr. Welles, however, it probably should not have done so. Like the early sketches of a master painter, the film in many ways points the way towards the greatness that was to come (in particular in Welles' use of elaborate make-up and in his practice of blending techniques gleaned from the German Expressionist and Soviet Montage movements), which makes it an invaluable piece of the Orson Welles puzzle.

The sole existing print of *The Hearts of Age* has been deposited with and preserved by the Library of Congress and is readily available in a good-quality DVD edition by Kino Video (the transfer of which is accompanied by a delightfully jaunty acoustic guitar score by Larry Morotta). Yet in spite of Orson Welles' reputation as one of the greatest directors of all time, it seems that even many Chicago-area movie lovers are unaware of his local filmmaking roots.

Appendix A:
SELIG POLYSCOPE'S POINTERS
ON PICTURE ACTING

Anyone appearing in a Chicago-shot Selig Polyscope production circa 1910 would have been given this handy, exceedingly amusing manual on "picture acting." Amazing but true:

ACTION — When the director gives you the word for action at the start of a scene, don't wait and look at the camera to see if it is going. That will be taken care of and started when the action settles down to where the directors think the scene should start.

LOOKING AT THE CAMERA — Never look toward the director when he speaks to you during the action of a scene and while the camera is running. He may be reminding you that you are out of the picture, or of some piece of business that you have forgotten. Glancing toward the camera near the finish of a scene to see if it has stopped is also a bad habit. The director will inform you when the scene is over.

EYES — Use your eyes as much as possible in your work. Remember that they express your thoughts more clearly when properly used than gestures or unnatural facial contortions. Do not squint. You will never obtain the results you are striving for if you get into that very bad habit.

MAKING EXITS — In making an exit through a door, or out of the picture, never slack up just on the edge; use a little more exertion and continue well out of range of the camera. Many scenes have been weakened by such carelessness.

LETTER WRITING — In writing before the camera, do so naturally. Do not make rapid dashes over the paper. You are completely destroying the realism you are expected to convey by so doing. When reading a letter mentally count five slowly before showing by your expression the effect of the letter upon your mind.

READING A LETTER — When a lady receives a letter from her sweetheart or husband she must not show her joy by kissing it. That is overdone and has become so common by usage in pictures and on the stage as to be tiresome.

KISSING — When kissing your sweetheart, husband or wife, do so naturally — not a peck on the lips and a quick break-a-way. Also use judgment in the length of your kiss. Vary it by the degree of friendship, or love, that you are expected to convey.

GESTURES — Do not use unnecessary gestures. Repose in your acting is of more value. A gesture well directed can convey a great deal, while too many may detract from the realism of your work.

STRUGGLING — Avoid unnecessary struggling and body contortions. Many scenes appear ridiculous by such action. For example, if in a scrimmage you are overpowered by superior numbers, don't kick, fight and squirm, unless you are portraying a maniac or a man maddened beyond control. Use common sense in this.

SHUTTING THE DOORS — Be careful in opening and shutting of doors in a set, so as not to jar the scenery. Carelessness in this respect causes make-overs, with a considerable loss of time and film, both of which are valuable.

IN PICTURE — Be sure that you stay in the picture while working. Mentally mark with your eyes the limitations of the camera's focus, and keep within bounds. You can do this with a little practice without appearing purposely to do so.

SMOKING — Don't smoke near the camera or where the smoke can blow across the lens. Take just as good care about kicking up a dust. If you are on a horse it is not necessary to ride circles around the camera. Throwing dust into a camera will cause scratches, and bring down upon your head the righteous wrath of the operator.

GOSSIP — Avoid discussing the secrets of the business you are engaged in. Remember that much harm is done by spreading the news of all the happenings of the day in your work. Revealing to outsiders the plots and names of pictures you are working on or have just finished is frequently taken advantage of and causes great loss to your firm, by some rival concern rushing a picture out ahead that they have on hand, of the same nature. All gossip of an injurious nature is deplorable, and will not be indulged in by any people who appreciate their position and wish to remain in the good graces of their employer.

PROMPTNESS — Come to work on time. An allowance of ten minutes will be granted for a difference in watches, but be sure it is ten minutes BEFORE and not ten AFTER. There are no hardships inflicted upon you, and you owe it to your employer to be as prompt in this matter as you expect him to be in the payment of your salary.

MAKE-UP — Regarding make-up and dress, do some thinking for yourself. Remember that the director has many troubles, and his people should lighten his burden in this matter as much as possible. For example, if you are told to play as a "49" miner, figure out in your own mind how you should appear, and don't ask the director if high-laced boots will do when you should know that they have only been in use for a few years. Don't ask him if pants with side pockets will do, when you know they were never worn at that period. A poor country girl should never wear high French heels, silk stockings and long form corsets; nor should her hair be done in the latest fashion. She would look very much out of the picture in such make-up carrying a milk pail. Do not redden lips too much as a dark red takes nearly black. Likewise in rouging the face, do not touch up the cheeks only and leave the nose and forehead white. The effect of such make-up is hideous in photography. Get in the habit of thinking out for yourself all the little details that go to complete a perfect picture of the character you are to portray. Then, if there is anything you do not understand do not be afraid to ask the director.

BEARDS — In the making of beards one cannot be too careful. This is an art that every actor can become proficient in, if he will only take the pains to do so. Remember that the camera magnifies every defect in your make-up. Just use your mental faculties to give some thought to your character studies and you will win out.

SLEEVES — Avoid playing too many parts with your sleeves rolled up. Cowboys and miners use the sleeves of their shirts for what they were intended. If you are playing tennis, or courting a girl at the seaside, you may display your manly beauty to your heart's content. Do not let common stage usages govern you in this matter.

PROFANITY — Let the gentleman exercise care when in the presence of ladies and children to use no profanity. It is just as easy to express yourself without it if you will only try it.

USE NO PROFANITY IN THE PICTURES — There are thousands of deaf mutes who attend the theatres and who understand every movement of your lips.

PARTS — Do not become peeved if you are not given the part you think you ought to have. The director knows what type person he wishes to use in a particular part, and if it is not given to you it is because some other person is better fitted for it. We should all work for the general good. By giving our employer the best we have in us, we are greatly benefiting him, and by so doing are enhancing our own value.

Appendix B:
A COMPLETE LIST OF
THE EXTANT CHICAGO-SHOT
FILMS NAMED IN THIS BOOK
AND WHERE TO SEE THEM

Tragically, more than 90% of all American films made before 1929 have been estimated to be lost. The further back into the silent era one looks, when the major Chicago studios were at their most prolific, the more that percentage increases. Nonetheless, some of the films discussed in this book do survive today and, through the preservation efforts of the Library of Congress, the George Eastman House International Museum of Photography and Film, the American Film Archives and other institutions, they are available to be viewed in 35mm prints, on DVD and Blu-ray, and online. The following is a list of all of the extant Chicago-shot films mentioned in this book as well as how and where they can seen.

The Adventures of Kathlyn, Chapter 1 (Pr. Selig Polyscope, Dir. Francis J. Grandon, 1913) — 35mm print, Eyefilm, Amsterdam, The Netherlands

Armour's Electric Trolley (Pr. Edison Manufacturing, Dir. James H. White, 1897) — 35mm print, Library of Congress Paper Print Collection, Washington, D.C.; http://www.youtube.com/watch?v=n3meO5UpwDQ

An Awful Skate; or, The Hobo on Rollers (Pr. Essanay, Dir. Gilbert M. Anderson, 1907) — 35mm print, George Eastman House International Museum of Photography and Film, Rochester, NY

Back to the Old Farm (Pr. Essanay, Dir. Archer McMackin, 1912) — Farmington Implement Co. DVD 5; http://www.youtube.com/watch?v=Bow99bzHfiM

The Battle of Santiago Bay (aka *Spanish Fleet Destroyed*) (Pr. Amet, Dir. Edward Amet, 1898) — Video exhibit, Lake County Discovery Museum, Wauconda, IL

Cattle Driven to Slaughter (Pr. Edison Manufacturing, Dir. James H. White, 1897) — 35mm print, Library of Congress Paper Print Collection, Washington, D.C.; http://www.youtube.com/watch?v=LjPL6EJUfa8&feature=relmfu

Chicago Police Parade (aka *Chicago defile de policemen*) (Pr. Lumière, Dir. Alexandre Promio, 1896) — The Movies Begin — A Treasury of Early Cinema, 1894–1913, Kino DVD, 2002; The Lumière Brothers' First Films, Kino DVD, 1998; http://www.youtube.com/watch?v=tt9aaIgm_P8

Chicago Fire Department Runs (Pr. Amet, Dir. Edward Amet, 189?) — Video exhibit, Lake County Discovery Museum, Wauconda, IL

The Coming of Columbus (Pr. Selig Polyscope, Dir. Colin Campbell, 1912) — 35mm print, Library of Congress, Washington, D.C.

Corner Madison and State Streets, Chicago (Pr. Edison Manufacturing, Dir. James H. White, 1897) — 35mm print, Library of Congress Paper Print Collection, Washington, D.C.; http://www.youtube.com/watch?v=CLlc40myPyQ

The Count of Monte Cristo (Pr. Selig Polyscope, Dir. Francis Boggs / Thomas Persons, 1908) — 35mm print, Library of Congress, Washington, D.C.

The Cowboy Millionaire (Pr. Selig Polyscope, Dir. Francis Boggs / Otis Turner, 1909) — 35mm print, Eyefilm, Amsterdam, The Netherlands

The Crisis (Pr. Selig Polyscope, Dir. Colin Campbell, 1916) — 35mm Print, The Library of Congress, Washington, D.C.

Dreamy Dud: He Resolves Not to Smoke (Pr. Essanay, Dir. Wallace A. Carlson, 1915) — 35mm Print, The Library of Congress, Washington, D.C.; The Origins of Film: Origins of American Animation, Image Entertainment DVD, 2001; http://www.youtube.com/watch?v=Oup5EnKMGxM

From the Submerged (Pr. Essanay, Dir. Theodore Wharton, 1912) — Treasures III: Social Issues in American Film, 1900–1934, Image Entertainment DVD, 2007; http://www.youtube.com/watch?v=Nbmh7CGjj40

The Gans-McGovern Fight (Pr. Selig Polyscope, Dir. ?, 1901) — http://www.youtube.com/watch?v=q9O9DlFq5FM

The Hearts of Age (Pr./Dir. Orson Welles/William Vance, 1934) — 35mm print, The Library of Congress, Washington, D.C.; Avant Garde: Experimental Cinema of the 1920s & 1930s, Kino DVD, 2005; http://www.youtube.com/watch?v=pXKIMag5hHE

His New Job (Pr. Essanay, Dir. Charles Chaplin, 1915) — Chaplin's Essanay Comedies Vol. 1, Image Entertainment DVD, 2004; http://www.youtube.com/watch?v=WIIuhlruc14

Mamma's Pets (Pr. Amet, Dir. Edward Amet, 189?) — Video exhibit, Lake County Discovery Museum, Wauconda, IL

Maud Muller (Pr. Selig Polyscope, Dir. Otis Turner, 1911) — 35mm print, George Eastman House International Museum of Photography and Film, Rochester, NY

Max Wants a Divorce (Pr. Essanay, Dir. Max Linder, 1917) — http://www.youtube.com/watch?v=rKvvaDivQ6Q
Mr. Flip (Pr. Essanay, Dir. Gilbert M. Anderson, 1909) — Slapstick Encyclopedia, Kino DVD, 2002; http://www.youtube.com/watch?v=Tc6k1GA3sA8

The Prince of Graustark (Pr. Essanay, Dir. Fred E. Wright, 1915) — 35mm print, George Eastman House International Museum of Photography and Film, Rochester, NY

The Raven (Pr. Essanay, Dir. Charles Brabin, 1915) — Grapevine Video DVD, 2006) Note: the Grapevine version, which appears to be complete, runs 59 minutes. Other circulating versions run shorter and do not feature the scenes in the correct order.

The Roller Skate Craze (Pr. Selig Polyscope, Dir. ?, 1907) — 35mm print, George Eastman House International Museum of Photography and Film, Rochester, NY; 35mm print, Library of Congress Paper Print Collection, Washington, D.C.; (Heavily edited Library of Congress version: http://www.youtube.com/watch?v=-Qw6SHcMSLg)

Sheep Run, Chicago Stockyards (Pr. Edison Manufacturing, Dir. James H. White, 1897) — 35mm print, Library of Congress, Washington, D.C.; http://www.youtube.com/watch?v=LjPL6EJUfa8&feature=relmfu

Sherlock Holmes (Pr. Essanay, Dir. Arthur Berthelet) — 35mm print, Cinémathèque Française, Paris, France

Tempted By Necessity (Pr. Selig Polyscope, Dir. Lem Parker, 1912) — 35mm print, George Eastman House International Museum of Photography and Film, Rochester, NY

Within Our Gates (Pr. Micheaux Book and Film Co., Dir. Oscar Micheaux, 1920) — 35mm print, Library of Congress, Washington, D.C.; Grapevine Video DVD, 2007; The Origins of Film: African American Cinema I, Image Entertainment DVD, 2001

The Wonderful Wizard of Oz (Pr. Selig Polyscope, Dir. Otis Turner, 1910) — *The Wizard of Oz* (Three Disc Emerald Edition), Warner Home Video Blu-ray, 2009; *More Treasures from American Film Archives 1894–1931*, Image Entertainment DVD, 2004; http://www.youtube.com/watch?v=F1MmaXcEI98

Appendix C:
SOME CENSORED SCENES OF CHICAGO FILMS NOTED IN LOCAL NEWSPAPERS

From 1914 to 1916, a popular portion of Kitty Kelly's "Flickerings from Film Land" column in the *Chicago Daily Tribune* detailed scenes that the censorship board ordered to be cut (as well as some movies that were rejected outright). Here are some Essanay and Selig films that were targeted:

5/5/1914
At Last We Are Alone (Selig) — Bedroom scene showing embracing of couple in night robes.
A Pair of Stockings (Selig) — Man entering and leaving room through window; shorten scene in which he rifles (through) dresser; cut out actual stealing of necklace and stockings.

6/4/1914
Broncho Billy: Outlaw (Essanay) — Shorten to flash struggle between Mexican and girl.
Finger Prints (Essanay) — Struggle between crook and girl; shorten scene between detective and crooks.

- 193 -

6/26/1914

The Count of Monte Cristo (Selig) — Subtitle: "To further his own end Dr. Villeford suggests robbery and murder." shooting woman; hitting man on the head with bottle; man stabbing himself; and the actual killing in duel.

Broncho Billy and the Sheriff (Essanay) — Drinking scene in church; "bad man" driving congregation from church; shorten scene showing sheriff giving money to the "bad man"; giving file to prisoner; showing file after escape; prisoner filing bars; prisoner escaping from jail.

10/14/1914

Escape of Jim Dolan (Selig) — Putting file in bottle; sawing prison bars; Indians attacking man; tying him to horse's tail; and horse dragging him; subtitle about Indians torturing man.

10/13/1914

Hearst-Selig Pictorial News Company No. 1 (Selig) — Subtitle: "A farmer shoes his horse by the wayside while the soldiers amuse themselves by making an effigy of the Kaiser."

Her Sacrifice (Selig) — Subtitles: "A little girl who loved not wisely but too well." "That man owes my little sister something."

5/21/1915

How Callahan Cleaned Up Little Hell (Selig) — Shorten gambling scene; shooting police captain; interior of dive from beginning to where doors in rear are closed; dive keeper with currency in hand; eliminate idea that politician was being paid for protection.

Beautiful Belinda (Selig) — Man with arrow sticking in his back.

2/16/1915

A Night Out (Essanay) — Man kicking woman; five scenes of man improperly clad in a strange woman's bedroom.

4/30/1915

Sweedie in Vaudeville (Essanay) — First half of gambling scene in which money is shown.

6/21/1915

A Woman (Essanay — Charlie Chaplin) — Woman kicking man; woman picking man's pocket in park; all scenes of man minus trousers; all scenes in bedroom showing him dressing up as a woman; all scenes showing extraction of hatpins from man's anatomy; man pulling skirt off woman and subsequent and subsequent vulgar actions; picture with father giving couple blessing.

11/11/1915
How Marjorie Won a Career and Lifted the Mortgage from Her Mother's Home (Essanay) — Rejected outright because the picture is a demonstration of a corset fitting on live models and is offensive to public modesty.

ENDNOTES

Introduction: Hollywood Before Hollywood

1 Phillips, Michael. "When Chicago Created Hollywood," *Chicago Tribune*, July 22, 2007
2 Parsons, Louella. *The Gay Illiterate*, Doubleday, 1944, pg. 18
3 Bordwell, David and Thompson, Kristin. *Film History: An Introduction*, 3rd ed., McGraw-Hill, 2009, pg. 31
4 Riesler, Jim. *Cash and Carry: The Spectacular Rise and Hard Fall of C.C. Pyle, America's First Sports Agent*, McFarland, 2009, pg. 53
5 *Show World*, June 29, 1907
6 *Billboard*, August 27, 1907
7 E-mail to author Michael Glover Smith
8 Lauerman, Connie. "Hollywood East," *Chicago Tribune*, March 5, 1995

I. THOMAS EDISON, INVENTION, AND THE DAWN OF A NEW CHICAGO

1. Edison Kinetoscope and Pre-Motion Picture Entertainment

1 *Chicago Daily Tribune*, June 15, 1878

2 Obituary, *New York Times*, October 19, 1931

3 *Chicago Daily Tribune*, March 2, 1878, reprinted from the New York Sun

4 *Chicago Daily Tribune*, March 2, 1878, reprinted from the New York Sun

5 "The Speaking Phonograph," *Scientific American Supplement*, March 16, 1878, p. 1828. Reprinted from the *New York Sun*.

6 "The Speaking Phonograph," *Scientific American Supplement*, March 16, 1878, p. 1828. Reprinted from the *New York Sun*.

7 "The Speaking Phonograph," *Scientific American Supplement*, March 16, 1878, p. 1828. Reprinted from the *New York Sun*.

8 Dyer, Frank Lewis and Martin, Thomas Commerford. *Edison: His Life and Inventions Volume 2*, Harper's, 1929, pg. 748

9 Miller Reese Hutchinson quoted in "Learning from Failures," *Munsey's Magazine*, Volume 58

10 Biographiq. *Thomas Edison: Life of an Electrifying Man*, Filiquarian, 2008, pg. 23

11 Pickover, Clifford A. *Strange Brains and Genius: The Secret Lives of Eccentric Scientists and Madmen*, HarperCollins, 1999, pg. 14

12 *Chicago Daily Tribune*, June 5, 1891

13 *Chicago Daily Tribune*, June 5, 1891

14 *Chicago Daily Tribune*, June 5, 1891

2. The Columbian Exposition

1 "Profits on the Side," *Chicago Daily Tribune*, July 15, 1894

2 "Profits on the Side," *Chicago Daily Tribune*, July 15, 1894

3 Musser, Charles. *Before the Nickelodeon: Edwin S. Porter and the Edison Manufacturing Company*, University of California Press, 1991, pg. 39

4 Clark, Herma. "When Chicago Was Young," *Chicago Daily Tribune*, April 19, 1942

5 Larson, Erik. *The Devil in the White City*, Vintage, 2004, pg. 247

6 "Burton Holmes' Third Talk.: Gives His Illustrated Lecture on 'The City of the Barbary Coast'," *Chicago Daily Tribune*, November 27, 1897

3. The Dawn of Exhibition

1 "Classified Ad 7," *Chicago Daily Tribune*, May 24, 1894

2 *Western Electrician*, January 6 - June 30, 1894

3 *The Motion Picture World*, July 15, 1916

4 Josephson, Matthew. *Edison: A Biography*, John Wiley & Sons, 1992, pg. 173–174

5 *Maguire & Baucus Fall Catalogue*, 1897, p. 10

6 "The Wonderful Kinetoscope," *Chicago Daily Tribune*, May 19, 1894

7 Bernard Tavernier, quoted from the commentary on Kino Video's *Lumière Bros. First Films* DVD, 1998

8 "Hopkins' South Side Theater," *Chicago Daily Tribune*, June 28, 1896.

9 "Amusements," *Chicago Daily Tribune*, July 7, 1896

10 The undated *Chicago Post* article on the cinematographe was reprinted in several regional papers; the text we have used comes from a printing in the January 7, 1897 edition of the *Trenton Evening Times*.

11 *Morning Olympian* display ad, August 7, 1897

12 "Show Life and Beauty," *Chicago Daily Tribune*, October 5, 1896

13 *Maguire & Baucus Fall Catalogue*, 1897, p. 9

14 "Kinematograph & Lantern Weekly," *The Film Index*, Vol. IV. No. 38, September 18, 1909, pg. 12

II. CHICAGO RISING

4. Colonel William Selig

1 Dengler, Eugene. "Wonders of the 'Diamond-S' Plant," *Motography*, July, 1911

2 Erish, Andrew. *Col. William N. Selig, the Man Who Invented Hollywood*, University of Texas Press, 2012, pg. 7

3 Erish, Andrew. *Col. William N. Selig, the Man Who Invented Hollywood*, University of Texas Press, 2012, pg. 11

4 Untitled Manuscript, Selig Folder 551, Margaret Herrick Library, Academy of Motion Picture Arts and Sciences

5 Untitled Manuscript, Selig Folder 552, Margaret Herrick Library, Academy of Motion Picture Arts and Sciences

6 "Chicago as Movie Capital," *Chicago Daily Tribune*, December 9, 1962

7 *Selig Catalog*, 1903

8 Musser, Charles. *The Emergence of Cinema: The American Screen to 1907*, University of California Press, 1994, pg. 255–258

9 *Selig Catalog*, 1903

10 Aycock, Colleen and Scott, Mark. *Joe Gans: A Biography of the First African American World Boxing Champion*, McFarland, 2008, pg. 69–70

11 "Knockout for prize fights," *Chicago Daily Tribune*, December 18, 1900

12 Musser, Charles. *The Emergence of Cinema: The American Screen to 1907*, University of California Press, 1994, pg. 290–291

13 *The Moving Picture World*, October 1, 1910

14 *Selig Catalog*, 1903

15 Bernstein, Arnie. *Hollywood on Lake Michigan: 100 Years of Chicago and the Movies*, Lake Claremont Press, 1998, pg. 56

16 Gaudreault, Andre. *American Cinema: 1890–1909: Themes and Variations*, Rutgers University Press, 2008, pg. 71

17 Erish, Andrew. *Col. William N. Selig, the Man Who Invented Hollywood*, University of Texas Press, 2012, pg. 18

18 Ramsaye, Terry, *A Million and One Nights*, Simon & Schuster, 1986, pg. 465
19 "Selig's Motion Picture Plant" Ad, *Chicago Examiner*, 1908
20 "Film Makers' New Industry," *Chicago Daily Tribune*, November 3, 1907

5. George Spoor, George Kleine and the Rise of the Nickelodeon

1   Statement of Edward Amet, filed March 24, 1897, federal archives
2   Undated (1940s) letter from Edward Amet to the Waukegan Historical Society
3   Letter from "Verne" to "Uncle," dated April 6, 1897, Lake Country Discovery Museum archives
4   Musser, Charles. *The Emergence of Cinema: The American Screen to 1907*, University of California Press, 1994, pg. 162
5   *Chicago Daily News*, October 9, 1943
6   Undated (1940s) letter from Edward Amet to the Waukegan Historical Society
7   Dretske, Diana. "Illuminating Lake County, Illinois History.": Edward Amet's Films, 1896–1898. Web. 22 June 2012. <http://lakecountyhistory.blogspot.com/2010/09/edward-amets-films-1896-1898.html>
8   Undated (1940s) letter from Edward Amet to the Waukegan Historical Society
9   *Chicago Daily News*, October 9, 1943
10 *Waukegan Daily Gazette Register*, November 15, 1898
11 *Chicago Daily News*, April 11, 1951
12 "First Movie Star Never in Hollywood," *Cleveland Plain Dealer*, June 25, 1939
13 *Chicago Daily News*, October 9, 1943
14 "Move A If Alive," *Chicago Daily Tribune*, April 4, 1897
15 Kiehn, David. *Broncho Billy and the Essanay Film Company*, Farwell, 2003, pg. 7
16 Grau, Robert. *The Stage in the Twentieth Century: Third Volume*, Broadway Publishing Co., pg. 125
17 "Reel Chicago." - Chicago Magazine. Robert Loerzel. Web. 17 June 2012. <http://www.chicagomag.com/Chicago-Magazine/May-2007/Reel-Chicago/>
18 *The Moving Picture World*, Vol. 4
19 *The Moving Picture World*, Vol. 29
20 Gaudreault, Andre. *American Cinema, 1890–1900: Themes and Variations*, Rutgers University Press, 2008, pg. 84
21 "The Origins of the Film Exchange," *Film History Vol. 17*, Taylor & Francis, 2005, pg. 431
22 *New York Clipper*, October 15, 1904
23 Laemmle, Carl. "The Business of Motion Pictures," in Tino Balio, ed., *The American Film Industry*, University of Wisconsin Press, 1985, pg. 163

24 Dick, Bernard. *City of Dreams: The Making and Remaking of Universal Pictures*, University Press of Kentucky, 1997 pg. 16

25 Rabinovitz, Lauren. *For the Love of Pleasure: Women, Movies and Culture in Turn-of-the-Century Chicago*, Rutgers University Press, 1998, pg. 110

26 Ringer, Ronald. *Excel HSC Modern History*, Pascal Press, 2005, pg. 148

6. Gilbert "Broncho Billy" Anderson

1   Bianculli, Anthony. *Iron Rails in the Garden Sate: Tales of New Jersey Railroading*, Indiana University Press, 2008, pg. 80

2   Musser, Charles. *Before the Nickelodeon: Edwin S. Porter and the Edison Manufacturing Company*, University of California Press, 1991, pg. 253

3   Brownlow, Kevin. *Hollywood, The Pioneers*, Knopf, 1979, pg. 35

4   Brownlow, Kevin. *Hollywood, The Pioneers*, Knopf, 1979, pg. 35

5   *Edison Films Catalogue*, No. 200, 1904

6   Lahue, Kalton C. *Winners of the West: Sagebrush Heroes of the Silent Screen*, A.S. Barnes, 1971, pg. 25

7   Kiehn, David. *Broncho Billy and the Essanay Film Company*, Farwell, 2003, pg. 7

8   Courtlandt, Roberta. "A Chat with G.M. Anderon [Broncho Billy]", *Motion Picture Magazine* Vol. 8, 1915

9   *Chicago Daily News*, October 9, 1943

10 Bowser, Eileen. *History of the American Cinema: The Transformation of Cinema, 1907 – 1915*, University of California Press, 1994, pg. 179

11 Essanay Ad, *The Moving Picture World*, July 27, 1907

12 Grisham, William. "Those Marvelous Men and Their Movie Machines," *Chicago Tribune*, December 7, 1969

13 Davis, Debra and Davis, Lon. *King of the Movies: Francis X. Bushman*, BearManor Media, 2009, pg. 36

14 "Announcement," *The Moving Picture World*, July 27 1907

7. The Edison Trust

1   Balio, Tino. *The American Film Industry*, University of Wisconsin Press, 1985, pg. 135

2   "Edison Gets $200,000 From Moving Picture Men," *Chicago Daily Tribune*, February 11, 1908

3   *Edison v. American Mutoscope & Biograph Co.*, 151 F. 767, 81 C.C.A. 391 [March 5, 1907].

4   "Suits Started By Edison on Moving Picture Patents," *Chicago Daily Tribune*, March 8, 1908

5   "A Plan to Reorganize the Motion Picture Business of the United States," unsigned, May 1908 in Tino Balio, ed., *The American Film Industry*, University of Wisconsin Press, 1985, pg. 163

6 "To the Exhibitors of Moving Pictures," *The Moving Picture World Vol. 4*, No. 4, January 23, 1909

7 "Declare War on Film Trust," *Chicago Daily Tribune*, January 16, 1909

8 Bach, Steven. *Final Cut*, Newmarket Press, 1999, pg. 30

9 Grisham, William. "Those Marvelous Men and Their Movie Machines", *Chicago Tribune*, December 7, 1969

10 "Kinematograph & Lantern Weekly," *The Film Index*, Vol. IV. No. 38, September 18, 1909, pg. 12

11 "Insurance for Picture Houses," *New York Dramatic Mirror*, April 10, 1909, pg. 14

12 "Motion Picture Patents Company: Their Policy and Procedure," *The Moving Picture World*, April 3, 1909

13 "Censorship Board," *The Moving Picture World*, March 20, 1909

14 Brief for the defendants, *U.S.A. v. M.P.P.C.*, pg. 94–95

15 Erish, Andrew. *Col. William N. Selig, the Man Who Invented Hollywood*, University of Texas Press, 1999, pg. 198

III. THE GOLDEN AGE OF CHICAGO FILM PRODUCTION

8. The Golden Age of Essanay

1 Davis, Debra and Davis, Lon. *King of the Movies: Francis X. Bushman*, Bear Manor Media, 2009, pg. 38–39

2 Boggs, Johnny. *Jesse James and the Movies*, McFarland, 2011, pg. 27

3 "Letter from W.C. Quimby to the Editor," *The Moving Picture World*, February 11, 1911

4 *The Essanay Guide*, March 15, 1910

5 Waterbury, Ruth. *Photoplay: the aristocrat of motion picture magazines, Vol. 11*, pg. 69

6 Davis, Lon and Davis, Debra. *King of the Movies: Francis X. Bushman*, BearManor Media, 2009, pg. 35

7 Parsons, Louella. *The Gay Illiterate*, Doubleday, 1944, pg. 26

8 Davis, Debra and Davis, Lon. *King of the Movies: Francis X. Bushman*, BearManor Media, 2009, pg. 36

10 Davis, Debra and Davis, Lon. *King of the Movies: Francis X. Bushman*, BearManor Media, 2009, pg. 37

11 Parsons, Louella. *The Gay Illiterate*, Doubleday, 1944, pg. 26

12 Grisham, William. "Those Marvelous Men and Their Movie Machines", *Chicago Tribune*, December 7, 1969

13 Bowser, Eileen. *History of the American Cinema: The Transformation of Cinema, 1907–1915*, University of California Press, 1994, pg. 64

14 Slide, Anthony. *Early American Cinema*, Scarecrow Press, 1994, pg. 23

9. The Golden Age of Selig Polyscope

1 "The Five Cent Theaters," *Chicago Daily Tribune*, April 10, 1907
2 *Chicago Daily News Almanac and Year Book for 1911*, published 1910
3 "News of the Theatres," *Chicago Daily Tribune*, October 3, 1908
4 "Voice of the People", *Chicago Tribune*, January 2, 1977
5 "Voice of the People", *Chicago Tribune*, April 6, 1969
6 "Hunting African Lions," *Chicago Daily Tribune*, May 23, 1909
7 "Kinematograph & Lantern Weekly", *The Film Index*, Vol. IV. No. 38, September 18, 1909, pg. 12
8 "Hunting African Lions," *Chicago Daily Tribune*, May 23, 1909
9 "Studio Janitor Kills Movie Director," *Los Angeles Times*, October 27, 1911
10 Erish, Andrew. *Col. William N. Selig, the Man Who Invented Hollywood*, University of Texas Press, 2012, pg. 98
11 Jensen, Richard. *The Amazing Tom Mix: The Most Famous Cowboy of the Movies*, iUniverse, 2005, pg. 47
12 *The Film Index*, Vol. IV. No. 5, January 30, 1909, pg. 4–5
13 Selig letter to William Renick, February 18, 1914, quoted in "If It's Not Scottish It's Crap: Harry Lauder Sings for Selig," Scott Curis. *Film History*, Vol 11, No. 4, 1999.
14 "Harry Lauder Pictures," *Variety* 34.5, April 3, 1914
15 McQuade, James. "Chicago Letter," *The Moving Picture World*, January 31, 1914
16 Kelly, Kitty. "Flickerings from Film Land," *Chicago Daily Tribune*, March 1, 1915
17 "Gossip of the Movie Plays and Players," *Chicago Daily Tribune*, June 28, 1914
18 Taken from an undated exhibitor's catalog, most of the copy was reprinted in "Kathlyn Williams' Great Success at the Pastime Theatre Today Only" in the July 27, 1914 issue of *The Bakersfield Californian*
19 "Film of the Week," *Cleveland Plain Dealer*, July 12, 1914
20 *Photoplay*, dated April 1914, but probably from later
21 "Answers to Movie Fans," *Chicago Daily Tribune*, April 26, 1914
22 "Green Room Jottings, *Motion Picture Magazine*, August, 1913
23 *Motography*, March 7, 1914
24 "Hearst-Selig Moving Picture" Ad, *Chicago Examiner*, 1914
25 Erish, Andrew. *Col. William N. Selig, the Man Who Invented Hollywood*, University of Texas Press, 2012, pg. 156

10. Essanay Signs Charlie Chaplin

1 Swanson, Gloria. *Swanson on Swanson: An Autobiography*, Pocket, 1981, pg. 44
2 Chaplin, Charles. *My Autobiography*, Plume/Penguin, 1992, pg. 125

3 Chaplin, Charles. My *Autobiography*, Plume/Penguin, 1992, pg. 126
4 Chaplin, Charles. My *Autobiography*, Plume/Penguin, 1992, pg. 330
5 Bell, Geoffrey. *The Golden Gate and the Silver Screen*, Associated University Presse, 1984, pg. 58
6 Chaplin, Charles. My *Autobiography*, Plume/Penguin, 1992, pg. 144
7 Chaplin, Charles. My *Autobiography*, Plume/Penguin, 1992, pg. 146
8 Chaplin, Charles. My *Autobiography*, Plume/Penguin, 1992, pg. 147
9 Chaplin, Charles. My *Autobiography*, Plume/Penguin, 1992, pg. 149
10 Chaplin, Charles. My *Autobiography*, Plume/Penguin, 1992, pg. 153
11 Chaplin, Charles. My *Autobiography*, Plume/Penguin, 1992, pg. 158–159
12 Arnold, James. *Seen any good dirty movies lately?*, St. Anthony Messenger Press, 1972, pg. 61
13 Chaplin, Charles. My *Autobiography*, Plume/Penguin, 1992, pg. 160
14 *Chicago Daily News*, October 9, 1943
15 Grisham, William. "Those Marvelous Men and Their Movie Machines," *Chicago Daily Tribune*, December 7, 1969

11. Chaplin in Chicago: His New Job

1 Chaplin, Charles. My *Autobiography*, Plume/Penguin, 1992, pg. 166
2 Chaplin, Charles. My *Autobiography*, Plume/Penguin, 1992, pg. 165
3 Swanson, Gloria. *Swanson on Swanson: An Autobiography*, Pocket, 1981, pg. 42
4 Chaplin, Charles. My *Autobiography*, Plume/Penguin, 1992, pg. 165
5 *Picture-Play Weekly* I, April 24, 1915, pg. 1–4
6 "Right Off the Reel," *Chicago Daily Tribune*, January 10, 1915
7 *Motion Picture Magazine*, March 1915, pg. 75–77
8 "Pursued by Silent Screen Ghosts," *Chicago Daily Tribune*, April 24, 1960
9 Grisham, William. "Those Marvelous Men and Their Movie Machines," *Chicago Daily Tribune*, December 7, 1969
10 Jaglom, Henry, Orson Welles, and Peter Biskind. *My Lunches with Orson: Conversations between Henry Jaglom and Orson Welles*. Metropolitan, 2013, pg. 143
11 *Motion Picture Magazine*, March 1915, pg. 75–77
12 Chaplin, Charles. My *Autobiography*, Plume/Penguin, 1992, pg. 167
13 *Chicago Daily News*, October 9, 1943
14 Kelly, Kitty. "Flickerings from Film Land," *Chicago Daily Tribune*, February 2, 1915
15 Chaplin, Charles. My *Autobiography*, Plume/Penguin, 1992, pg. 124
16 Chaplin, Charles. My *Autobiography*, Plume/Penguin, 1992, pg. 168
17 Chaplin Jr., Charles. *My Father, Charlie Chaplin*, Random House, 1960, pg. 32
18 Milton, Joyce. *Tramp: The Life of Charlie Chaplin*, Da Capo, 1998, pg. 87
19 Milton, Joyce. *Tramp: The Life of Charlie Chaplin*, Da Capo, 1998, pg. 97

20 Chaplin, Charles. *My Autobiography*, Plume/Penguin, 1992, pg. 173

21 "Looking at Hollywood With Ed Sullivan," Ed Sullivan, *Chicago Daily Tribune*, Oct 9, 1938

22 Witter, David. "Chi Lives: Mack Sennett's Motorcycle Stuntman." *Chicago Reader*, January 5, 1989

IV. IT ALL CAME CRASHING DOWN

12. The Decline of the Chicago Studios

1   Witter, David. "Chi Lives: Mack Sennett's Motorcycle Stuntman." *Chicago Reader*, January 5, 1989

2   *Motion Picture Patents Co. v. Independent Moving Pictures Company of America*, 200 F. 411, 2nd Cir., 1912

3   Original petition, *United States v. MPPC*, 247, U.S. 524, 1918

4   Balio, Tino. *The American Film Industry*, University of Wisconsin Press, 1985, pg. 149

5   J.A. Berst to George Kleine, July 8, 1914, George Kleine Collection, Box 4

6   *U.S. v. Motion Picture Patents Co.*, 225 F. 800, D.C. Pa., 1915

7   Swanson, Gloria. *Swanson on Swanson: An Autobiography*, Pocket, 1981, pg. 48

8   Swanson, Gloria. *Swanson on Swanson: An Autobiography*, Pocket, 1981, pg. 53

9   "Voice of the People," *Chicago Daily Tribune*, March 24, 1969

10 Bell, Geoffrey. *The Golden Gate and the Silver Screen*, Associated University Presse, 1984, pg. 62

11 "Max Linder Coming to America," *The Moving Picture World*, Vol. 29

12 *The Moving Picture World*, Vol. 27, January 8, 1916

13 "Selig Company to Shut Down Big Chicago Plant," *The Morning Telegraph*, July 21, 1914

14 Kelly, Kitty. "Flickerings from Film Land: Tells How The Name of Selig Grew Famous," *Chicago Daily Tribune*. April 30, 1915

15 "Monkeyshines," *Chicago Daily Tribune*, October 5, 1917

16 "Aha! Sherlock is Outdone!," *Chicago Daily Tribune*, April 22, 1916

17 "Casino Stars Stage Thriller," *Chicago Daily Tribune*, May 13, 1916

13. Major M.L.C. Funkhouser and the Chicago Censorship Code

1   Couvares, Frances. *Movie Censorship and American Culture*, University of Massachusetts Press, 2006, pg. 33

2   McCarthy, Kathleen. "Nickel Vice and Virtue: Movie Censorship in Chicago: 1907–1918", *Journal of Popular Film* 5/1, pg. 45–46

3   Haberski, Raymond. *It's Only a Movie!: Films and Critics in American Culture*,

University Press of Kentucky, 2001, pgs. 34–37

4   "Movie Censor Chief 'Jumped' Over Two Women," *Chicago Daily Tribune*, March 17, 1916

5   "Freak Dances Betold in Moving Pictures," *Chicago Daily Tribune*, October 23, 1913

6   McQuade, James. "Chicago Letter," *The Moving Picture World*, January 31, 1914

7   Kelly, Kitty. "Flickerings from Film Land," *Chicago Daily Tribune*, February 2, 1915

8   "All Nation Sees Eastland Film," *Chicago Daily Tribune*, July 29, 1915.

9   Kelly, Kitty. "Flickerings from Film Land," *Chicago Daily Tribune*, August 3, 1915

10 McQuade, James. "Chicago Letter," *The Moving Picture World*, February 7, 1914

11 Koszarski, Richard. *An Evening's Entertainment: The Age of the Silent Feature Picture, 1915–1928*, University of California Press, 1994, pg. 203

12 Koszarski, Richard. *An Evening's Entertainment: The Age of the Silent Feature Picture, 1915–1928*, University of California Press, 1994, pg. 203

13 "Yo Ho! And the Censor Is On Rampage Again," *Chicago Daily Tribune*, August 24, 1917

14 "The Police and Social Vice," *Chicago Daily Tribune*, July 19, 1918

15 Haberski, Raymond. *It's Only a Movie!: Films and Critics in American Culture*, University Press of Kentucky, 2001, pg. 37

Epilogue

1   *Chicago Daily News*, January 9, 1929

2   "Essanay Lot Gone, Not Its Guiding Hand," *Chicago Daily Tribune*, December 21, 1947

3   Hayner, Don and McNamee, Tom. *Chicago Sun-Times Metro Chicago Almanac*, National Book Network, 2003, pg. 186

4   Adams, Mike. *Lee De Forest: King of Radio, Television and Film*, Adams, Springer, 2012, pg. 213

5   "'Bronco [sic] Billy Recalls Films of 1911," *Los Angeles Enquirer*, June 28, 1943

6   "King of Comedy," *Tonawanda News*, January 12, 1955

7   "Veterans of Films Honor Ben Turpin," *Prescott Evening Courier*, July 4, 1940

8   Display Ad, *Chicago Tribune*, Jan 19, 1927

9   Mahar, Karen. *Women Filmmakers in Early Hollywood*, JHU Press, 2008, pg. 190

10 Golden, Eve. *Golden Images: 41 Essays on Silent Film Stars*, McFarland, 2001, pg. 209

11 "Reel Chicago." - *Chicago Magazine*. Robert Loerzel. Web. 17 June 2012.

<http://www.chicagomag.com/Chicago-Magazine/May-2007/Reel-Chicago/>.

12 "Death Takes Funkhouser at Lunch Table," *Chicago Daily Tribune*, September 19, 1926

13 Ramsaye, Terry. *A Million and One Nights*, Simon & Schuster, 1986, pg. 101

14 Baldwin, Neil. *Edison: Inventing the Century*, University of Chicago Press, 2001, pg. 407

Postscript: Oscar and Orson

1 "Within Our Gates," *Chicago Defender*, January 17, 1920, pg. 12

2 "Eighteen Years Old, Scores Hit in Shakespeare," *Chicago Daily Tribune*, December 24, 1933

3 McBride, Joseph. *What Ever Happened to Orson Welles?*, University Press of Kentucky, pg. 152

4 Welles, Orson and Bogdanovich, Peter, Jonathan Rosenbaum ed. *This Is Orson Welles*, Da Capo, 1998, pg. 41

INDEX